AF380096

Willem Sandberg
Portrait of an Artist

Ank Leeuw Marcar

Valiz, Amsterdam
Werkplaats Typografie, Arnhem

INTRODUCTION

In this book, which is compiled from interviews taken more than 30 years ago, Sandberg looks back on his life, particularly on the period from around 1945 until 1970, during which he was active as a typographic designer and as director of the Stedelijk Museum in Amsterdam.

The question arises whether 30 years later a reprint is justified. Sandberg had distinct ideas about art, how to deal with artists, about working as a typographic designer and managing a reputable Museum of modern and contemporary art. A younger generation may perhaps know the name of Sandberg, but is less acquainted with his ideas, his work, and his life. This book offers a first-hand insight into questions that are still relevant today: what does the job of museum director entail; how does art criticism function; what is the role of art or artist; what does the ideal museum architecture look like? Many of Sandberg's ideas about such issues are still fresh today and very challenging and can give new impulses to discussions about them and especially place them in an historic perspective.

After the Second World War, Willem Sandberg (1897–1984), with great creativity and passion and often in close cooperation with artists and architects, turned the Stedelijk Museum into a dynamic centre of modern and especially innovative art and culture. Something new for this time was his aim to bring this art closer to the common man, 'the passerby and the man in the street', and furthermore to involve young people in it. He did this from the conviction that art has a social function and that a museum director should show 'the creativity of a period'.

Unlike his predecessors, Sandberg did not see art
as an independent development or tradition but as
something that organically, 'like a plant, a flower on
a stem', arises from society, as something that comes
from 'the growth of our society, the relationship of
human-being to human-being'. He considered it his
task to exhibit in his museum that which pointed for-
wards: 'in the direction in which our society is moving'.

The basic material for the book is the interviews
that art critic Paul Aletrino held in the years 1970–1971
with Sandberg for the VARA radio "Staalkaart" [Colour
Card] he made at that time. Then, text fragments were
added from the TV portrait that Theo van Haren
Noman and Aletrino compiled in the following year for
the NOS. It was also possible to use the conversations
that Aletrino held in March and April 1981 with Sandberg to evaluate a number of subjects and make an
addition. A wonderful support in this was the documentary biography that Ad Petersen and Pieter Brattinga
made in 1975 on the occasion of the Erasmus prize,
which was awarded to Sandberg together with the art
historian E.H. Gombrich.

That biography was equally a big support for me
when, in 1981, I was given the task to compile this book
from the material that had been collected. I arranged
the chapters according to the most important themes
which were raised in the interviews. In addition, I
turned the spoken language of Sandberg into reading
language and reflected as faithfully as possible his own
word usage. The text was authorised by Sandberg for
the first edition.

Each of the chapters discusses a different facet of

Sandberg's comprehensive and lively vision on twentieth-century art and society. He participated actively in this as typographical designer before, during and after the Second World War.

Sandberg recounts and contemplates his life, in which he quickly set aside his idea of becoming a painter, because he needed interaction with people and wanted to stand in the middle of society. He talks about health, vegetarianism and fasting; and about Herman Gorter, who explained Marxism to him in countless conversations.

He talks at length about the museum as institution *and* as building for the public, and about the city as working and living community. He mentions many major artists and architects, most of whom he knew personally. These include Piet Mondrian, Picasso, Kandinsky and Le Corbusier, Mies van der Rohe, Gerrit Rietveld. He also talks about artists who participated in the Russian Revolution (1917).

Referring to his activities, Sandberg's controversial exhibitions are reviewed: "Cobra", "Bewogen Beweging" [Moving Movement] and "Dynamisch Labyrint" [Dynamic Labyrinth] or Dylaby. And also art criticism, which he believed should rather approach art with a question of where this can lead, what it expresses about the direction in which we are going, than with a judgment. According to him, those who experience it themselves write best about it. The book ends with a postscript by Sandberg, written in October 1981.

Ank Leeuw Marcar
Summer 2004 / Spring 2013

It is striking how Willem Sandberg's work has inspired many generations of designers both within and outside the Netherlands, and continues to do so. In the next generation as well I perceive renewed interest in his work. This shows that his work is timeless and of a rare quality and consistency.

Personally, I find especially the attitude demonstrated by the work appealing. With Sandberg designing is an organic process. It does not stand alone, but is part of a larger involvement with society. He shows how design, without being ostentatious, can be distinguished and yet playful and musical at the same time. From Sandberg I learned that the answer lies in the question. Form is a logical consequence of content, without violating its meaning. Form can in itself represent content.

In their wording and meaning, Sandberg's texts show the same intrinsic naturalness that distinguishes his design work. Therefore I think it is important that these texts are being reissued in an inspired and more personal form. Their content deserves this and a great number of people will benefit from it. I also think it's in Sandberg's spirit to have the reissue designed by a young designer from the next generation, showing his personal views. Louis Lüthi (Bastia, 1980), who in 2002–2004 participated in the Werkplaats Typografie, designed the original Dutch edition. He had studied Sandberg's graphic design and said: "Sandberg's work is beautifully honest, perfectly imperfect and strikingly simple… Art has a function in and for society, graphic design has a function in and for society. Ideally perhaps, good graphic design is the result of an honest

reflection of clear viewpoints which go beyond the field
of graphic design."

I am pleased that now an English edition is available too. This time Rutger de Vries (Zwolle, 1987),
in 2011–2013 participant in the Werkplaats Typografie,
has designed the book in his own way and says:
"Playfulness and simplicity I find typical of Sandberg's
work. By working on this book I was drawn to his ideas
and designs. For me this was very inspiring and I am
convinced that his work and attitude are still significant,
also for my generation. Fortunately, with this English
edition of the book Sandberg's legacy is now available
to a wider audience".

Karel Martens
Spring 2013

The Sandberg Instituut in Amsterdam, the master programmes of the Gerrit Rietveld Academie, was named after Willem Sandberg, former director of the Stedelijk Museum Amsterdam, designer and charismatic champion of all things new and different in art. To many artists and designers he is a huge source of inspiration. His 'scheursels' (rippings), his work at the Stedelijk Museum and his close ties with artists, architects and designers are widely known.

The Gerrit Rietveld Academie and the Sandberg Instituut both have a special bond with Willem Sandberg. His attitude and work method contain many elements that we consider important for our own practice and art education: the natural way in which he combined various disciplines, his devotion to the public interest, his commitment and political stance, the interweaving of art and social responsibility, the fun and passion of working with very divergent groups in the field of art: all these are aspects of a highly contemporary, critical attitude that we hope to instil in our students as well.

We wholeheartedly support this publication in the hope of encouraging students, artists, designers, politicians and many others to study Sandberg's work and be inspired by his unconventional, socially conscious way of thinking.

The directors of the Gerrit Rietveld Academie
and the Sandberg Instituut
Spring 2013

Ank Leeuw Marcar (1939, Medan, Indonesia) is an art historian. During the 'sixties she worked at the Stedelijk Museum Amsterdam and taught at the Rijksuniversiteit Groningen. Thereafter she worked freelance for several museums of modern art (including Museum Boijmans Van Beuningen, Rotterdam).

She is the author of several articles and publications, such as the major artist's book "Woody van Amen. Crossing Worlds" (Rotterdam, 2003), for which she collaborated with artist and graphic designer Karel Martens and wrote the biography.

Karel Martens (1939, Mook en Middelaar, The Netherlands) graduated from the Arnhem School of Art in 1961. Since then he has worked as a freelance graphic designer, specialising in typography. In addition to commissioned work he has always made 'free' work such as prints and three-dimensional work as well. Today he is widely recognised as one of the most important professional artists working for major clients, including publishers, architects, and institutions.

Martens has taught at the Arnhem School of Art, Jan van Eyck Academie Maastricht and Yale School of Art and in 1998 he co-founded the Werkplaats Typografie, a two-year master's programme for graphic design.

WORK BY SANDBERG

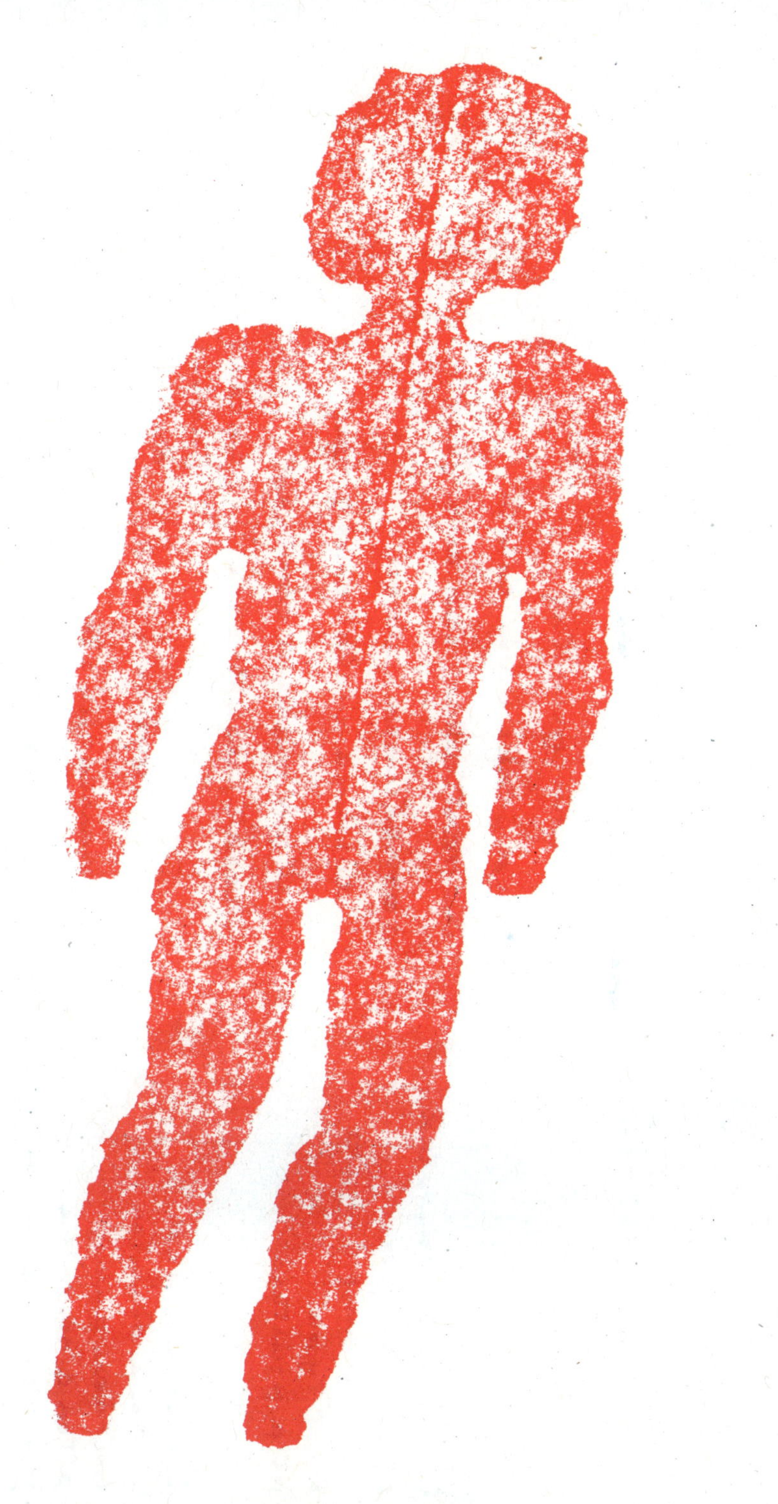

i was never schooled
as a designer
only during 6 weeks
i set Type
at a printers

i had wanted
to be a painter
but ran away
after 6 months
from The academy

i did not become
a painter

i believe
in warm printing
and i like vivid colors
in particular red and Blue
sometimes yellow
i dislike violet and green
but for violent contrast
i rarely use Brown   except
                            Tobacco scrap iron
                            or wrapping paper
i love square forms
romanesque structures
and mondrian
equilibrium between
The spiritual and the material

to produce
something useful

at the age of 30
i became a designer
because somebody
wanted a calendar

at 40
i became a museum man
because a director
wanted an assistant

i had never thought of
becoming a designer
or a museum director
but i dont believe in accidents

The use of gold
or brilliant paper
i prefer the rough
in contour and surface
torn forms
and wrapping paper

as a freelance designer
i did not feel free
to experiment

as a museum man
designing
my own catalogues and posters
every design
became experimental

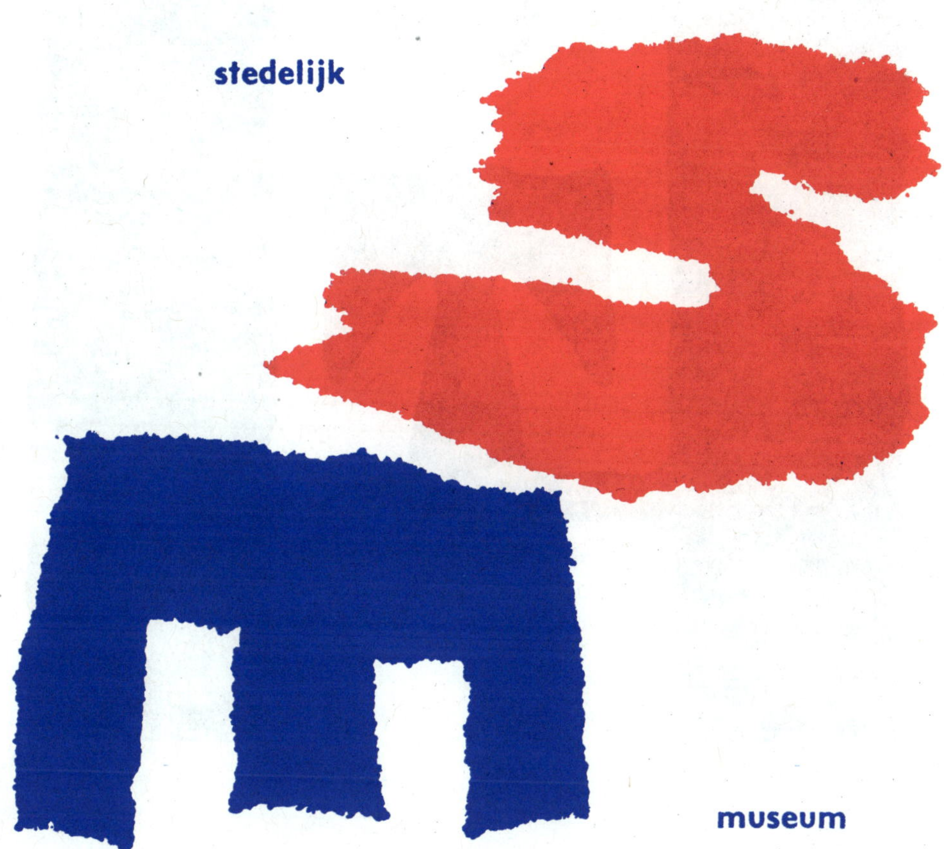
stedelijk
museum

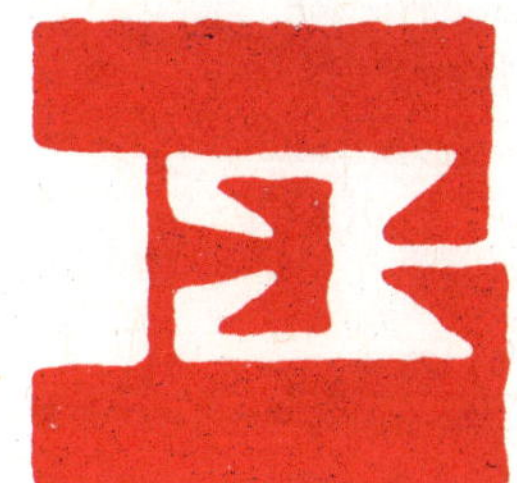

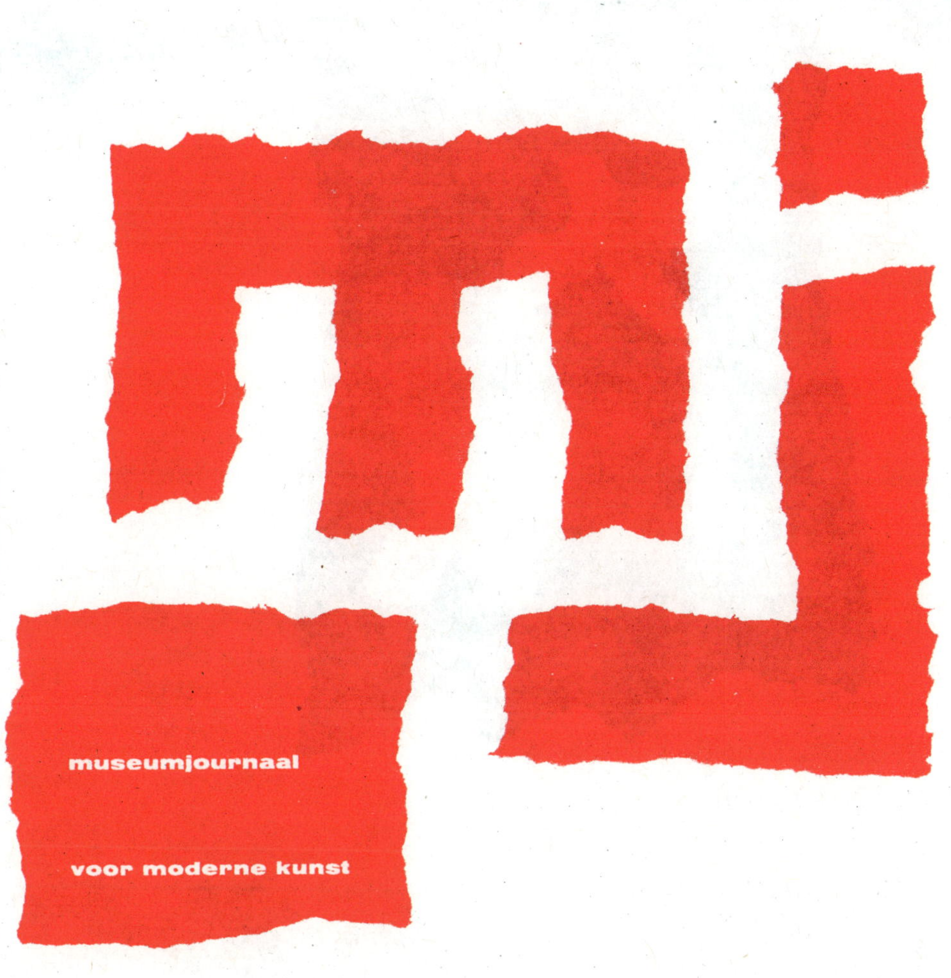
museumjournaal
voor moderne kunst

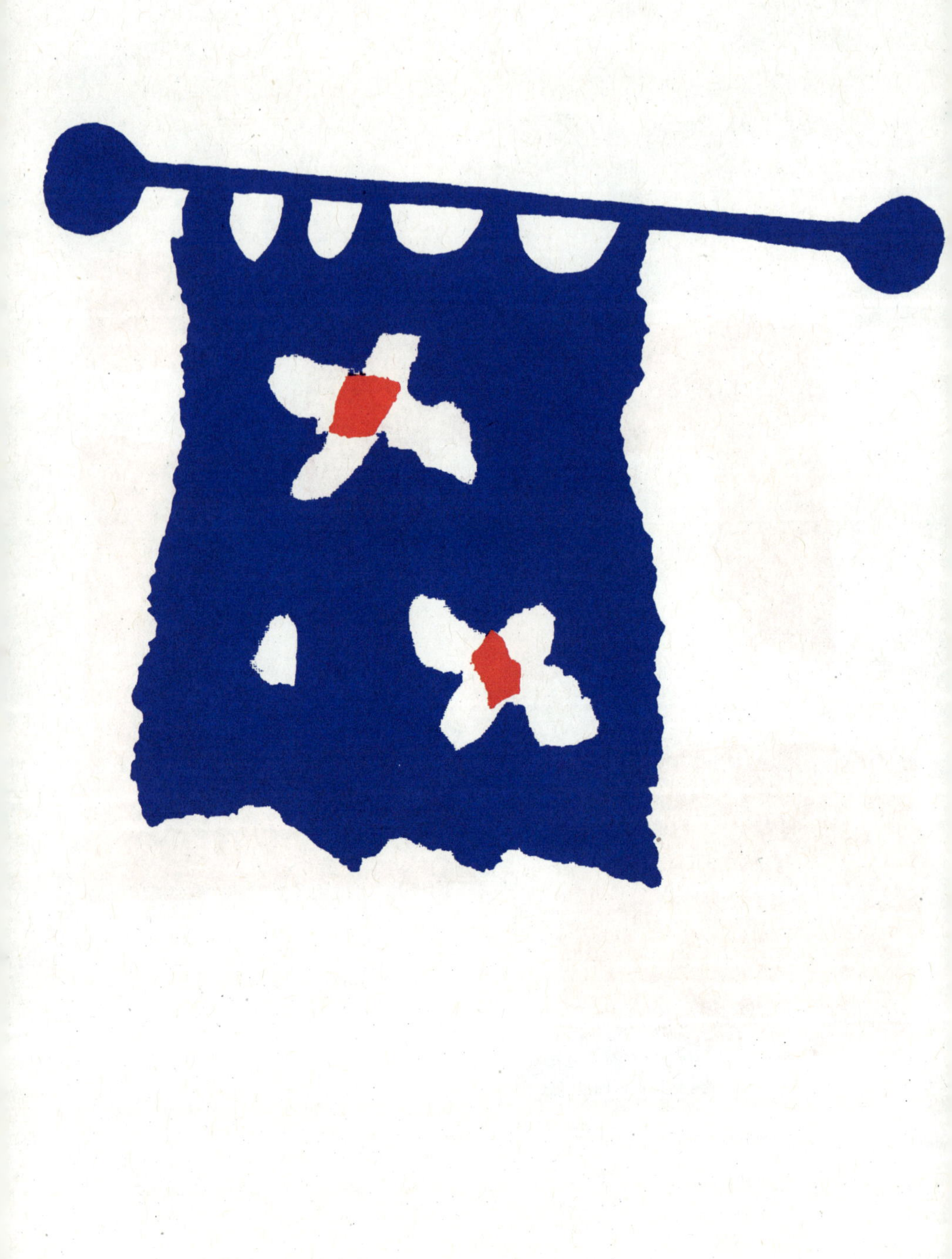

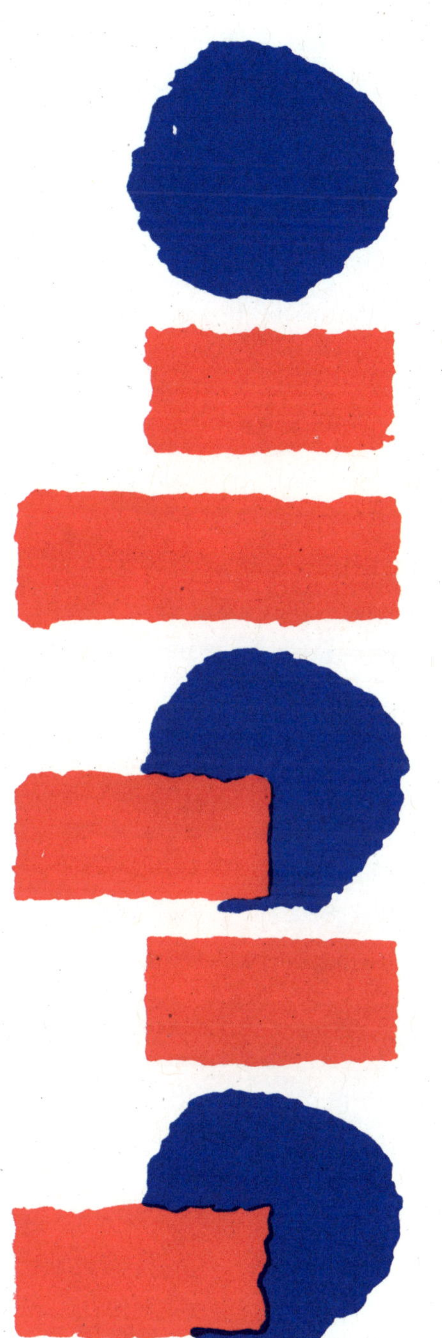

theek
teca
thèque
thek

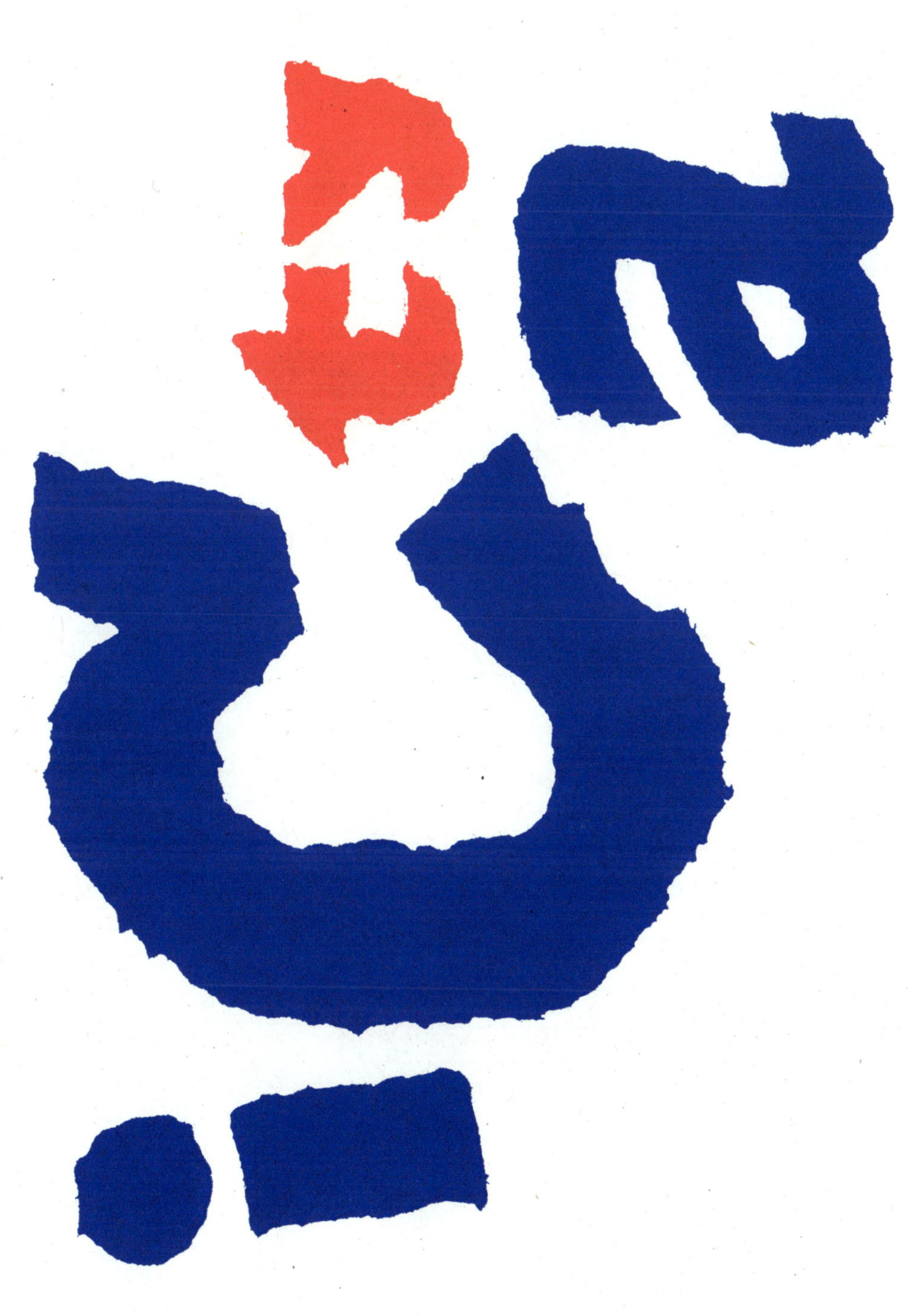

avantgardecahier 1

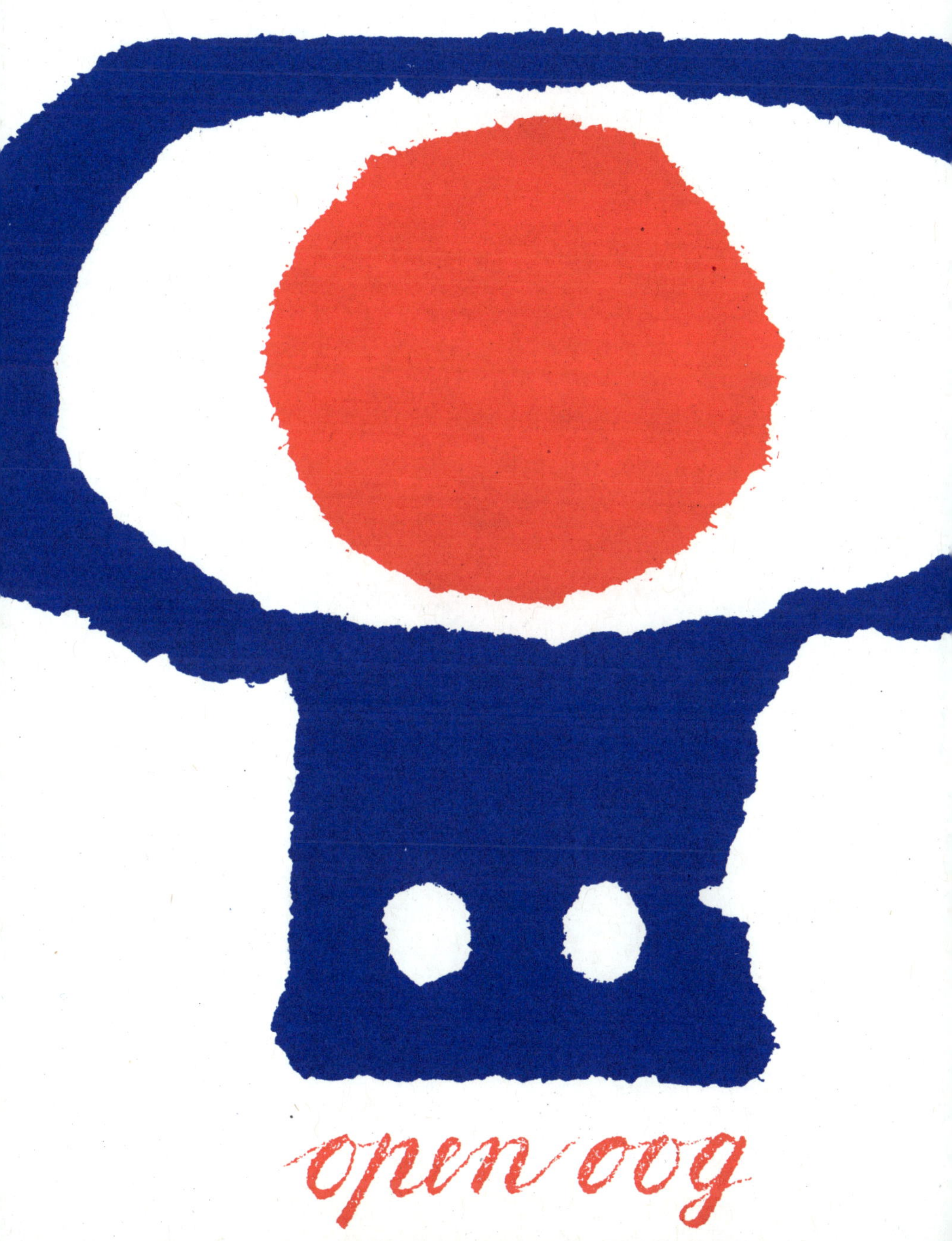

open oog

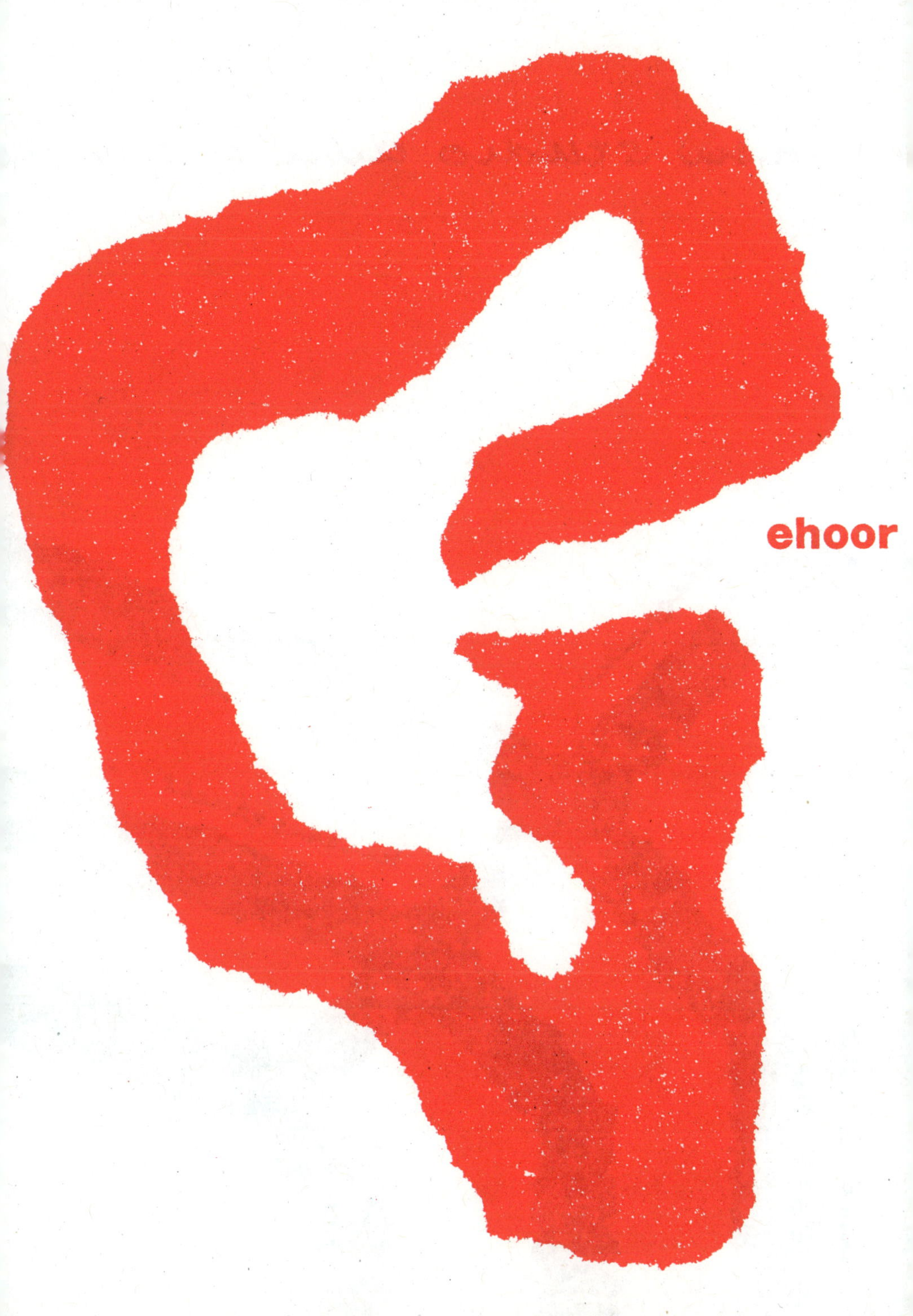
ehoor

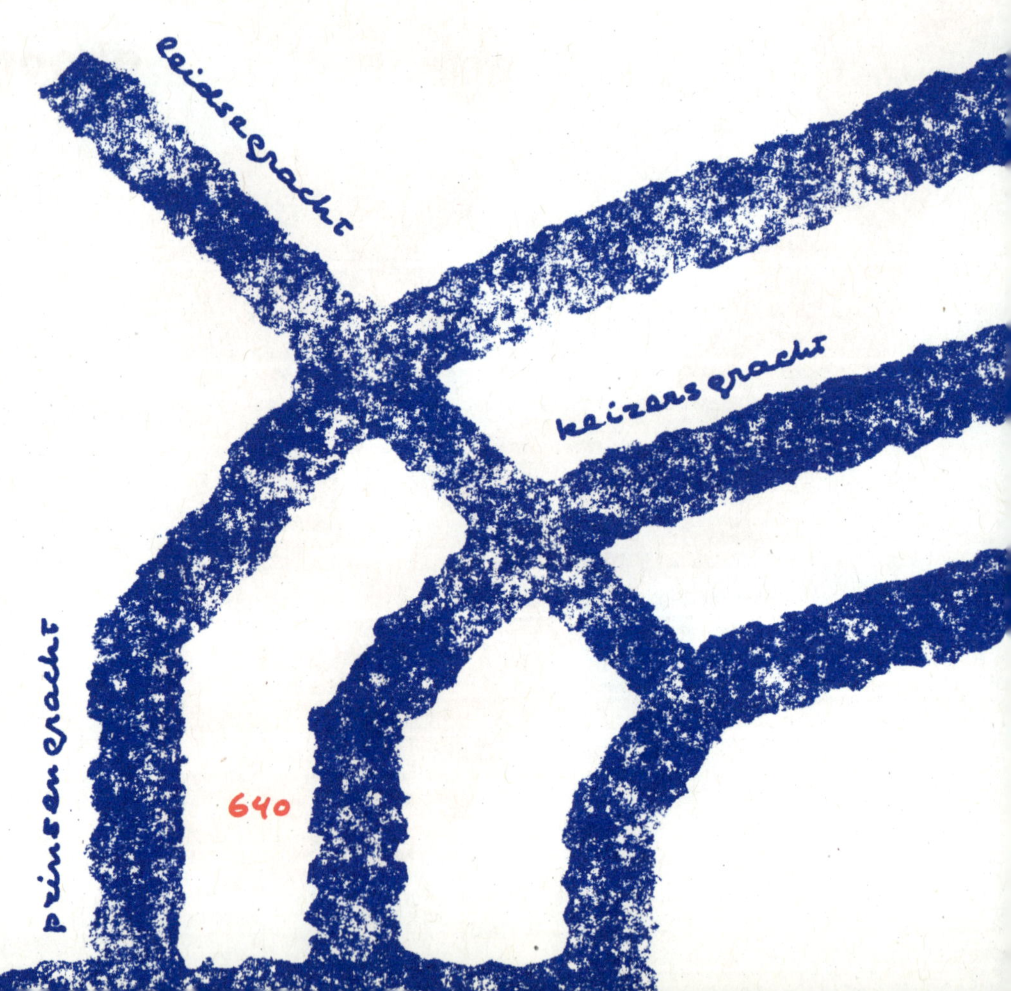
new studio adress sand
leidsegracht
keizersgracht
prinsengracht
640

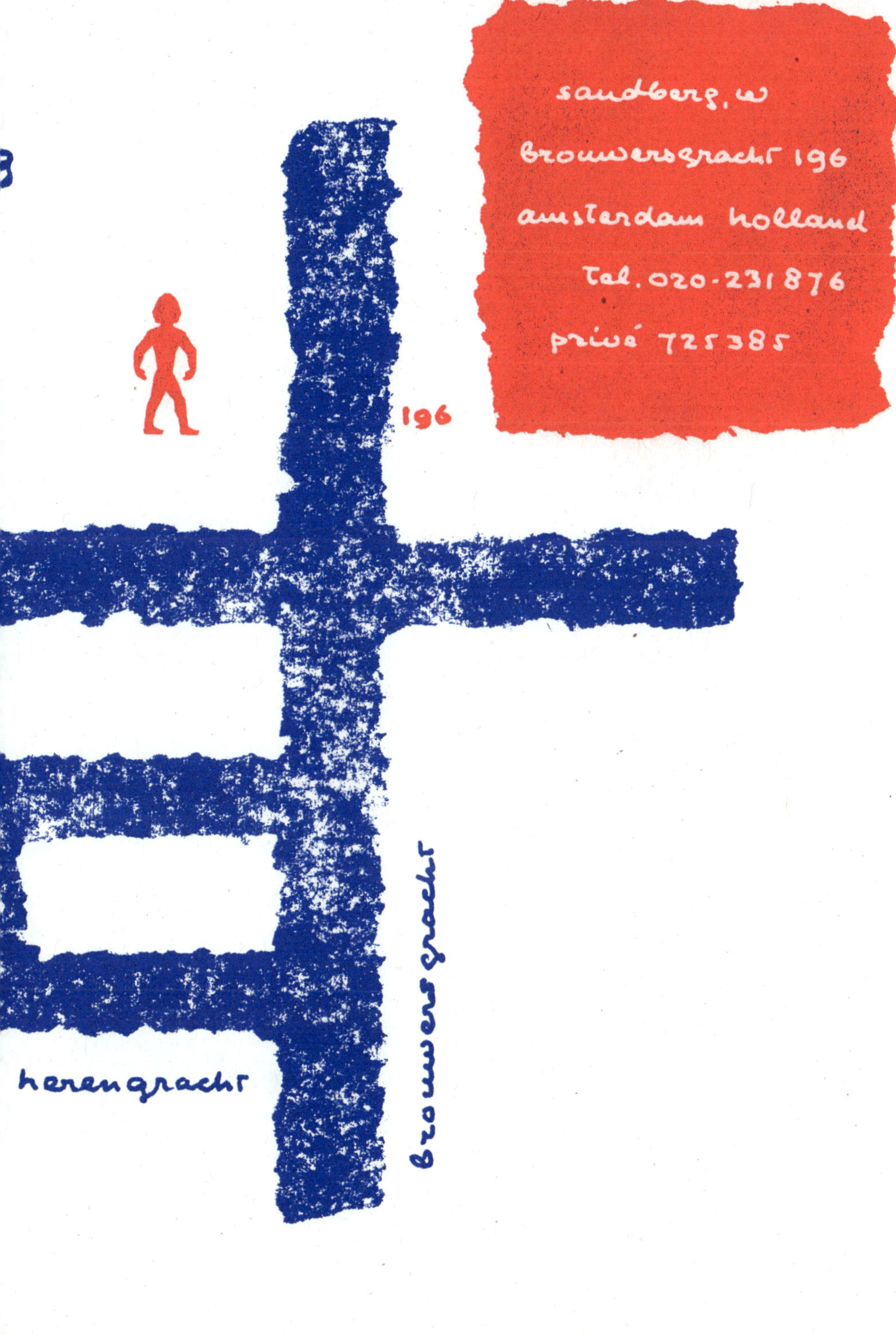
sandberg, w
brouwersgracht 196
amsterdam holland
tel. 020-231876
privé 725385
196
brouwersgracht
herengracht
central station

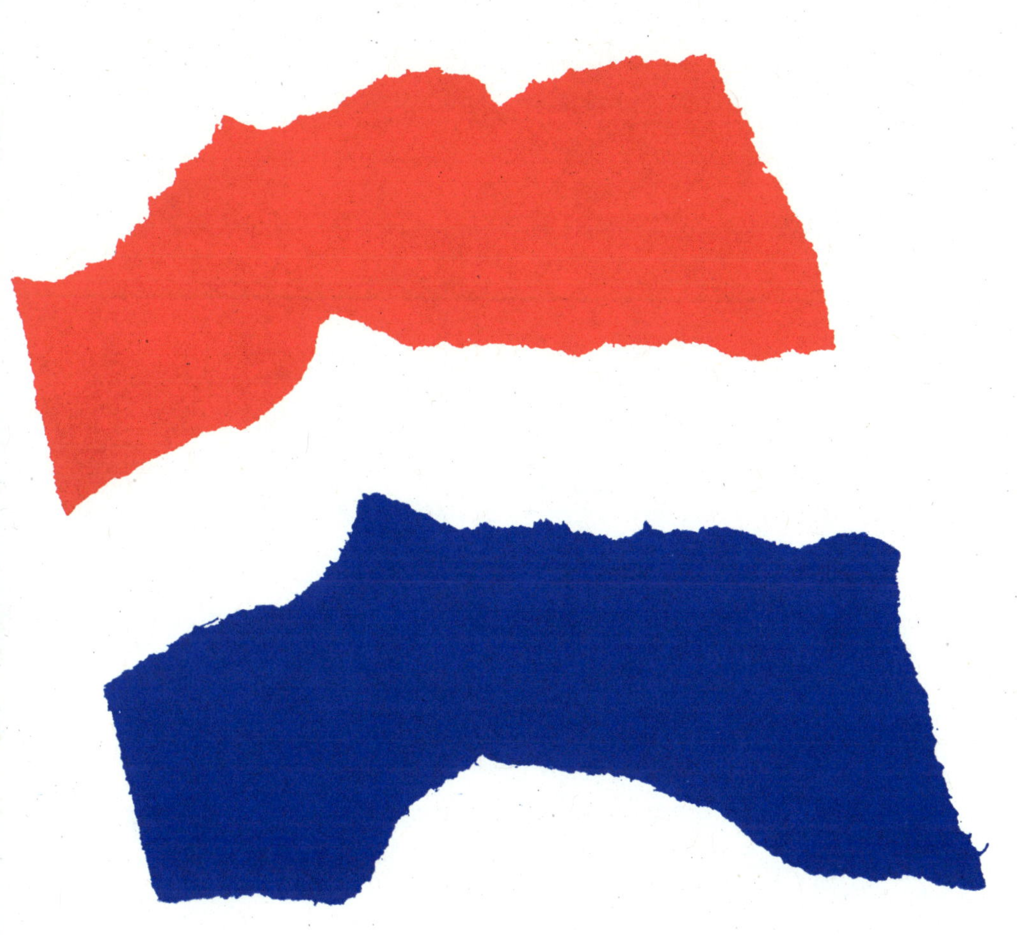

art and sport in holland

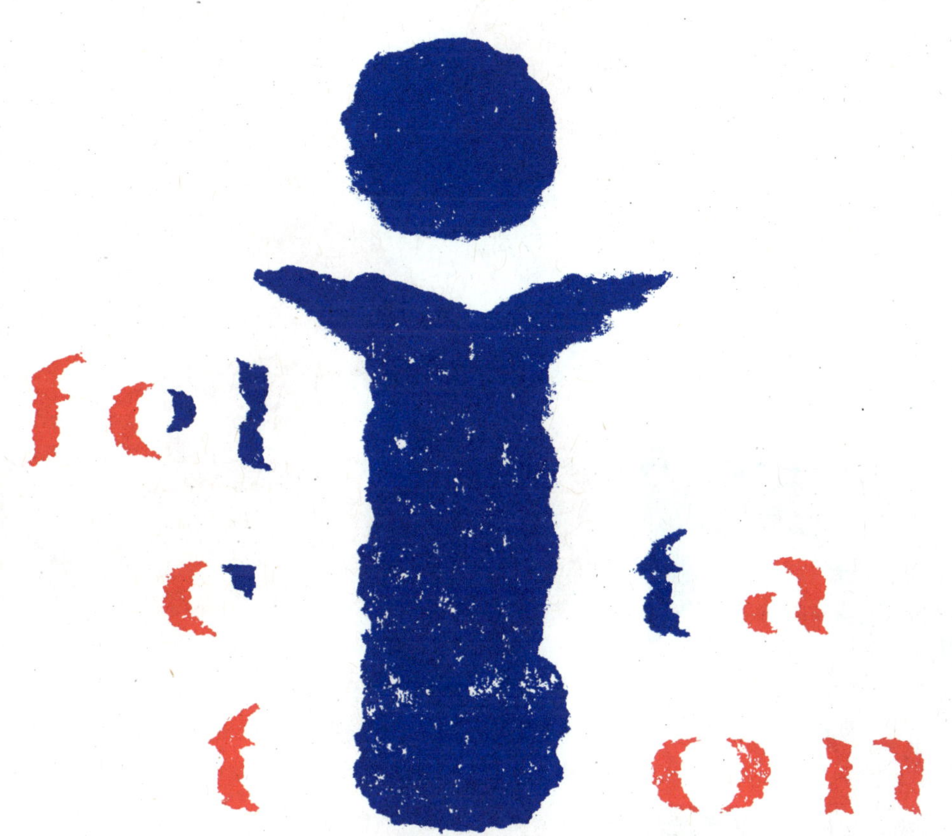
fel
ci
t
ta
on

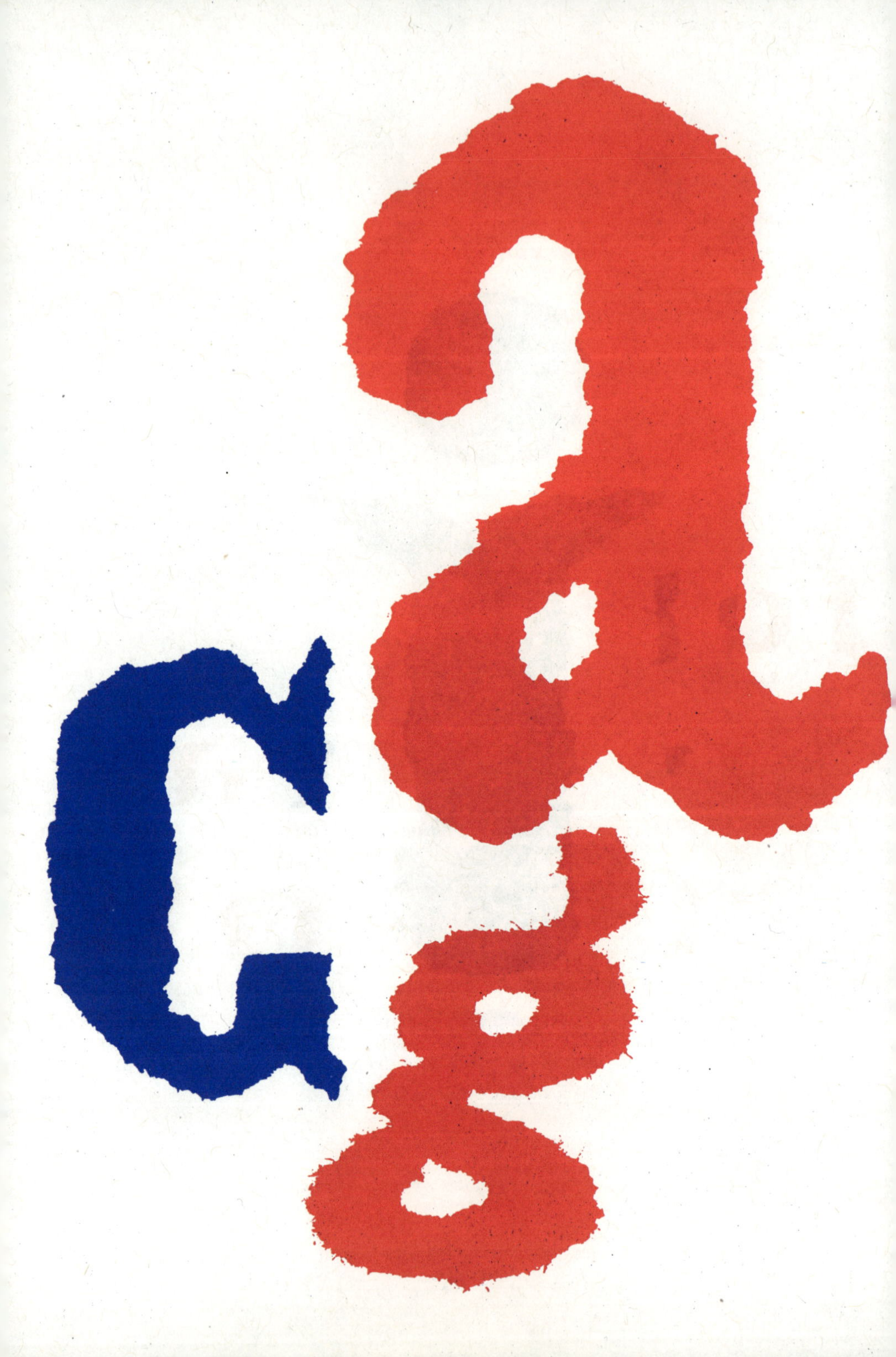

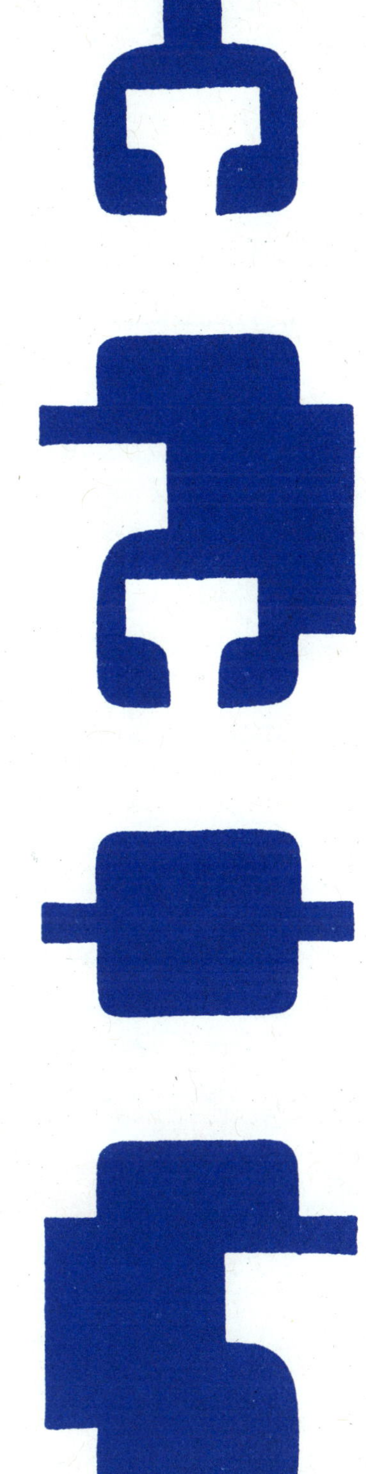
the inner
principle

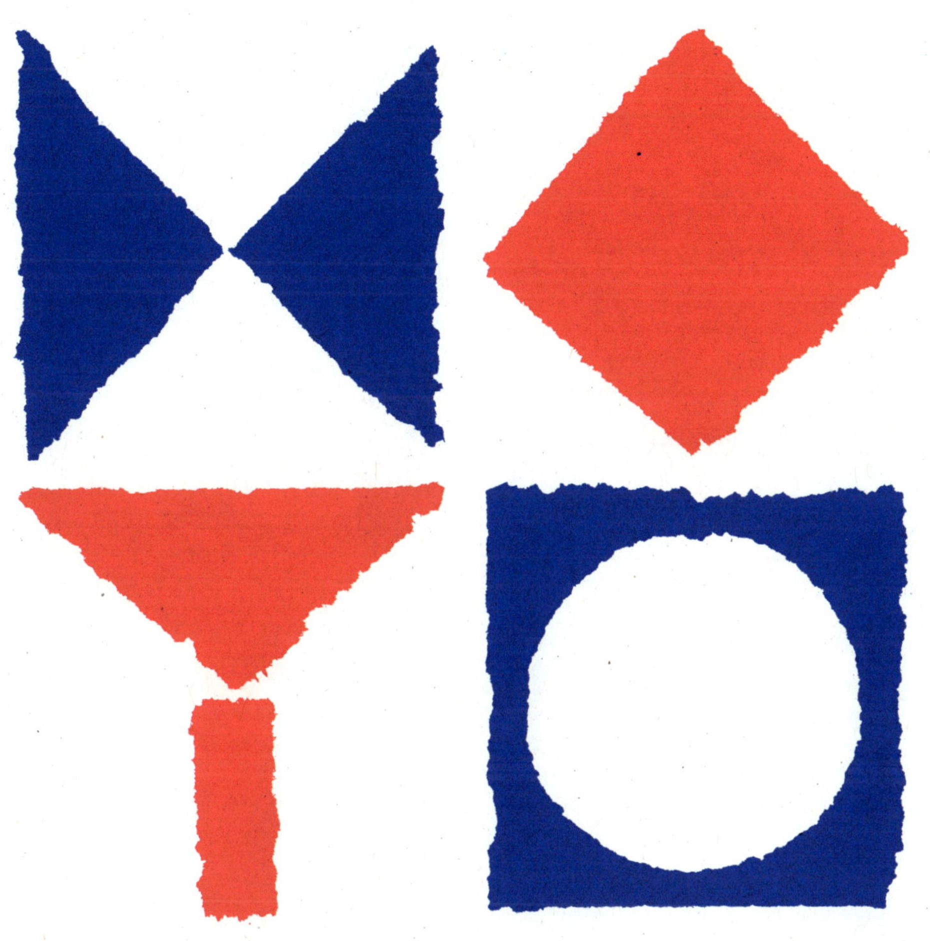

the israel museum

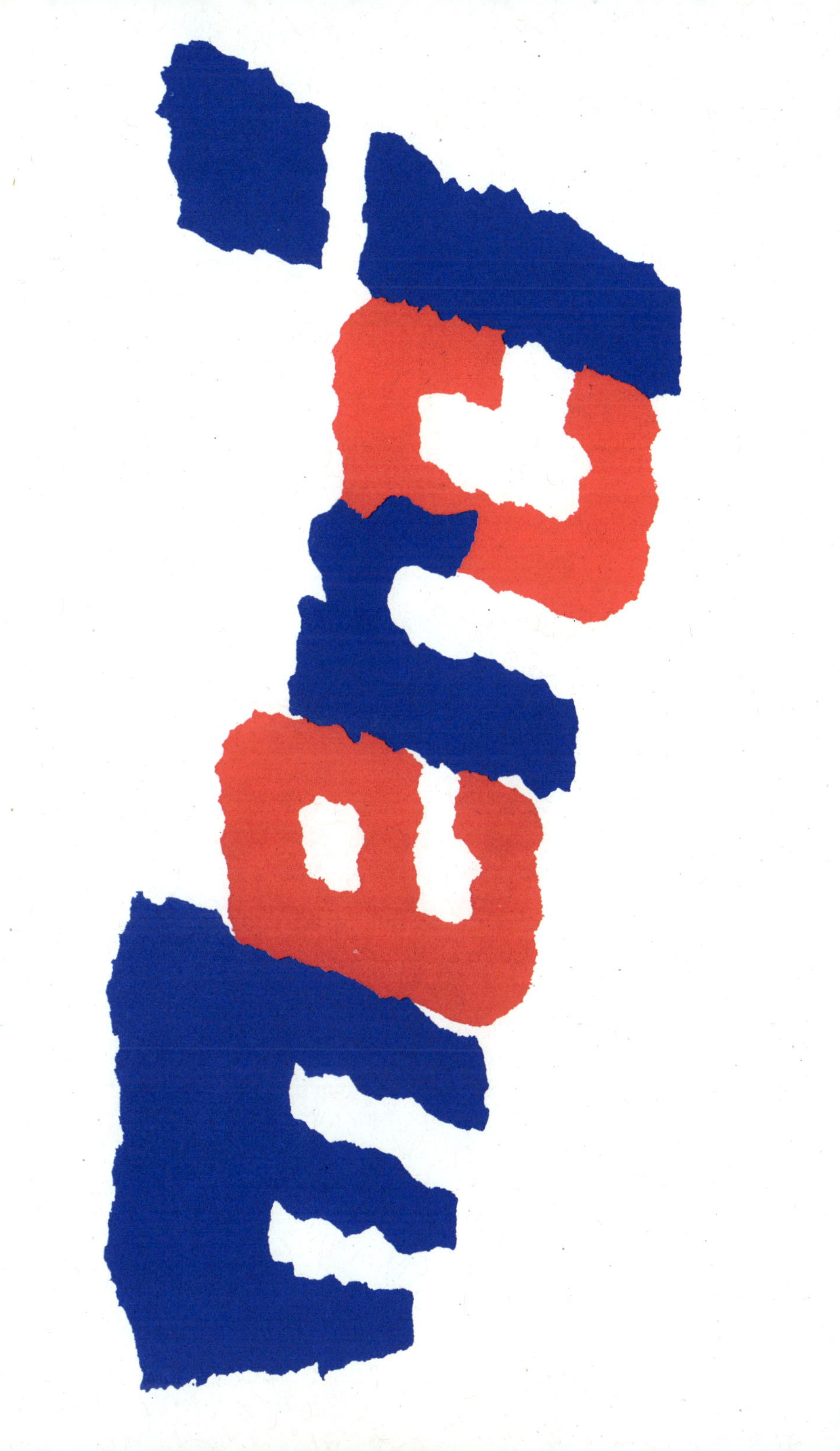

LIFE STORY

As a kid, I probably wanted to be a liveried driver of a horse-drawn cab. Today, that would mean a taxi driver, but they didn't exist at the time. For me, taxi drivers have always been a certain type of person, who, practically speaking, have little to do with their boss. In almost every job you have a boss, somebody you have to take into account. As museum director, you have a local council, mayor, alderman and councillors who find fault with you. As taxi driver, you have nothing to do with your boss, as long as you hand over the money on time. It is what you could call a free profession. A free profession of people, of ordinary people. That means there is a certain type of person who chooses that profession. I have used a lot of taxis, because I don't drive myself anymore. I always sit next to the driver and talk to them. When, for example, I was in the museum, I often discussed it with them. Generally that conversation started with Pierre Janssen[1], for he had the gift of making everybody listen to him. Intellectual or blue-collar worker, it didn't matter. Everybody is interested in what he has to say and the way he says it.

And so I discussed my museum policy, the building of the New Wing and the like with taxi drivers. You need a correcting influence when you live in the company of intellectuals, who view things completely differently than the man in the street. And yet, as

1. Pierre Jansen (1926–2007) was a Dutch reporter, art critic, curator, and director of the Gemeentemuseum Arnhem from 1969 to 1982. He pioneered art programmes on television and was popular and successful in explaining art to the general public.

museum director, you want to do things for that man in the street. For that you need an audience — even though you talk to your own staff, with your attendants and so on — and for me that audience was always taxi drivers. I have also had interesting experiences with taxi drivers abroad.

I remember in the summer of 1968 taking a taxi early in the morning to go to Los Angeles airport. The driver was Porto Rican. He had just got married and told me a whole story about it. Then we spoke of the place Porto Ricans have in American society. They are really lumped together with negroes, but they don't really mind that at all because it means that they are not alone in their fight. Our conversation went so well that when we arrived at the airport he said: *Sir, I have enjoyed this conversation so much that I don't want to take any money from you.* I have always learned a lot from taxi drivers. But I think I soon gave up the idea of becoming a liveried driver of a horse-drawn cab.

When I was at grammar school, I had to choose between alpha and beta — between the classics and the sciences — but I didn't choose, and studied both. I attended a small grammar school in Assen. Altogether I think there were only 45 pupils, and there were only five or six in our class. I was the only one who chose the beta subjects as well, and so those were almost private lessons. I remember the biology lessons that were given by the director of the Secondary School. We wandered through the Assen Woods and looked at plants and animals. For mathematics, I always had to go to the mathematics teacher's office for lessons. Later, in 1920, I married her, but that didn't last long.

I have always tried to keep all my options open and it took me a long time before I found my own direction. I first thought of becoming a painter. Actually I was predestined to become a lawyer. That was a tradition in our family, there was no escaping it. You began by reading law and then later you became a barrister or a civil servant or whatever. That was how it was. But since I often lived at odds with my surroundings, I didn't want to accept that. I wanted to become a painter, something we had never had in our family before.

My parents let me have my way; they saw that they couldn't do anything with me and acquiesced. After my military service I went to the Rijksacademie [National Academy] for visual arts in Amsterdam. I passed my entrance examination with honours, because I could draw a very attractive plaster head, with all the difficulties that involved. The difficult thing with a plaster head is that it is white, and the white has to come through. What's more, the plaster heads were extremely dusty, so you had to draw both the shadows and the dust. Quite a work of art, but apparently I completed the task well.

Once I was at the academy, I didn't like it one little bit. The professor always wanted to scribble in my drawings and his handwriting was not at all like mine. After about five, six months I simply walked away. I got married and went to Italy. I thought: Italy is the country of painters. I was 22 years old when I went to live in Italy. Later, in Paris, at the Académie de la

Grande Chaumière, I drew a lot of nudes and if I didn't like the models, I would draw my colleagues, the other people who sat there working. That was in 1923 and something like 25 years later, I think, I bumped into one of the models I had drawn a lot. That was the sculptor Alberto Giacometti, whom I got to know personally in 1948. I knew his face very well, but didn't know the man himself at all.

In the years that I attended the Rijksacademie, I got to know Herman Gorter[2]. That was in 1918–1920. I returned to civilian life at the end of 1918, after two years military service. I took a room in Amsterdam on the Herengracht near the Blauwburgwal. It was the only house that was bombed during our four-day war from 10–14 May 1940, but by then I had already been gone for twenty years.

During my military service I had got to know a boy from Haarlem and we saw each other regularly. After the war he came to Amsterdam to read law. One day he came to me and said: *Look. I attended Secondary School and then I passed my state certificate. I was trained for that certificate by Herman Gorter. I wanted him to tell me more about Marxism. But Gorter always said: 'Yes, but first pass your state certificate and then we can talk about it. First you have to learn Latin and Greek.'* (Gorter had been teacher of classic languages

2. Herman Gorter (1864–1927), was a Dutch poet and socialist. He is particularly famous for his epic poem May, which is considered by many the pinnacle of Dutch impressionist literature. He was an active member of the Social Democratic Labour Party, which later, in 1918, changed its name to the Communist Party of Holland.

in Amersfoort, before he freed himself to dedicate himself entirely to art. I remember that my father, at the time Council Secretary of the municipality of Amersfoort, moved house. When he moved out of the first home he had had after his marriage, Herman Gorter moved in. My father always said to me: *I never understood anything about the man and I don't know what 'summer gossip' means.* That was my first memory of Herman Gorter.)

My friend continued: *Gorter would naturally like to give me some idea of Marxism and Communism here in Amsterdam. Could we use your room for that? I answered: Of course, on condition that I can be present as well.*

From then on, Gorter and my friend would regularly visit me and we would spend two hours reading Marx. We did that very punctiliously. First we had to prepare the text. We weren't tested on it, but I remember that we read 'The Historical Materialism' by Gorter himself, and 'Das Wesen der Menschlichen Kopfarbeit' by the German cobbler Jozef Dietzgen. We delved deeply into them. Those were the first years of the Russian Revolution. Occasionally Gorter disappeared to Russia. He was a good friend of Trotsky and Radeck, but he didn't talk much about Lenin. Of course he knew him, but Gorter had been expelled from the Communist party here, and that presented some difficulties.

Gorter was a fantastic speaker, an impassioned man, and he could sweep us along with him. What was remarkable was that after an hour or two of communist theory, he would always say: *Now we have to*

relax. Now we are going to read Shakespeare or Shelley.
In this way we read 'The Tempest' by Shakespeare
and 'Prometheus Unbound' by Shelley, who greatly
influenced him in his 'May', as did Keats. These meetings with Gorter — he always stayed on to drink coffee
and I would fry him an egg — remain among the
strongest memories in my life. We were very left in
our ideas. It was a reflection of the time and people
really thought that the revolution in Russia was the
start of a whole new era.

I believed that for years, but I must honestly admit
that I have since changed my mind. It is not that I
deny that capitalism is not only old fashioned, but also
played out and no longer sustainable, but I do not
believe that the Russian solution to this issue is the
right one.

The great U-turn began in 1920. Lenin's health
was poor. I assume that Stalin already had increasing
influence at that time. Sternberg and other people
wanted to follow the new course, which had become
so incredibly important in Russia thanks to people
such as Malevich, Tatlin, Majakowski and others.
Gorter was very effected by that. He was completely
on the side of the new direction in literature and visual
arts, but it was actually in the middle of this issue that
we stopped. I got married in 1920 and went to Italy
and that brought our meetings to an end.

Those meetings didn't always take place in my
room in Amsterdam. We often went to Bussum. Or we
went walking in the dunes in Bergen. Whenever we
went out with him, it always turned into a long walk,
he really enjoyed that. He already had problems with

a weak heart, and this was the cause of his death in
1927 in Brussels. I don't know under what circumstances, but it is a fact that he was taken to the ceme-
tery on a handcart. And I think, if he had witnessed
it himself, he would have enjoyed that a lot.

Gorter was a typical intellectual, but an enthusiastic intellectual. Somebody who could sweep you away,
a man, I would almost say, who embodied everything
he stood for. I think he had considerable financial
problems. He had married a rich woman. She had
already passed away and I had the impression that he
had given most of the money to the party. He had to
earn his living by giving lessons. He went from one
lesson to the next, although he was never in a hurry.
He came at 10 in the morning, and if he left by 3 in the
afternoon, that was early, for he never looked at his
watch when he was occupied with something.

I don't think I ever saw Gorter in anything other
than a blue suit. A somewhat casual blue suit, with
very heavy brown shoes, a detachable collar, at that
time made of celluloid — you never needed to wash
them — as was the fashion then. And a long black tie,
which was fixed to some metal contraption, so you
just pulled it through and never had to knot it. He had
reduced his clothing to the absolute minimum, it became almost standard equipment. I never saw him
in anything other than those heavy light brown shoes
from pigskin or calfskin and that blue suit. It may
perhaps have looked rather odd. On his nose he wore
a 'so-easy', a small pair of gold spectacles that stayed
in place with a clamp. That was expected in those
days. He had a perfect bald head; any hair that grew

there he had cut or shaved off.

I still see that face before me and I shall never forget the impression that it made on me nor what I got from him. I am still very grateful for that.

I had slowly come to realise that painting was not for me. I needed interaction with people, I wanted to be part of society. Spending my life at an easel with, perhaps, a still life or a landscape on it, that wasn't right for me. I radically turned my back on it. Yet it was probably good for something, because years later — that was in 1928 — a publisher contacted me for a calendar. Okay, I could put together a calendar for him, I made it. This is how I became a typographic designer. I began learning about typography in 1922, at a printer's in Herrliberg, near Zurich.

One thing led to another and I found myself designing. I did it for ten years and I enjoyed it. It was a free profession. You sometimes had to deal with clients who could prove difficult. For example, I once had a client who said: *Yes, I want something like Jo Spier makes.* I said: *Then, sir, you should go to Jo Spier; I shall look up his address for you and you can phone him. I don't make what Jo Spier makes.* Or another said: *I want to have a calendar like those Paul Schuitema makes for Boele & van Eesteren.* (That was a very beautiful calendar; I always used it myself.) And to that I said: *Then you must go to Schuitema.* That is how I selected my own clients. In the end I worked mainly for government institutions, such as the post office, for which I made shop windows in the Zeestraat in The Hague.

I took over that job from Piet Zwart. That was how

— it was in 1933 — I got to know Piet Zwart, who had just received a major commission from the Dutch Post Office to produce a book. I think he spent four years on it. It was a very nice book. He had previously always made the window displays together with his pupils, and I took over that work from him. I did ask him: *I'm not stealing the work from you, am I?* But Piet said: *No, I want to see the back of it, I've had enough of it, you take over.* That was how we first met.

I had the National Insurance Bank, the Labour Council for which I would mount exhibitions; later I had the Concertgebouw and the Conservatorium. I had a small group of clients for which I worked regularly, and that went rather well. You didn't earn very much, but I could earn a living and that is, after all, the main thing.

In 1927 I went to Vienna where I got to know Otto Neurath, the sociologist. Neurath was director of the Institute for Society and Economy there. He had set up an area in the basement of the town hall, where, using visual statistics, he showed the developments and the connections in Socialist Vienna: the Gesellschafts- und Wirtschaftsmuseum. I was fascinated by the visual statistics and later frequently used that method — but I had actually gone to Vienna to study the drawing methods of Cizek and Richard Rothe. They were not part of the Bauhaus. Later I found more of what I sought with Johannes Itten who had given the Vorkurs [Preliminary Course] at the Bauhaus and who I had met five years earlier in Switzerland. In addition, I attended lectures in psychology by Karl Bühler and Alfred Adler.

I could also have made use of those visual statistics — that was in 1928 or 1929 — for the PTT [the Dutch Post and Telecommunications company], but then the crisis came and all those commissions dried up. Everybody kept their purses tightly closed.

There was also the exhibition "Arbeid voor Onvolwaardigen" [Work for the Handicapped]. That was in 1928, just before the crisis, under the chairmanship of that minister with the beard, Slotemaker de Bruïne. The congress about this was held in the Tropeninstituut [The Royal Tropical Institute] and the exhibition was in the Stedelijk Museum. I designed a room there with visual statistics. They asked me to take care of this because I had worked previously with such material. I had to supply all the pieces myself. Those panels were about two metres high and one hundred and twenty centimetres wide.

That I was then already doing things in the Stedelijk Museum came about as follows: in former times, associations such as the Dutch Watercolour Circle, the Independents, were allocated a certain exhibition area per year. The VANK[3], the Vereeniging van Ambachts- en Nijverheidskunst [the Association of Arts and Crafts] — people practising applied arts were members — were able to make use of the lower rooms, at the back right. I was invited to become a member of VANK in 1932. There was an exhibition committee in the VANK, and Paul Bromberg and I were alternating chairmen. Erna van Osselen was the

3. The VANK was set up in 1904, later focusing on graphic design with the emphasis on art rather than craft.

60

secretary. Almost immediately, I became a member of the Committee for Non-Permanent Exhibitions, in 1934 or thereabouts. Then the school and the associated museum in Haarlem were discontinued and the Stedelijk got a lot of things from them. It was a very good school, there in Haarlem. It produced Ben Merkelbach, who would later become city architect and Charles Karsten. They had both studied architecture there.

The Stedelijk didn't have any arts and crafts, but started with it at that time. A committee was set up to supervise it, including Ir. De Bie Leuvelink Tjeenk, the chairman of the Association of Dutch Architects — he was also general commissioner for the Dutch department at the World Exhibition in Paris — and H.K. Westendorp, who, in Amsterdam, was chairman of almost everything to do with art: the Society of Asian Art, the Society for the Formation of a Public Collection of Contemporary Art in Amsterdam and so on.

The so-called experts in ceramics always turned a plate over and looked to see which stamp it had. But I always first looked at the plate as a whole, and only then did I look for the stamp. That impressed the museum's director, the old Mr. C.W.H. Baard; he involved me in all sorts of jobs. He progressed from attendant to director there in a good thirty years. He was the father of the Baard who was later the director of the Frans Hals Museum in Haarlem.

Baard only spoke French; he made use of me for all other languages. Once, in 1935 — the museum would then be forty years old — he wanted to hold an exhibition of Dutch monumental art, with Heinrich

Campendonk and several artists who had worked in
Hagen, such as Jan Thorn Prikker. Whether I could go
and select things for that. He thought I was due a
holiday, that I should take 14 days off and, in the meantime, work on the exhibition. He did not speak a word
of German; he didn't even dare to go there. I said that
I wasn't in need of a holiday and also did not have
any time, but that I would put things in order in a few
days. He also asked me to make the poster and the
catalogue. And so I became more and more involved.

Within the framework of the non-permanent exhibitions of the VANK, I also organised in 1935 the
exhibition "De Stoel" [The Chair], which showed
the history of the chair until that time. For that occasion, Mart Stam brought me his famous floating steel
chair. That is how I became acquainted with and
befriended the architect Mart Stam. He also helped
me set up the exhibition. He had just returned from
Russia and had nothing else to do. And so we also
organised several other exhibitions. I remember that
in 1934, when Moholy-Nagy had fled the country, I
made an exhibition of his work, including 'The Light
Machine', which caused so much commotion. But
then it didn't work. We borrowed it again in 1961 for
"Bewogen Beweging" [Moving Movement] and then
it did work. I also made an exhibition about the initiator of De Stijl, Theo van Doesburg. That was five years
after his death, around 1936. So we didn't just con-
centrate on organising exhibitions for members of the
VANK, but did all sorts of things. I always worked very
closely with Paul Bromberg for that, and it was a very
enjoyable collaboration.

So when I later actually became curator of the museum, I already knew the staff and I remember that one of those people said to me: *Well sir, I would never have thought it, you becoming a civil servant.*

One day in 1937, I received a message from Baard's successor, D.C. Röell[4], who had become director of the Municipal Museums, that he would like to talk to me. I went to him and he said: *Look here, my curator, Van Regteren Altena, has been made a professor. So I am looking for a replacement. Do you have any ideas?* Well, I listed everybody I knew in the museum business and each time he said: *No.* Then I said: *I've delved into my memory and named everybody in this business, but you don't want any of them. So, I can't help you.* As I left he said: *Think about it.* I said: *There's nothing to think about. I've listed everybody I know.* Well, I arrived home, my wife had just started cooking and I told her my story in the kitchen. Then she said: *Now you're the one being dense. He meant you, of course.* I said: *Me? In a museum? No, I really can't imagine anything like that. And becoming a civil servant? No, no.* The next day, Röell phoned me: Have you given it any thought? I said: *Yes, but I really can't help you. Only, my wife thinks you mean me. — Well, didn't you understand that?* I said: *But you didn't say that?* To which Röell said: *Will you*

4. Jhr. David Cornelis Röell (1894–1961), was director of the Stedelijk Museum from 1936 until 1945. He was well-known for his innovations, international exhibitions and purchases. From 1945 until 1959 he was director of the Rijksmuseum.

give it some more thought? And I thought about it. For three days. Then I said to him: *Well, as long as I don't have to apply, and if I can continue doing my design work alongside the work for the museum if that's possible, then I'll do it.*

Röell was a man with very special qualities. He was somebody from the nineteenth century, who called his staff by their first names and devoted a large part of his life to the museum. Also with the major exhibitions that he made himself: "Twee eeuwen Engelsche Kunst, Honderd jaar Fransche Kunst, Rondom Rodin" [Two centuries English Art, One hundred years French Art, Around Rodin] and so on. He thought these up and implemented them. He was our director from 1936 to 1945, five of those years during the war. He did speak up for himself then. At first he studied, if I remember correctly, law in Utrecht, but did not finish his degree. Then he went into training in the Louvre and after that he became Curator of the Rijksmuseum. He succeeded Baard as director of the Municipal Museums.

I actually rolled through everything, I would almost say, through the war and the occupation, for I naturally had the inclination to flee when I started at the museum, but there was so much else to do, I will come back to this later. I went to Spain during the Civil War, I made all sorts of trips and then there was the matter of storing the art treasures during wartime and so on. Anyway, the museum profession, the real museum profession, had become something completely different. Then came the occupation. I spent two years in hiding. Then came the liberation and after the libera-

tion I became director. So I really just rolled into the
museum business. And since I came from outside,
had had no training for it, possessed no history, I was
able to do things in my own way. It was not until I was
thirty–five that I somehow found my feet. That's why
I understand the youth of today so well… you don't
know where you are. You don't know where you're
going, where you can apply that strange complexity
of talents and non-talents that you have in your possession. In any case, it took me a long time before I
found my feet. In my graphic designs and so on, which
gradually and very unexpectedly transformed into a
museum job. I had doubts for a long time: *where will
this take me, what will happen to you, where will you
end up. But I wouldn't want to call it fear.*

For us, money was extremely tight, but I always
thought: I can still earn a living. I did not know how or
where, but that's why I did all sorts of strange things.
I gave a lot of lectures about natural medicine and I
also started studying psychology — I was then 33.
I trod a lot of paths that led nowhere, simply because
you didn't know where the knowledge would fit in.

As subsidiary study to psychology, I did art history.
For that I attended the seminars of Professor Vogelsang for two years. This made me see very clearly
that that kind of art history meant absolutely nothing.
Vogelsang simply showed you a magic lantern
picture which you had to describe from top to bottom
and he occasionally interrupted. If for example you
said: *In the middle of the table, there is a beaker,* then
he would correct you: *Goblet.* Things like that. It was
purely describing art works. I still hear that now. I

mean: that's the whole point, that kind of description has nothing to do with art. Nothing about the emotion, the encouragement, about the stimulus that might be expressed, which in my mind was the only important thing.

From all the different paths I followed and which proved to be dead ends, I was slowly able to conclude what I *should* do. In fact, all those odd jumps were very important. I had a bachelor's degree in philosophy, I had studied old Netherlandish law and I had learned there what teaching was. The professor followed the classic manner. He had seventy students in front of him and he never knew where he had left off last time. He had no idea whatsoever of where he was going, but he held a conversation and developed a theme and made people think. So everybody had to take part in that conversation, had to answer. And he knew how to lead the discussion. That is the platonic method, but Plato said that he had learned it from Socrates. But I had never seen it done. Never experienced it.

The man later became a Nazi, unfortunately, just like my other professor, but I was deeply impressed by what I learned there. How you can clarify something for a lot of people. He was dealing with old Netherlandish law, something which in principle didn't interest me one bit, but the way in which he knew how to develop it! I thought it was wonderful.

When I retired from the Stedelijk Museum in 1962, I said to myself: I will never take another job. I have done this for 25 years, that was enough and I simply just wanted to be a designer again. Until, a year later,

I received a letter — I hadn't been in Canada long at the time — whether I would like to come to Israel for two or three weeks, to Jerusalem. They were building a new museum. They had a whole lot of questions and whether I could give them some advice. Then I wrote back: *Yes, please!* I was invited with my wife. When I had replied *yes, please,* I received a second letter which said: *We asked you to come here for two or three weeks, but after further consultation, we could actually use you permanently. Would you like to come for two years?* Then I said: *We'll have to talk about it.*

We reached agreement on the condition I wrote in my agreement: *You may fire me any day, I may go any day.* But when I arrived in Jerusalem in 1964, they said: *Yes, we talked about two years, but we actually meant five.* I answered: *That's too long, let us stick to two years. We can always see how things turn out.* Well, those two years turned into four and a half.

Then I returned here. I had made a trip around the world and meanwhile letters had also arrived in Jerusalem. Whether I would like to come to Harvard for six months and give lessons and lectures there and to work with students. On the one hand, I didn't want to do it. I think earning your living by talking to people is boring work. But on the other hand, the contact with young people and particularly because so much was happening at the universities in America — here as well, by the way — that appealed to me. I really wanted to know what students in America looked like, how they reacted, how you could work with them. So I said yes.

I went there in 1968 and introduced myself with

the words: *Born in 1897 in the provincial city of Amersfoort, in Holland. 25 years earlier, Piet Mondrian was born in the same city. Christened Protestant, conceived and born in sin, and inclined to all evil. Grew up in the shadow of sin. Until I rebelled and became an unbeliever. I was then sixteen. I am still inclined towards evil. The servants at home were called by their first names, but they didn't call my parents and us children by our first names. In this way, I was inducted into the existence of class, and fascinated by the problems of equality. When I was twenty, during the First World War, the Russian Revolution took place. I was a soldier at the time.*

With these words, and naturally a lot more, I introduced myself to my students at Harvard. I thought, in fact, that they had the right to know who I was, where I came from, and what I could perhaps tell them. For them, I was a complete oddball. I knew the professors, but I couldn't expect the students to have ever heard of me. That's why I thought it right to start with an explanation of myself and my life, my ideas, my work etcetera. I think it hit home. At least, many felt the need to listen to what I had to say.

REGIMEN

I was often very ill as a boy, I always suffered from headaches. At the same time, I also played a lot of football and I went to bed very late, because I read at night, right through my time at grammar school. But I really had the feeling that I wasn't very healthy. I didn't like meat, I had once seen a chicken slaughtered. I like animals very much. I had always wanted to be a vegetarian. But that's quite a step, particularly when you live in lodgings. At the time, I lived in Amsterdam, on the Herengracht. Then you don't easily get round to it. It was very difficult to get vegetarian food. I'm talking about 1918–1919.

I got married in 1920. I left the Academy and went to Italy. We went by foot all the way along the Riviera, from Genoa. When we got to Pisa, I thought it was such a beautiful city and wonderful surroundings, that we rented an apartment nearby, on the coast. It cost 25 guilders a month, a furnished apartment on the beach, in Marina di Pisa. I think that was in October, November. It was beautiful weather, and it stayed that way throughout the month of November. In December, it suddenly turned cold. I looked to see whether there was some sort of stove, but there wasn't even a hole in the wall through which you could stick a pipe. It was, quite simply, impossible to heat. The Italians, particularly at that time, were far more impervious to the cold than to the heat. The people sat in the street and it wasn't so very cold there. But in the houses, which were completely constructed against the warmth, with their stone floors, walls and attics, it was cellar temperature. We made do with a primus stove, but I have never in my life been as cold as in the winter of

1920–1921, when we lived there near the beach.

Until, around February, it started to get warm again and I could go swimming. Then it was over. But in those few months I suffered endless cold and what's more, you were overrun by fleas. For as soon as it turned cold, all the fleas came from the beach into the house. And in our house, thanks probably to the primus, it was slightly warmer than on the beach. I know that you could easily catch forty fleas in the morning from off your shirt. They had been stunned by the cold at night. Then they couldn't jump away so quickly and you could easily catch them. But in any case, it was a most unpleasant experience. In Pisa, I started painting and in particular drawing. I made a lot of portraits at that time. A whole series of self portraits. Highly academic, neat portraits. It is strange how an academic training restricts one, it is difficult to break free of it. Later, I often spoke of this with Campendonk. You actually learn to draw so well that it is extremely difficult to conquer it. Similarly, at the start of my typography I would draw my letters so neatly and that's why I began to tear them. Then they couldn't be so neat anymore. That is one of the reasons why I later always tore letters, because I could draw them so well.

Anyway, in the spring I felt terrible and I went to Switzerland, to Locarno. I really wanted to undergo treatment there, but I had something against doctors. During my military service, I had a nose operation, because the doctors said that this was the cause of my headaches. My nasal septum was crooked. They sawed in my nose and the doctor said: *Good, come back in fourteen days.* After fourteen days I went back and he started sawing in my nose again. Then he said: *Come back in fourteen days.* I came back again, and he set to work and said: *Come back in fourteen days.* Then I never went back. That is actually the last time I ever saw a doctor, because it started to annoy me.

So I didn't really know which path to follow in Locarno. I don't believe in coincidence, but one evening I met a German opera singer, who had settled down there after he retired. He said: *Gosh, aren't you feeling very well? But then you should go to Jungborn in the Harz. They cured my mother-in-law with an apple cure and it cured me of goodness knows what. Why don't you go there?* Anyway, he gave me the address in Jungborn in the Harz. The next day, I wrote to that place and requested a prospectus. I received it several days later and it said that there were all sorts of nature parks where people could walk around naked. You also had all sorts of diet possibilities and there was a little sentence: *People who fast for more than three days, pay half board.* I laughed myself silly at that, but thought: well, I won't find it here, so I might as well go there. So we went there. I don't really like the Harz, all those bushes and the rather shabby woods, but the surroundings are very beautiful. I loved the gentle slopes of the hills. I did a lot of walking there. There were around three hundred guests in that Naturheilsanatorium. But I really didn't like the conversation at table.

Just imagine: it was the summer of 1921, people had endured hardship for years and now they were on holiday. They thought they were entitled to a steak and all sorts of tasty things, and there they were on a diet: they had to crack nuts and eat wholegrain bread and stuff like that. The whole conversation at table revolved around these things and how at home they fried delicious things in butter, etcetera. So, I looked around a bit and went to the nature parks, where the people walked around naked, and I saw people who were never at the dining table. Then I asked them: *What do you do exactly? — Well, we're fasting.* I spoke to the people and thought: maybe that's something. I found a library and there was a whole shelf with books about fasting and about the Mazdaznan natural healing method[5]. I read them all in fourteen days and then I said to my wife: *You know what? I'm going to fast.* And so I fasted for ten days. Now I should say that after all those operations, my nose never healed properly. The wound was still open, and if I sat in a train — in those days the trains were terribly dusty — then the next day I had a swollen nose. In addition, I had a thyroid disorder and I hadn't the least idea what to do about it.

After ten days of fasting, that had improved slightly, but when I slowly started to resume eating, the first day a bowl of soup, the second day two bowls and the third three, I noticed that I still didn't feel how I wanted to feel. But I progressed slowly. I ate for fourteen days. Then a few friends came to visit from Holland and we

5. Mazdaznan, founded by Otto Ha'nisch or Hanisch, is a religious movement focusing on physical and mental well-being through various comprehensive and varied therapies.

went somewhere and ate strawberries and cream. The next day I felt really awful, it came out of every orifice. Then I said to my wife: *You know what, I'm going to fast again.* And I fasted for twenty days.

Now that fasting is, in itself, nothing to speak of. You don't eat, you only drink a little water, and that's it. Hunger? Well yes, for the first two days you feel hungry, because you are used to the rhythm of three meals a day, but you soon forget it. The odd thing is that when you begin to eat again you feel terribly hungry after your first bowl of soup. Then you really have to control yourself. Then you have to realise that you'll have to wait for the next day when you may get two bowls of soup and the day after that three. If you violate that, it naturally could be dangerous, but other than that, I don't think there is any risk involved. And if you die from it, you can be sure of a painless death. For if you haven't eaten anything for some time, you don't feel anything, and you aren't bothered by pain or the like anymore. But what I did learn is that, during such a fasting cure, the body eats itself. Digestion continues and you live off yourself. You have to be a little careful with that. Naturally, you gradually become a little weak in the knees. After you've been fasting for a week, you shouldn't climb a lot of stairs. But I can tell you that after twenty days of fasting, I could take a fifteen minute walk, if the road wasn't uphill. Then I slowly resumed eating and with that, I was freed of all my problems. My nose healed, my thyroid condition cleared up. I could wear a collar two sizes smaller, and since then I have always felt fine. A result of that fasting, which I hadn't expected and about which I had read nothing, was that you felt so incredibly clear in your head and that before making a decision you saw things so very clearly. If you want to work something out, fasting is a wonderful aid. At a later age, I took my bachelor in law. Now I used to get very anxious and nauseous when sitting examinations, but when I sat my bachelor papers, I said to my wife: *I'm going to fast.* Then she said: *Yes, but there in Utrecht you'll have to climb all those stairs to sit the exam. What if you only ate fruit?*

Then I only ate fruit for ten days and I wasn't the least bit nervous about the exam and got through it easily. Another, completely unexpected result of fasting was that I no longer stuttered. I always used to stutter, particularly when I was nervous. Let's say, when I was standing at the ticket window in a station and had to buy a train ticket, then I would begin to stutter and couldn't say the name of the place I was trying to go to. That disappeared completely. A third thing was that, whereas previously my school German didn't get me hardly anywhere, after the fasting cure I spoke fluent German and I have always kept it up to scratch since then.

You can actually best learn languages while you're fasting and while you constantly hear the language all around you. It becomes a part of yourself and you speak it easily and automatically. There are really two methods for learning a language. I don't mean the school method but: either you fall in love with a woman from that country, or you fast. Naturally the first method is awkward if you want to learn two languages at once. Two women at once is not very practical.

That reminds me of an old gentleman who told such a story at the opening of an exhibition. He was a lace collector from London. We exhibited his collection and he came here to open the exhibition. Then he began in the same way and said, without us having spoken about it: *Look, I have, I think, learned ten languages in my life, but I am now over eighty. I know that if you can fall in love with a woman from that country, that's the easiest way to learn a language and to address you here in Dutch. But there is also an age limit to it.*

As I have already mentioned, I became a vegetarian in 1920 — I was 22 at the time — but after the fasting cure, I couldn't bear the sight of meat. There was no question about eating meat. I remember, many years later, ordering a mushroom croquette in Brussels and somehow or other they had put mince in it. I immediately burst out in a rash all over my arm. So I had gradually become allergic to meat.

Now I think there's a whole lot connected with that way of life. I have always been affected by what Gandhi said about it. Gandhi, when talking about doctors, said: *I first felt very attracted to the profession, but I soon saw that it was not an honourable profession. The medicine of the West is only concerned with alleviating the complaints, and not at all with dealing with the causes of diseases. Those causes are generally bad habits — he called them sins — to allow a patient to give himself over to those habits without danger. That is why medicine demoralises people. They weaken them and prevent people from keeping their body and mind under control. Illness is not just a consequence of our actions but also of our thoughts. It is*

May I give a small example to illustrate this,
I would almost call it Gandhi's aggressive condemna-
tion of the medicine practised by doctors? I had close
acquaintances with a weak stomach, but whenever
they saw a good meal in front of them, they couldn't
resist eating everything and drinking enough with it.
Then they would have to swallow carbon tablets or
something similar. This is exactly what Gandhi meant
when he said that medicine is primarily intended to
allow people to sin. It is remarkable that, several centuries earlier, Voltaire also spoke of this. Voltaire said:
our health depends on three things: frugality, sobriety
and exercise. It is sufficient to give nature a helping
hand, for it is always ready to cure us of our complaints. And Hippocrates, a few thousand years earlier,
around 500 BC, speaks of the Egyptians, who believe
that all illnesses are caused by incorrect food. I don't
believe it is as simple as that, but I have to say that I
did apply it to myself. And that I always fared well by
doing so. In the years between 1924 and 1926, I gave
a lot of lectures throughout the country about natural
medicine, in all the small provincial towns. There was
a lot of interest and I told people what was possible,
but I never tried to convert people or to persuade
them to follow my example. Not even in my own family. If my children or my wife wanted to eat meat,
I always thought: that is up to them. For I don't believe
that everybody is born to be a vegetarian. I believe
that I was born that way, as herbivore, but that other

people are born as carnivores, and that you can't simply impose it on people. But for me, this has been the way to live my life.

So, whenever I didn't feel well, I always turned to fasting. I helped myself overcome it and never saw a doctor for any illness. Except, much later in life, I went to the hospital twice for a check up. I always felt fine. Without recommending anybody to do the same, for you have to decide for yourself. I did, for example, when they asked me to take on the museum in Jerusalem, think things over very carefully. For when I took my leave of the Stedelijk Museum, I promised myself never to take another job. On the other hand, I adopted the principle you should respond to every request, that you must always remain available, amenable for things. So those two principles came into conflict with each other. Then I fasted for ten days and I took the decision to go to Jerusalem. And I have never regretted that decision.

After Jungborn we first returned to Italy, but my wife didn't want to have our child in an Italian hospital — she thought they were all very dirty. That child was Helga. And so we went to Herrliberg in Switzerland. The European centre of the Mazdaznan movement was located there. That is a movement based on natural medicine, but it also included a philosophy, with a religious background. There was a leader, who lived in America, Dr. Ha'nish who was addressed as 'Master' by his disciples. Now first of all, a leader and what's more somebody who is addressed as 'Master' is something to which I immediately object. But I knew the man well and I felt that there were a lot of good ideas in that Mazdaznan movement. It was in the context of that movement, which I introduced here in the Netherlands, that I gave those lectures. Until I had had enough of it all. For you found yourself in an environment of disease and that is exactly the environment that I dislike. I prefer to live among the healthy.

Probably also as a consequence of my fasting, I had acquired some sort of gift of being able to read somebody's disease in their face. If you're sitting in a tram or in a train and you see the people opposite you with all their illnesses — of which they are hopefully unaware — it becomes something of an obsession. So for me it felt like salvation to stop. I completely lost that gift. It would require considerable effort to regain it.

But there are all sorts of occult matters that were involved in this. I remember for example one experience. I was in London, it was in 1924. It was my first time in England, at a congress for natural medicine. Then the chairman of that congress suddenly said: *Yes, we have among us today Mr. Sandberg from Amsterdam, and he will tell us about the situation on the continent.* Well, all I had to do was to stand up. It was the first time I had to speak English and so I stood up. I told my story and sat down again. At the exit there was a fat lady with a red face, who jovially pumped my hand. (Recently I saw her photograph in the newspaper. She turned out to be Annie Besant, from the circle around Krishnamurti.) The following summer I met her on a terrace, somewhere on the lake of Zurich. I was sitting there with a few friends and she said to me: *Mr. Sandberg, I heard you in Lon-*

don and you have a gift for speaking. You only have to stand before your audience, have no intentions and then everything will be all right. Well, I never believed in that and it is certainly not true, but I was impressed by it for quite some time. Apparently so much so that when I held a lecture shortly after in Delft — that was in a small crowded room on a canal — two gentlemen approached me afterwards on the canal outside and said: *Were you inspired this evening?* I said: *Inspired? Inspired? Well, you must have heard it, yes or no? I wasn't aware of it. — Yes, we're spiritualists and, as you were speaking, we saw a woman standing behind you.* Then they described the woman to me — a fat lady with a red face. *You occasionally moved forward, and then the lady was standing behind you, and when you leant against the wall she disappeared.* I then said: *Well, the lady you describe once told me that I should simply stand in front of my audience and start talking. Then it would turn out well. Perhaps in some way or another I unconsciously thought of that lady, when I was standing there in front of you, but I certainly never took it into account.* I found it a remarkable experience. I also thought it remarkable that some ghost or other or, I don't know, an apparition was also linked to a body and needed room for the corpulence. When I moved forward, she could stand behind me, and when I stood against the wall, she disappeared. This was one of the many experiences I had with the lectures I held during those years.

I think it was in that same summer of 1922 that Johannes Itten of the Bauhaus in Weimar came to Herrliberg, with some twenty students. Of those, the

ones I still know are Mordechai Ardon and Paul Citroen.
I had then, in Herrliberg, just learned composing and
printing. And I made use of that, from 1924 to 1926, to
publish a Mazdaznan magazine.

Those Itten pupils from the Bauhaus in Herrliberg
were all dressed the same: wide trousers and Russian
shirts, with short hair and a bang fringe in front,
almost a cap. I joined in their lessons — we drew with
both hands at once using charcoal, with the narrow
or sharp end and the broad end. All shadings, all ways
to express something in charcoal. At certain times,
the lessons were interrupted to do other exercises
with movement and breathing and so on. My wife
(this was still my first wife; we divorced in 1926 and I
remarried a year later) later invited Itten to come to
Holland to speak about Mazdaznan. At the time he
also worked on the New Art School of Paul Citroen.
In 1938 he was in Holland, because he had to take
refuge since his Itten School in Berlin had been closed
down by the Nazis.

THE TASK OF THE MUSEUM DIRECTOR

When I retired as director of the Stedelijk Museum in 1962, I was presented with the so-called Sandberg collection and I gave this to the museum. I believe that that collection arose from friendship. They were all gifts. It was an idea of Ger Lataster and Bill Couzijn who had discussed it with a whole lot of other artists. Some made a gift of magnificent items, others gave less important things. The only link is that I have been friends with a whole lot of artists. Lataster and Couzijn brought everything together. They proposed all sorts of names and then came with new names. They said that I only had a veto in the matter. I didn't draw up the list in the sense of: you should approach these people. They did that all by themselves.

I think it is a very nice collection, because it contains all my friendships and because I think that a museum director must really first and foremost live with the artists. If he wants to understand anything about a museum, so actually show the creativity of a period, then he must try to uncover the secrets of creativity. What intrigued me most during my career as museum director is: how is it possible that certain people make something in a spirit that has never been expressed before? How is it possible that people make a contribution to the development of art, or let me put it another way: on making something visible that inspires us all? Now there are many different theories about making something visible that inspires us all. Is it the artist who depicts in advance what is going to happen or is it that which is in the air every-where, but which nobody has yet given form, which has not yet become visible and which is suddenly given shape by the artist?

I believe it is the latter. I do not believe that an artist is a prophet, who sees the future, but he does have longer feelers than the normal person and therefore feels more clearly what is happening at any given moment. He knows how to find a form, a sound, a colour and a story for that and to express that, to make it visible, audible, tangible. That whole puzzle, on the one hand, often has little to do with the character or the lives of the people who bring this about, but on the other hand, it demands an enormous strength of character to persevere. For when we look at the careers of the great masters of painting and sculpture, then the majority only developed art further at a certain moment, mainly during their youth. A very small minority has gone further and continued to develop right up to their deaths. For me, those are the truly great artists. And by that I mean: somebody who makes a contribution to the development of art. The others I would simply call painters and sculptors.

I have gained in all those years a whole complexity of experiences by speaking with many of these people. I entered this world late in life — I was forty — but I still have had the opportunity to speak to all sorts of people who were, at the time, considered great masters. I think of Kandinsky, Léger, Brancusi, Mondrian and many others, who I have known personally. I became intimate friends with some of them. The conversations, the work and how the work slowly arises and develops, are all issues that have intensely occupied me.

I have always tried to acquire the core works for

the museum: if you pick the right moment, when somebody begins a new development and becomes himself, the moment at which he makes his contribution. There are, as I said, only a very few people who have continued to do this throughout their lives. One of those people is Mondrian. Mondrian was always able to develop further right up to his death, because he had set his aim so far away. It was probably an unreachable aim: to recreate the space, actually: to create a new space.

He hesitated for a long time — until he was nearly forty — about which direction to take. He first painted small still lifes and landscapes, made portraits. He then became an expressionist. After his expressionism, he began painting as a cubist, after he had seen the cubists in Paris, around 1909. (He made something very personal of cubism, but it remains based on what Picasso had discovered.) Until suddenly, after he had come to Holland on holiday in 1914 and became imprisoned here or rather, could not return to France because of the First World War. Then he set to work here in his loneliness and he came upon abstraction. He actually became the great leader of abstract art, what people in America call the 'hard edge painting'.

It is remarkable that in those first works after 1915 a great liberation took place. Those are large colour planes which were first isolated from each other on the white canvas and then slowly the black lines come in. But they remain large planes which he wants to separate with lines and the colour of which, actually the purity of the colour, is retained by the black lines. But then, particularly in the 'thirties, the lines begin to

dominate and it is almost — and perhaps that is the
whole constellation of the era, the emergence of
national socialism, the reaction that was then vented
— as if he felt as if he were in a cage and for more
than ten years that cage grew gradually smaller.
Those black lines were simply bars. They became the
bars of a cage, until, in America, he found an environment that perfectly suited him. There everything is
built based on the square, the rectangle. If you look at
the street map of New York or if you imagine New
York by night and you see all those square illuminated
windows in the dark, then you understand the enormous inspiration that Mondrian experienced. And
when, in 1943, he saw that the war was really taking
a turn for the better and when the allies gained the
upper hand after Stalingrad, he painted, without ever
knowing peace, his 'boogie-woogies'. Maybe the
"Victory Boogie Woogie", his victorious boogie-
woogie, is indeed one of his masterpieces. Gradually,
the bars are disappearing. They turn grey and there is
a wonderful flourishing of colour. Of course they still
remain squares and rectangles, but the paintings are
fascinating. It is almost as if Mondrian is cheering at a
late age. I think it's wonderful. If we look at the developments, particularly from his cubist period from
1909–1920 to the end, in 1944, we see that the man
grew constantly.

And when you knew the man and knew how simple
and modest this man was — which is exceptional
among artists — how full of admiration he was for
people who made things completely different to those
he made himself… For example, the first time I spoke

to him, he suddenly began talking about Kees van Dongen.

Now Van Dongen was, as somebody who was completely focused on effect and advertising, in essence the greatest contrast, the greatest antithesis to Mondrian. I was therefore very surprised and expressed as much, and then Mondrian said: *Yes, but look at it. Van Dongen did begin to simplify things, simplify the colours, the lines. He went in the right direction and that is important.* This modesty shown by the man Mondrian, who lived as it were as a sort of monk in his white cell, with all those paintings in primary colours, red, blue, yellow, and white of course, all this makes the image of the man wonderfully complete. And it is extraordinarily rare.

One of the other people who continued growing right through to the end is, perhaps, Paul Klee. He too started developing late. He was already in his thirties when as soldier in the First World War he was allocated to an air force division deep in Germany and found himself. Then he became the Paul Klee we all admire so much. For the largest part of his life he made tiny paintings. Somebody who had visited him – I think it was Campendonk who told me this – in the years before the First World War, I think in 1911, he said: *yes, he couldn't have made large things in that small apartment he had.* He only had a small corner of a desk on which to paint. He had no room to put his colours. They hung in the attic. Most of the space was taken up by his wife's grand piano, because she earned the family's income by giving piano lessons.

This man continued to work in a tiny size until,

at the end of the 'thirties, he fled Germany and arrived in Switzerland. He was never granted citizenship there, because he had no means of support. Now they would be proud if Klee had been Swiss. Then he contracted a disease. I don't know what disease it was, but his skin tightened. This meant that his movements were no longer supple and he couldn't make tiny things any more. He could no longer draw those precise lines. And so he then used, to his mind, those very large canvases and I would almost say his illness had made him greater. I believe his last canvases are among his very best. He did not live to an old age I believe, he was sixty or sixty–one when he died, but he was one of those people who kept growing until the very end.

The third example I would like to mention is Pierre Bonnard. He was also a very modest, very private man. I didn't know him, but he was often described to me by friends. Bonnard was a man who lived completely in colour. For him, colour was everything. Except when he was working on a painting, he always had one of the walls of his studio covered with a long canvas. When he had found a new colour, he would walk along that wall to see where he could apply that new colour from his palette to the painting. When he had progressed a long way with that very large canvas, he would cut it into pieces and transform those pieces into paintings. A very unusual way of working.

He is also somebody who continued developing until the end of his life — and he lived to be eighty — but he didn't have a very early development. Perhaps that is one of the solutions. I have seen so many

others attempt to get going and then, after a short
period of years, after the 'Sturm und Drang', fall away
to nothing. One of the remarkable experiences is that
you discover that the tendency of the artist is not
what matters, but that it far more depends on, how
shall I put it, on character: how a person only lives for
what he does, concentrates on that, and doesn't in
the slightest yearn for success or publicity or anything
else. There are, of course, always exceptions that
prove the rule: I think that Picasso occasionally
indulged in publicity. He was still a great master. The
people who really were great masters and continued
to develop until the very end, were all people of strong
character, who lived for their art. They may perhaps
have wanted to become well known or famous, but
they didn't do anything about it.

We must talk as well about the museum itself and
about its history. I thought the exterior of the building
was appalling. The only good thing about it, to me,
was the contrast. Older people still remember how,
when you entered the building through those heavy
wooden doors, you found yourself in a hall, a hall with
a staircase leading to an upper hall. This was made
completely of bricks, red with yellow stripes, and there
were green tiles in the arches above the doors. And
the fan-light, at the top of the stairs, was made of
yellow glass.

And this treatment was not restricted to the
entrance hall and the stairway; many other rooms on
either side, upstairs and downstairs, were decorated
in an identical way. When I entered for the first time
on 1 January, 1938, I thought: this is the first thing that

will have to be changed. I raised it with Röell, my director, and he said: *Yes, I'm working on it and we have made some tests for it and also for new corridors.* The doors were extremely tall. Riders on horses could have passed through them, or people riding on an elephant, they could go through without ducking their heads. The doors were also often in the wrong place. Only, the thing I noticed at once was that the light in the upper halls, the light from above, was fantastically good. I have never seen a museum anywhere in the world where the top lighting was so excellent. The old Mr Weissman, the architect of the museum and founder, I believe, of Heemschut[6], had calculated it superbly. He had visited various museums in Europe and in particular studied the lighting there. He made all sorts of sketches about the light incidence and even wrote a brochure about it. He looked at it exceptionally well, so that the light did not fall on the floor but on the walls and was at its strongest exactly where you would hang something. He had also taken a close look at artists' studios. It is very similar to that, with this distinction, that studios at that time never had top lights. They had light from the side. High side light, and if the artists were poor, they worked in a normal small room with side light. I knew a sculptor's studio with top light, but knew of no painters' studios with top light.

We have to pause here for a moment, for this later

6. The Heemschut association was founded in 1911, to protect and preserve national monuments. It is still active today and mainly run by volunteers.

inspired me when I built the New Wing. Especially when artists produce slightly fatty paintings, with a lot of brush oil paint, the paint forms something of a relief. These reliefs cause shadows, and they were really intended to do this, just think of Van Gogh. Van Gogh never painted with top light but always with side light. I believe that he never actually owned a studio. He simply sat in a room and painted. So if you want to view a real Van Gogh properly, you have to imitate that light. Then the shadow thrown by the stroke of paint is in the right place. The paint stroke was often curled in his work, or in any case had a curve, for Van Gogh probably painted from his wrist. You can paint from your wrist or from your elbow or shoulder. This gives you completely different strokes. It is, of course, true that later generations mainly painted from the shoulder and moved the whole arm. He only moved his hand and this causes the typical twist of the brush on the canvas.

And that was also the intention. You see the same thing with Rembrandt, and Hercules Seghers did it very emphatically. It is almost as if he modelled the paint and you sometimes have to see the stroke of the hairs of the brush. He used this to express more clearly what his intention was. I think, for example, of a small painting by Rembrandt in the museum in Krakow, a small landscape, very typical and somewhat in the style of Hercules Seghers, where it is exactly the relief of the paint stroke that makes an incredible contribution to the total effect of the thing. Good, just a side remark about that top light, but if you accept top lighting for a museum — which I do not, but we'll get to

that later — then this is, in my opinion, ideal top lighting. There have been several museum builders who
have visited the Stedelijk Museum to study how
Weissman had made the top lighting. And also the
northern light in the galleries at the front, both on the
ground floor and on the first floor. That is fantastic.
But what I want to say: the design of the rooms was
good as it was. Weissman had an unusual feeling for
space. When, for example, you turn right at the top of
the stairs — or left, for it is completely symmetrical —
you first enter a square gallery. From there you can
reach the rooms to the left and right. Then you walk
straight ahead and for that he made rectangular
rooms. And when you reach the corner and have to
make a turn, he made a square room and then again
rectangular rooms. He thought of these things
according to the direction you had to take. He had a
feeling for proportions and space. The halls were as
I described them, but the rooms also had panelling
and that was painted in a purple brown. Above it there
was a rather impoverished green grey velvet.

The various rooms were exactly the same and
then you looked up to the whole mechanics of lighting. We have tried to eliminate the wrong things and
to accentuate the good things. My first idea was to
paint over the bricks. I did some tests for this with the
architect Eschauzier[7]. Then I said to Röell: *Is it alright*

7. Frits Adolf Eschauzier (1889–1957), was a Dutch architect, in the 'forties and 'fifties mainly known as museum
architect and for the redesigning of the Rijksmuseum and
the Stedelijk Museum.

with you if I go over it with the whitewash brush? Well, that made him slightly jumpy. He rather liked the idea, but he was scared of doing it just like that without asking the mayor and aldermen for permission first. Then I said: *I know how to get round it, you take a week's holiday and when you come back you'll see for yourself.* And that's exactly what happened. When he got back from holiday, the whole inside of the museum was painted white. Mayor De Vlugt, who had also been a building contractor himself and thought he knew a lot about building, and who considered the Stedelijk Museum an architectural masterpiece, was furious. He knew I was the guilty one.

At an opening of an exhibition, he came up to me in the evening under full sail and said: *Mister Sandberg, you have painted all this white and I have even heard that you have done this with a paint which can never be removed.* That paint had a specific name.
I then replied: *I have indeed painted it completely white. But you can remove it. And I'll prove it to you.* Then I took him to a corner behind a fire extinguisher and there I removed the paint with a wet finger to prove that it could be removed. Then he was slightly appeased and later we became good friends, particularly during the occupation. For during the occupation — I will return to that later — I was the liaison man between the resistance and Mayor De Vlugt. After he was retired by the Germans, I often visited him in Aerdenhout. He was a terribly nice man, honest, with a certain grandeur. He never meddled with childishness or trifles. He had a certain allure and you miss that sometimes in the current city council. I also got

on well with Wibaut[8]. I know that Wibaut could never
be Mayor for he was a socialist and that was pretty
awful at the time, but Wibaut was called 'the powerful
one' in Amsterdam. And he gave a whole lot of things
to Amsterdam, things we can still be grateful for today.

So that was the story of painting the museum
white. Then we started on the galleries. We first removed the panelling and stretched ordinary jute over
the walls. We then painted it white. There was wood
behind it, so you could always knock nails in it. The
jute was so coarse that when you pulled out the nail
again, you couldn't see the hole. I thought it was a
fantastic wall covering, it is slightly coarse. It comes
closest to a white painted wall, which is always the
finest for paintings. And the fact that there was wood
behind it and you could use nails made it unneces-
sary, as is often seen in so many museums, to hang
the paintings on metal bars or use some other impossible way of hanging them. Then we changed the
doors and slowly — although that only took place a lot
later — we started on the central heating, which stood
in the middle, with those elephant-like seats around it,
laying the pipes under the floor. The parquet flooring
is still the same as it was, but the look of the interior of
the museum has, through the years — and that had
progressed a lot by 1950 — become that of a modern
building. It has the neutral character that allows the

8. Florentinus Marinus Wibaut (1859–1936), Dutch busi-
nessman and politician in Amsterdam for the SDAP (Social Democratic Labour Party), known for his activities as
alderman for residential housing.

art works to speak, it does not speak itself.

I think that is because of the awnings that are stretched above the halls, under the top lights. They have a very restful effect. Sufficient light comes through and the extremely bright light has disappeared. In the past, in the time of director Baard, this was done in the spring by painting the sky-lights in the roof with whitewash — a mixture of chalk and buttermilk. The rain washed it off as the year progressed. By the autumn it was clean again. At that time the light was less bright and you could get through the winter time. The following spring the coating was applied again. The skylight in the hall originally had yellow glass. That was very characteristic. Röell called the upper hall the urine bath. That said it all. It was a really nasty yellow. You couldn't put anything there or hang anything up, because all the colours were distorted and falsified by that infectious yellow. We removed that yellow glass immediately after we had painted the rooms white, and we replaced it with white glass, but then the light was much too bright and we needed a large awning.

At that time, Johannes Itten was in the country. He had fled Germany in 1938. He was one of the first 'Meister', masters of the Bauhaus, from 1919 to 1923. Then he quarrelled with Walter Gropius and with others, because he was somewhat obstinate. Later he founded a Johannes Itten school in Berlin, and at the same time he was a teacher at the textile academy in Krefeld. He was Swiss by birth, not a German. He couldn't stand that Hitler Germany. He had a dictatorial manner himself and two dictators never get on well together, so he came here. He was an old friend of mine and destitute because he had had to flee in a hurry. Then I thought: *gosh, it's nice to have Itten here, let us help him earn some money and get him to design an awning.* And that is exactly what he did. First he thought of making something with Japanese paper and to stick coloured silhouettes on it. We did a test with this. It would have been too heavy, because an awning like that would weigh a lot. Our paperhanger then came up with the idea that we could use very thin gauze, sometimes two layers, sometimes three, to translate Itten's drawing. I think there were blue and red dolls in it, very systematic and also from gauze. That was then held up by a zigzag stretched rope, in the same way we now stretch the normal awnings.

I must stop here for the moment to interject another story. One day, Röell said: *Can't you help us find an upholstery company?* I then phoned my friend Paul Bromberg and he said: *Yes, you should get in touch with mister De Waal.* The first thing had to do with this: we had just dismantled the large seats around the heating, but the heating elements stood on ordinary poured concrete. The parquet flooring started a bit farther away and that concrete surrounding the heating was very ugly. So mats had to be placed over it. The first job for the upholsterer was to make mats for that and so I booked Mr. De Waal. Then two large gentlemen arrived wearing hats, they looked like directors of a fairly large company. Good, Röell explained to them what the mats should look like and how it should be done. Then the men removed their hats and said: *Yes sir. That will be fine,* and they left.

And then Röell said to me: *Yes, but I had expected workers to come, normal upholsterers. This is a business with two directors, how is this going to turn out?* Well, I said, *just you wait and see.* I knew a little about the ins and outs. It will get under way tomorrow and it will be completed by such and such a date, so let's just wait and see what it's like.

Well, the following morning I come upstairs with Röell and there are the two gentlemen, laying on the floor in shirt-sleeves, making the mats. They were De Waal senior and his son. They did a fantastic job and for years on end they recovered all the walls, made all the awnings and also the awning designed by Johannes Itten. That had to be ready by a certain date, for the opening of the exhibition "Honderd jaar Fransche Kunst" [One hundred years French art]. That went from Ingres up to the Impressionists. Picasso wasn't included at the time — you must remember it was 1938. It was a fantastic exhibition. It was opened very officially by ambassadors and I think even Prince Bernhard[9] popped in, or the queen. In any case, it was something magnificent and the awning had to be ready. Day and night, the whole De Waal family, the two gentlemen with their wives, sat at large sewing machines in the Room of Honour in the Stedelijk Museum to get it finished and it did indeed hang there in time for the opening of the exhibition.

9. Prince Bernhard van Lippe-Biesterfeld (1911–2004) was the husband of Princess Juliana, who later, after the death of her mother Wilhelmina, became Queen of the Netherlands.

'Those were in fact the first steps to make the interior of the museum more 'up to date' and through the years we continued this. We always did it together with the architects but never said to them: *Now, I must have it like this or this,* but instead left it to them. We have always managed to bring about a very close collaboration between museum man and architect. I think that is one of the secrets of why it turned out rather well. At the start we had Eschauzier, who later became professor at Delft. He did it until 1956, I think, and then one of his assistants, Bart van Kasteel, took it over. He also modernised and restored the Burgerweeshuis, now the Amsterdam Historical Museum, together with Schipper.

Immediately after the war, there was talk of two museums being built on the Ice Club Ground, as it was called at the time — now Museumplein — on either side of the Museumstraat. At the time it was simply the Ice Club Ground, where grass grew, with a high fence around it. Two museums were to be built opposite the Concertgebouw: one for antique, classical art, so Greek, Roman and perhaps Egyptian — and the East Asian art would also be included — and opposite it, a new municipal museum would be built. In this plan, the current Stedelijk Museum was destined to become the Maritime Museum and the Dutch Museum. Fortunately, I would almost say, nothing came of these plans. There was no money. There wasn't the courage at the time, immediately after the war, to do something new with it. There was still so much to be built and on the other hand I would not have known at the time — 1945–1946 — exactly what

a museum of today should look like. For that I had to
gain a lot of experience. I had to study and look everywhere before I got any idea about that. I learned a lot
from foreign museum directors, in particular Alfred
Barr, and how he fitted out the Museum of Modern
Art in New York. There he included all sorts of things
in the programme: film, photography and manifesta-
tions as regular features, and a decent facility for the
visitors — all things that were still new and you had to
adapt your design to accommodate them.

I was not at all unhappy that I first had to experiment with the old building and later could work on the
New Wing. That became our experimental model for
a new museum and we said: no top light, but side
light. Side light that you can adjust. You could namely
— and this is something that happened here for the
first time — lower the blinds in front of the windows
all the way down and then from the top, lower them
with the rails to which they were attached, so that you
only had high side light. That was therefore one possibility. Then there was my plan for free-standing
partitions that you could move around, standard partitions so that you could have the paintings at right
angles to the windows and never needed to hang
them opposite a window. In that way, you wouldn't get
very much reflection and you could, in my opinion,
easily create a route. I always feel that when you come
into a square or rectangular room, you really have to
walk round it twice. I find that inconvenient and what's
more, you always have paintings behind your back
which you also want to look at. That is annoying.
Of course, when you have top lighting you can fill the

walls with paintings on all sides, but when you have side light, the windows at least stop you from completely filling the walls. I think in general museums crowd things together too much. So I wanted to achieve a more ethereal arrangement for exhibitions. The width was, in relationship to the height, calculated to give enough light in the middle of the room. You could still hang a painting high enough there so that it could be seen clearly, while the windows themselves were far enough apart, with around fourteen metres between them. You're not hindered by them and you can always cover them with the aluminium blinds. It is an exhibition set-up that is as elastic as possible and we worked it out and carried it out together with Eschauzier. It was difficult, at first there was a lot of money, then little. Then they scaled down again and afterwards it turned out that there was more money again. Whatever, it was often subject to change. Eschauzier was only allowed to do the interior and the city architect had to be responsible for the exterior.

At first, the city architect was Ir. Hulshoff, and later Leupen took over from him. Anyway, we worked together quite well, we just didn't understand each other. We spoke two different languages. The city wanted those big windows, but then divided into small panes which could, if you wanted, be covered with cardboard instead of closing them off with blinds. I didn't like that at all. I wanted large panes of glass and it took me a year to convince the city that the windows belonged to the interior, not to the exterior. A fortunate coincidence was that we wanted, together with Eschauzier, Leupen and with Sargentini, who I believe was also with us, to take a look at the sculpture room in the Kröller-Müller Museum in Otterlo, to see how it was done there. I wasn't particularly happy with that sculpture room, but we drove there together in the museum's van. And on the way, the engine broke down. We were stranded and couldn't go any further. Then we found a taxi and that took us to Kröller-Müller. But because of this we were far too late and we stopped on the way back to get something to eat. And we accompanied that meal with quite a few glasses of old jenever and that brought us into the mood that the windows were deemed part of the work of the interior designer and not of the exterior architect.

About the New Wing: okay, there are all sorts of things that could have been better, for example the pillars in the lower floor could have been eliminated. You could have constructed things so that no pillars were required. You could span that fourteen metres. I saw a span in Paris of 34 metres. But at the start there were all sorts of financial difficulties. We went from a steel construction to concrete, from concrete back to steel, and then again from steel to concrete, all because the Korean war had made steel so expensive. That is why the pillars that weren't there at first were introduced later. But I still think that the principle of the building is very good — when it is used properly and people hang as few paintings as possible opposite windows, in other words give them side light. Then I think it suffices well.

Since 1954, when the New Wing was opened, I was overrun by museum directors and architects

who wanted to build new museums. I think of the
Museum Folkwang in Essen, the Maison de la Culture
in Le Havre, the museum in Vienna and Scandinavian
museums. Everybody first came to visit the Stedelijk
Museum to see how it was done here and adopted the
principle either fully or partially. Actually it was adopted in its purest form for the Museum of Modern Art in
Rio. I was in Rio in 1953 as commissioner of the Dutch
department of the Biennial in São Paulo and then the
architect Alfonso Reidy asked me to look at the model
of the new museum with him. We looked at it together,
it was still rather schematic. Then he said: *What do
you think about the light and what should it be like?*
Then I told him what I thought about it and later he
thought that was the best solution. Later, when I
returned there in 1955, he had completely redrawn it
that way. After that, he came to Amsterdam to view it
here and also to look at the artificial lighting. We
worked together on the museum in Rio in an extremely
convivial way. It is a very big museum and it is located
in the centre of the city. In earlier times, it had been
sea, but they sawed off the top of one of those sugar
breads, the large mountains that stood on the water,
and threw it into the sea. And there, in the middle
of the city, at the end of the Avenida Rio Branco, they
built the Museum of Modern Art. It took a very long
time. When I last visited Rio, in 1966, it still wasn't
finished, but I later heard that it was completed and
that it was very satisfactory. I believe it is one of the
very good modern museums. For in South America
you see a lot of very large and expensive buildings,
but the study of museum techniques is, actually,

not used very much.

Another museum that adopted the principle of our New Wing is the Musée des Arts Populaires, the Museum of Folk Art in Paris. They started building it in 1952. The curator was George Henri Rivière and we spoke a lot about what that museum could look like. It has not become an ideal building; in my opinion, the architecture is somewhat too classical. But it is, in any case, a building of our time. In this museum, the emphasis is not on art works, but on objects of handicraft, cottage industry and tradition. And everything we could possibly find out about exhibiting and allowing those objects to come into their own was studied exceptionally well there. All the accessories are superbly executed. It is one of the best studied museums I have ever seen. That is because the whole thing here came about in a close collaboration between architect and museum man.

A museum is simply not a subject for a competition. You may perhaps be able to create a multiple commission by calling for idea sketches so that you can choose the architect, but the whole execution of the museum plan has to be done by the architect and museum man together. As long, of course, as the museum man is able to read architectural drawings, which is not always the case. Look, the large windows in the New Wing of the Stedelijk Museum were not only intended to provide light for the paintings and objects on display there. They were also intended to allow people to look in and see what was happening inside. If they didn't like what they saw, they could remain outside and if they saw something that appealed to them, they could come in. So they could also profit from things without paying any entrance fee.

One of the main principles of museum policy was that I wanted to involve the passer-by and the man in the street in the museum. That is why the heavy wooden doors at the entrance to the old building were removed. We put in glass there, so that people could look inside. And we also made the New Wing completely from glass so that people can see everything from the Van Baerlestraat and from the other side, the museum garden, which they can also enter free of charge. I naturally slowly arrived at this after I heard what people had to say.

Taxi drivers were always my counsellors, but I also remember something else: I had my barber in the Van Baerlestraat opposite the museum and I talked to him about it once. He said: *Yes, it's a very beautiful building, but I've never been inside.* I said: *How long have you been here?* He had been there for thirty years. And he had never felt the desire to come in. *No, he said, I wouldn't know how to behave, it's something for the gentry and has nothing to do with me.* And then, in the summer of 1954, I had the idea of building a platform on the corner of Paulus Potterstraat and Van Baerlestraat, so that people from outside could mount the platform and look inside. And inside I had put on the exhibition "Wonen & Wonen" [Living & Living]. After the exhibition had just opened, I drove past the museum at eight o'clock in the morning, and the first person I saw on the platform was my barber. And because he had looked inside and saw that perfectly normal things were taking place and nothing extraordinary, he became a visitor to the museum.

I have always listened to other people, but I have always done things in my own way. I have certainly allowed myself to be influenced by them. For example, by opening up the museum, the doors of glass, the New Wing of glass. That I then built that platform around the museum is naturally the result of the fact that I spoke to people, people in the street, barbers, taxi drivers, whoever. I have spoken to a lot of people, mainly ordinary people, and also with my own staff, with the attendants. I have asked about their experiences with the public and we have talked about it in depth.

I certainly took all that into account, but I have always had the feeling: what I must bring is that which looks ahead and not that which looks back. That which heralds in something new, which goes farther than what we know. That has been my guideline. Not just any old new thing or something different, but something that points in a certain direction. I thought it was the direction in which our society was moving, even though I could not describe it. It is something that naturally is ahead of society, because artists have different antennae and sense what is going to happen earlier than the 'man in the street' or many intellectuals. For most people, the truth is that they look at what is happening around them and try to act accordingly. That is the way fashion arises, isn't it, but I didn't try to follow fashion. I tried to find out the direction in which art was moving. I focused only on that and not on incidental opinions of people who just wrote something in the paper or something like that. Because my

experience had not given me a particularly high opinion
of that.

I believe that management — which includes,
according to me, museum directors — should really
manage, lead. They shouldn't follow or think: what
can I do that will make me look good? What would
attract people? I have in any case thought: it is necessary to show this here. And in general, I became the
first person in Europe to do this. A very large number
of museums have followed me. I also believe that this
gave a certain impulse to the whole world of Dutch
museums. I know that, when they needed a new
director in The Hague, they said: we must look for
somebody who can compete with Sandberg. That in
itself is an indication that it had worked. I believe
that I gave that development an impulse. That may
also have been my intention and this gave Amsterdam
with its Stedelijk Museum international significance.
Yes, if the building meets the demands, it can become
a centre for a lot of arts and cultural aims. We adopted
photography as early as 1957 and in my time it was
the librarian Kloet who promoted this.

And we brought music into the museum with
museum concerts, when Eschauzier's auditorium was
completed. Jan Martinet worked hard on this. The film
museum also made use of the auditorium for a long
time, because there was a projection booth at the
back. That was in 1952. Four years later, the restaurant and terrace — which took the place of the garden
room — were completed. They provided visitors with
comfort and convenience. But we didn't have dance
or theatre, and you really had to have those if you

were to talk of a 'mouseion'. There has to be vivacity and comfort. I also think that such a centre must also be housed in a centre in the city or in a place where people are. It must be a meeting-point, such as the Centre Pompidou or Beaubourg in Paris. Originally that was supposed to be located where Les Halles were, but it was built on the other side of the Boulevard Sébastopol, where a large number of old houses had been demolished. A public library and a large exhibition area were built there. The Museum of the 20th century was built there.

I was very pleased that I was invited to be a judge in the competition for this, because I had been working with those people from the very start. I tried to get them to move in my direction. I didn't really believe in competitions, but this was an idea competition in which well-known architects could submit their ideas and the execution of those ideas would take place in close collaboration with the museum people and the architects.

ART AND SOCIETY

The background to my museum policy has always been that on the one hand I tried to encourage the staff to think of it as their museum, that they participated in it, and that on the other hand I wanted to give young people the feeling that it was their museum and that they belonged there. Immediately after the liberation we said: we have to involve the youth in it, the school children. Fortunately, the Alderman of Youth Affairs was also the Alderman for Education, and he was very much in favour of it. We then got all public schools and later also a lot of special schools to take a tour, once a month, and to visit the museum. They went to the Rijksmuseum and the Stedelijk Museum, five times a year to each.

The problem was whether we should have the tours given by the teachers, to whom we would give a special course in art, in aesthetics, or by artists, to whom we would give a bit of training in pedagogy. Fortunately, we opted for the latter and when I left there were some 22 artists affiliated to both institutions. They took over the classes from the teachers. The classes were divided in two. Unfortunately, there are forty children in one class in Amsterdam, and twenty seems to me the maximum for a tour.

I said to the artists: *Look, you know what the children are going to see. You are free to go where you like and show them what you want, but try to keep your mouth shut as much as possible. Avoid trying to teach them anything. The ideal situation would be for you to say nothing and for them to discuss what they see among themselves.* That was our intention. Schultink, a former teacher, was also involved. He was one of the mentors of this idea.

I believe that not everybody can do it precisely like that and control it, but the best tour guides were those who were simply there and answered any questions, who got the children to discuss all sorts of things among themselves. We were able to give children this stimulus in tours. That was one of the things we aimed at along with — and that is naturally a lot better, but something we weren't able to do on a large scale — helping the children to express themselves freely, and in the past we even had classes in the museum for that.

Later that developed on the one hand into the Werkschuit and on the other into a completely different movement. The Werkschuit[10], of which I too was chairman for some time, tried to bring the expressive element into all parts of education. To permeate not only drawing lessons and the like with this element of self expression, but also throughout education as a whole. I believe the Werkschuit is doing well. It is one of the best known institutes abroad, because it was joint initiator of this whole action of not just telling the youth or confronting them with things, but of giving them a chance to express themselves freely in different materials, with colour, with form, with voice, with movement and whatever else.

Our education especially is, I believe, something

10. Founded in 1950, the Werkschuit operated originally from a sand barge. The goal was to enhance development and education, especially geared towards children, by stimulating creative expression.

that we can use to achieve much in the use of spare time, which is causing difficulties for so many people. Not for me, I don't really have any spare time, but a lot of people talk of it. And they are bothered by it. They don't know what to do except watch TV, which of course is also very useful. But they actually don't know how to use their spare time productively.
I assume that if we could influence education in this direction, the children would be more themselves, would know better how to achieve things and so also know what to do with their spare time.

One of the other principles that the Stedelijk Museum has adopted is that you must take the artist as starting-point. Art naturally is based on the personality of the artist. The museum of living art in particular must grow and organise itself completely according to art and the artist. I believe we must give precedence to the artist.

I am exceptionally intrigued by what artists make today and try to see that as an expression of our society. I try to see the lines, the connecting lines between our society and their creation. But what will happen from here? I can't see into the future. It is the artists who look into the future. They have longer feelers than we do, which allow them to pick up vibrations much earlier, which are transmitted from that which is going to happen. They anticipate this and try to give it shape. That is, after all, the essence of art: each time giving shape to what is most current.

Art is a social function. We are not always aware of it but I believe that if we see things on a large scale and trace the line through to today we would then

have to realise that art is a social function. The artist
expresses things that are not yet at that moment visible for us. The change, the development, the evolution that he brings about in his art, naturally shocks us,
because it is something that has not yet been seen, is
not yet familiar; it is something our eyes are not used
to. Just as new music can sometimes seem unpleasant to our ears. But if we listen frequently to new
music, we grow accustomed to it. For a new generation that is immediately born into it, it is completely
self-evident. We, the older ones, may rear up against
it, when we take what already is as our starting point.

When we assume that the evolution of art depends on or combines with the making, the
designing of things that are not yet at the moment
visible to us, then, when we see the work of young
artists or new work by people, the question is not: how
must we judge this in the light of what we know about
Rembrandt, Cézanne or Picasso, but rather: what
connection does this have to our life? What can this
work tell us about the shape of our society, in which
we eat, drink and are happy or sad? I believe that that
attitude towards art prevents people from stagnating
and makes sure they do not get stranded in something that is past, but that they always remain open.
That they see in it a prelude to what is going to happen and what we may perhaps experience.

This has also been the starting point for my acquisition policy. I have always hunted for things that were
unknown; for new forms, new expressions, unknown
artists. I was frequently one of the first purchasers.
And I also paid the price that was asked. I remember

once visiting a colleague in Germany. He was General
Manager, and he said to me: *You know, I never buy
anything under the ten thousand. For if you buy something that has reached a price above the ten thousand,
you know that it has already gained social value.*
I replied: *I never buy anything above the ten thousand.*
That is not completely true. Later, I sometimes sinned
against this rule, particularly when devaluation took
place. But I have the feeling that, exactly because I
was early and didn't bargain, I purchased things much
more cheaply than the people who came too late, who
followed the movement. Once things have taken root
in society and have arrived in the hands of the art
trade, they naturally become a lot more expensive.
I have the idea that I bought things very cheaply.
People could perhaps accuse me of buying too cheaply, that I acquired too few expensive things for the
museum, but then they should also realise: I was ham-
pered a little by the start. When I became director of
the Municipality Museums in 1945, my acquisition
budget for the Stedelijk Museum was four thousand
guilders. Of course you couldn't do much with that. As
the years progressed, that fortunately rose with leaps
and bounds, but I have always been confronted with
budgets that were somewhat too tight. When I purchased those forty or forty–five small bronze sketches
by Jacques Lipchitz, I didn't have the money to pay for
them. It wasn't all that much, but I didn't have it. Then I
have, I think, paid for them over five years. And shortly
afterwards, I acquired the 'Still Life' by Cézanne. That
was sixty thousand guilders. Now it would be a million
or something like that, and certainly more than six

hundred thousand. I then had to pay that off over many years and that blocked my budget for other things.

 I bought that Cézanne relatively quickly, I know that, for its owner — Ina van Bladeren, who had a children's class in self expression at the time — used that money to build the Werkschuit and that is why we immediately agreed on the price, which was not high, but also not low, for the time.

Now I turn to something else. It is natural that the art trade occasionally discovers some young flop or other, who, to shock the citizens, makes some horror or other or in any case something conspicuous that therefore attracts publicity. Of course that happens, but for me I always followed the rule: when I was dealing with the work of young artists I always wanted to see the man himself before I bought anything by him. For I wanted to find out whether this was really something created by an inner drive. You soon discover that in a conversation. When an artist, for example, produces newspaper clippings, you know exactly how the land lies; the same applies when you notice all he wants to achieve is having success and making money. I actually always tried to purchase from unknown talent, or rather, I didn't care whether the people were well known or not. If something struck me, if I noticed something, I would examine it closely. Then I sometimes thought it wonderful or I saw the man and it wasn't genuine. In general, you don't have to do this with older artists. But on the other hand, this gave me the opportunity of buying early from a whole lot of artists. This meant that price did not play such an important role, for there wasn't any market price yet, no supply and demand price, because there was supply, but no demand. That is why I never really bothered myself about how high the price was, because if I had confidence in the man, I knew the price would increase in the future. Of course, I could not say with any certainty whether he would develop further. But I knew that he was, in any case at that moment, a completely honest and genuine person, who was posing himself a problem and finding a solution, and then I bought from him. Naturally, I often also made mistakes, but then the amount involved was never particularly high, because they were early works, most of the time. I actually believe that you must try to grasp the start, the beginning of an artist. As I mentioned earlier, for me Picasso begins with cubism. The blue and pink period and certain things preceding them, were also made by other people. Picasso was, perhaps, more of a genius, but it wasn't as yet completely original. At the moment, it is art for millionaires. They can afford it and they want a Picasso before Picasso was really Picasso. The same also applies to other artists. And then Picasso, because he paints in a naturalistic style, is acceptable for every Tom, Dick and Harry, and thus also for millionaires. Yet the person who really delves deeper into art tries to acquire the work from the moment when Picasso becomes Picasso, or Mondrian becomes Mondrian or Paul Klee becomes Paul Klee.

In 1946, I staged an exhibition in the Stedelijk of works Picasso produced during the war. It actually featured both Picasso and Matisse. By Picasso: all the portraits he made of Dora Maar. Those deeply tragic

portraits where you always see Dora Maar 'en face'
and 'en profil' and where the hunger and tragedy of
war plays a leading role. One of those things, 'The
woman with the fish hat' was very precious to me at
the time. I tried to buy the thing, even though I didn't
have any money for it, but I thought: I can pay for it in
instalments. But Picasso didn't want to sell it, and
that was that. In 1957, eleven years later, I met the
art dealer Kahnweiler at the opening of a Picasso
exhibition in Munich and what do you know? That
painting was hanging there again. And it still belonged
to Picasso. I said to Kahnweiler: *Can't you now coax it
out of him for me?* And Kahnweiler was optimistic,
which he generally wasn't, and said: *Well, I think I
could do that.* I asked him: *What does it cost?* And he
said: *Well, it costs around forty thousand francs.* I said:
That's fine, and I set aside a much higher amount,
since I didn't at all believe that I could get it for forty
thousand francs, because at the time the market price
was well above the hundred thousand. But indeed,
I acquired that painting for forty thousand, because
Picasso knew that our museum would not be able to
sell it anymore, so it would never appear on the
market again. Then it really no longer mattered to him
what he got for it. It was the same with those sculptures he made from the models he designed, he never
charged anything for them because he knew they
weren't commercial items. They were located on a
square somewhere or near a house or you name it,
and they could never be sold. A foundation had to be
constructed for them and they became immovable.
And because of that, they lost any commercial value.

And Picasso didn't need any money for that either.

Yes, I would also like to say something in response to what has happened in art in the last few decades. It seems to me that there is no longer a distinction between beautiful and ugly. That is of course something very difficult for art criticism. For centuries, people have continued to elaborate on that Greek basis and have viewed everything as beautiful or ugly. Although perhaps the work of newcomers was always in the beginning considered ugly by those who saw it. Until the moment that their eyes grew accustomed to it and then they thought it beautiful. That was frequently long after the death of the painter or sculptor. But now I believe we have completely done away with the concept of beautiful and ugly; we simply look and ask ourselves: is it stimulating, does it say something to us, does it do something with us? I believe that is the criterion you must use to judge art.

I'd also like to exterminate the word 'art', because it gives rise to all sorts of misunderstandings. Everybody who smears paint on a canvas with a brush is called an artist. And the result is called a work of art. I would like to reserve the title 'artist' for the innovators in that field, the people who go further, who develop things. And about that word development I see again a difference of opinion. Most art historians and so-called experts want to derive art from art. They think there is a certain tradition that continues and that that is the development. I see things slightly differently. I see social developments and each time I see a plant, a flower on a stem, arise from society. That is the art, the culture. Now people want to trace a line between those flowers, so on the level of art, but I believe you can only trace a line on the level of society: the growth of our society, the attitude of man towards man. That is frequently, perhaps even always the result of economic relationships and there is, in my opinion, the rub. Because there is a development in society, there is also a development in art, but only for that reason.

We cannot derive Mondrian from Van Gogh. We cannot derive Picasso from the impressionists, although he did start as an impressionist — I would almost say from the school of Renoir and Lautrec. What makes Picasso Picasso is that he starts something new. First by building on the technique and the way of expression used by his predecessors, he suddenly came across something new: cubism, or other directions, and particularly the 'Guernica', which doesn't derive from anything, even though it is maybe the 'Night Watch' of the twentieth century.

I believe that only when we see art in relationship to our society and how it has grown from it that we have a possibility of making a judgement for today. We must see whether it is moving in a direction, whether a direction can be found in the development of the artist. It is not that which Van Gogh learned from the impressionists that makes him Van Gogh, but exactly that which deviates from them. That is that Van Gogh discovers his fellow man and then always looks at him, not from afar, from outside, but looks at that person, whether he is a labourer or wherever he comes from, as his equal and dresses himself as that labourer. But he also knows how to express, even in his landscapes or in his still lifes, the drama of life, of society. I believe that is where his greatness lies and not in what he derived from others and which he perhaps perfected. It becomes important there, exactly where he breaks with his predecessors.

And the same thing happened with Mondrian. It is not what Mondrian painted before 1911 that is important. Mondrian only becomes Mondrian when he gives his own vision on cubism, and then slowly returns right to the elements of painting, the colour, the line, the shape. When he only knows the straight line, the rectangle and the primary colours, and so brings art back to its elements. The same is true of Kasimir Malevich. Malevich did it in 1915, I believe that Mondrian began in 1916 or 1917. They knew nothing about each other — one was deep in Russia, the other in Laren (NL). They had no contact with each other, because it was in the middle of the First World War, and yet they both, at the same moment practically speaking, reacted in the same way. The Russian dynamically, the Dutchman statically , constructively. The Russian with a certain tragedy, mysticism perhaps, when I think of the paintings where he ended: white on white and movement. But there again we see the great tragedy in the life of the Russian artist. Malevich is one of the few great Russian artists who was forced through family circumstances to remain in Russia. He couldn't go any further and ended his life painting portraits. Those portraits did, however, have character, but still, in the context of his complete oeuvre, they represented a decline. While Mondrian, from 1915 onwards, perhaps even from 1910, continued to develop in a straight line. Each work developed directly from the other. It is a very direct development that continued until his death — in 1944 — and he actually never deviated from his aim.

Now we are starting to feel the difficulties of criticism with regards to art. People have always been inclined to work with norms from the past. To compare art with other art. Instead of trying to understand what the artist felt was emerging in this society and which he tried to express. It is exactly this quality of the artist, which cannot be encapsulated by the battle between beauty and ugliness, which we cannot explain, understand or judge according to the Greek or classical principle. We can only assess their value based on life itself.

There are but few who are gripped and built as such, few geniuses who, by something or other, are lifted across the threshold of life. Those could be exceptional experiences, it could be illness or fever. Quite a few geniuses have suffered from syphilis, it seems that that is in one way or another something that carries people over the threshold, but those are, of course, exceptions. In addition we have the school. We have the master and we have the school. In this school, the pupils translate the work of the master into a digestible form. They are immediately dubbed wonderful by the critics and the audience, because — and I mean nothing discriminatory here — they parrot what the public wants to hear. They are immediately accepted, while the great artists are so shocking that initially they are hardly acceptable. We must therefore

realise that an artist actually directs himself to his
contemporary public via his school. Sometimes he is
assimilated by the school and is hardly discovered.
Only later does it transpire that he had actually provided the stimulus. For example, many artists collaborated in cubism. It wasn't only Picasso, it was also
Braque, Juan Gris, Le Fauconnier. It was a whole
phalanx of artists, but the pioneering personality was
Picasso, and perhaps, in a certain sense, Le Fauconnier.
But Le Fauconnier quickly got bogged down and later
he inspired the Bergen School here. I remember
being on Texel in 1918 and that two artists were wan-
dering around there, they could clearly be recognised
as artists from a mile away. They were Conrad Kikkert,
who also did a lot for the Bergen School, and Le
Fauconnier with his red beard. You could always find
him outside holiday time on the terrace of the American
Hotel, with his big dog and his girl friend.

   There is always a majority that does not succeed
in creating something new, but that is able to develop
a theme once it has been discovered, to expand it
and to make it acceptable, digestible for a large audience. But I believe that without a school there is not a
great artist. He is frequently inspired by that school.
I remember stories about people who worked in Paris
during the cubist period. I am thinking, for example, of
Jacques Lipchitz who related that one of the artists
had invented 'le compotier' — the fruit bowl, mainly
with grapes — and that immediately, the next day
even, all the cubists everywhere were painting fruit
bowls. They were, in that early period, actually limited
to two subjects: still life and portrait (a person). For

what is the great discovery of cubism? The existing perspective was broken down. The perspective of the man who sees his subject in front of him and draws lines so that what is near becomes large and what is farther away, smaller. He draws all sorts of lines to the horizon, or parallel to the horizon, and with these he constructs his illustration. The perspectives that were started by Mantegna, Leonardo da Vinci and Dürer were broken down. The artist leaves his chair, as I would like to call it, the chair on which he sits in front of his easel and walks around, around his subject, his object. He tries to capture the different sides or aspects of that object on one canvas. He therefore leaves the photographic perspective and finds a new relationship to his object. A new distance, a new relationship.

This is actually the great discovery of cubism: changing the point of view. Just as our whole society changed its point of view at the beginning of the century. I think of Einstein, who discovered relativity. Formerly, only the sun revolved around the earth and he saw all that suddenly moving. We were just a pin prick and also the sun became just a pin-head in that self moving universe. Einstein engaged the time — something Bergson did in philosophy. The relativity plus the tremendous blossoming of the socialist movement, the equality of people — which I just spoke about concerning Van Gogh — the changed and changing relationship between employer and employee, all such things suddenly changed people's point of view with regard to that which they saw, with regard to the outside world. I see the expression of this in cubism.

126

That was why cubism, particularly in the beginning, was restricted to objects you could walk around. You could use the still life particularly well for this and that was actually always the same time and again: some stringed instrument or other, a newspaper on a table and a fruit bowl, as I have mentioned. That was simply viewed from all sides and then combined together on the canvas. Or the human face or torso, generally never complete people. That was once again dissected into its facets and this meant you saw the person simultaneously 'en face' and 'en profil', from the front and from the side. That is something we now see flourishing in all forms of painting — trying to view a person simultaneously from the front and from the side, and thus combining both views on the canvas at the same time. That was a cubist discovery. These things meant that we got a completely different view of our surroundings. To propagate this, a complete school was required. That school really does have a social function: to make something like that digestible. In cubism, you had two schools, that of Montmartre and that of Montparnasse. The former was headed by Picasso, the latter by Le Fauconnier. Le Fauconnier has had a lot of disciples, but as leader — at least, as far as I know his work — he soon gave up. While Picasso constantly renewed himself and always shocked us time and again with his new vision on people and things. In the years around 1910, Picasso and Le Fauconnier were actually equal, you could say, but history, the distance shows what the one did and what the other did.

TYPOGRAPHIC DESIGNER

The museum — which used to be something for which
you would dress up in your dark suit and enter
aristocratically, with or without your wife and children
and mainly on Sunday — had, in my opinion, to become something that is for a normal weekday. It had
to become some centre of life. That that ultimately
became one of the aims, was why I enjoyed taking
charge of that museum. I was after all a designer and
I also tried, by being a designer, to bring everything
into one hand and to give one colour, one character to
the whole propaganda and to the building itself, at
least on the inside. I tried to impart an open and clear
character to everything I could change so that people
could immediately recognise it. If they saw a poster,
they could see from the colour and the letters that it
came from the Stedelijk Museum and if they received
an invitation, from the stationery. Everything that was
issued by the museum, even a catalogue, must have
the same character, normal and vigorous. I am actually a fierce enemy of high-brow. I was very pleased
that I could be my own client and did not have to follow somebody with all sorts of strange ideas. You can
experience strange things if you do not take any freedom with regard to your client. It happens frequently
that when you try to design something, you feel the
eyes of that man in your neck. That is debilitating.
That was why I was so pleased that I could simply do
my own thing at the museum. I was my own client and
could make catalogues the way I wanted. I was sub-
jected to a lot of criticism, because of the packing
paper I used in them. I wanted the pictures to be printed on the highest quality paper, but the text could

easily be printed on packing paper or on normal newspaper. It didn't have to be precisely right, just so. I am anti-perfectionist. At the same time, this allowed me to give those catalogues a personal face. Each catalogue was initially inspired by the subject I was dealing with. I remember a Schwitters catalogue. For that, I tried to work as Kurt Schwitters and a Picasso catalogue therefore looked completely different. Each catalogue could be given more or less its own character. You could use a classic font or a sans-serif, very bold advertising letter.

One of my favourites, which I especially used for posters, is an 'Egyptian'. That is a letter with a bold serif, a type of chocolate letter you could almost say. It is a font — as the name implies — inspired by Egyptian paintings. It was designed after Napoleon conquered Egypt. It was a large wooden letter. With this font, thanks to the thick serifs, the white inside the letter is sometimes more important than the shape of the letter itself and also the white between the letters. I used that frequently in my Typographic Experiments. My posters were printed at the Municipal Printing Works. They had a large number of those letters. They were not available in smaller sizes. For that I used the 'Volta'. But I made a lot of use of 'Egyptian'. And then I received a letter — or was it a visit, I can't remember anymore — from America, from the Museum of Modern Art in New York asking whether they could use my letter on all their inscriptions. I said: Fine, and then they wanted the whole alphabet. I went to the Municipal Printing Works and they printed the whole alphabet for them. They used this for years on end for their inscriptions and when, many years later, I visited the museum again, they started to talk to me about the 'Sandberg Font'. I said: What do you mean by 'Sandberg Font'? That is a normal Egyptian. — Oh, we thought you had designed it. I said: *No, it was in stock at the Municipal Printing Works; it is an old font.* Anyway, when I got home I started investigating and it turned out that the font was made by Hamilton in Chicago in 1860. It therefore returned to America via Amsterdam.

Designing those catalogues was relaxing. You did something completely different. But it was also quite demanding. Such a catalogue took some fifty to a hundred hours. And try and find these outside museum hours, often in just one week. Those catalogues were all created on Sunday or during the night. Only right towards the end did I find someone among my own people who could work on them and could, to a certain degree, take the execution of them out of my hands. But I did it all by myself for fifteen years, de-signed catalogues at my own initiative. But not all of them. Sometimes Otto Treumann or Dick Elffers or other people made them. I think that 328 catalogues were made under my auspices. I assume that around 275 were made by me and the rest by other people. Just guessing.

I have designed countless posters, mainly letter posters. On a rare occasion, they had some illustration or other. But I really enjoyed working with the Municipal Printing Works and particularly with the printers on those posters. They usually arose on pieces of paper from a writing pad that I kept in my pocket. I would design them during boring meetings and I knew exactly what number each letter had at the Municipal Printing Works, how wide it was and so on. I wrote that down and jotted the numbers of the letters and also the colour in the margin. Then I received a fantastic galley proof; I generally didn't have to change anything. Over the years, we had come to know each other pretty well. I never spent much time on those posters, but I did on the catalogues.

I have also designed enamel poster boards which, in certain areas of the city, point in the direction of the museum. These featured red, blue and yellow panes of colour, separated by white bars, with the names of the most famous artists of the time, and between them, in white, the name of the museum. Those enamel signs were made in 1954 and they are still very dear to me. The names of the artists are, of course, rather dated. They are from thirty years ago. We would have liked later to put other names on them. De Wilde[11] actually asked me to do this. Perhaps I brought up the subject myself. He then said: *Yes, but the difficulty is that you don't want to design for the Museum any more.* For when I left the Museum, I wanted to make a clean sweep of things and give my successor the chance of starting with a clean slate. It was already difficult enough. But then I said:

11. Edy de Wilde (1919–2005); in 1946 he became museum director of the Van Abbemuseum in Eindhoven but his interest in modern art was not shared by the board at the time. From 1963 to 1985 he was director of the Stedelijk Museum. His final exhibition "La Grande Parade" attracted much attention.

Well, it was my creation, I would like to put other names on it. But then I would like you to give me a list of names that should appear on them. Later, we got around to the subject again and I asked: *Have you got that list?* Then he said: *No, the sufferance tax is becoming so enormously high that I will have to take down the boards. We can no longer afford to pay to have them on the masts.* I was very sorry to hear that, because I thought they added a cheerful note to the Amsterdam streets. I also thought it ridiculous that a municipal institution was required to pay so much sufferance tax.

I remember that if we made arrows for Van Gogh or for some summer exhibition or other, the rent alone would cost us one guilder fifty per week per arrow. So with fifty or a hundred arrows for three months — that cost quite a bit. It is a significant budget post. I didn't know how much the enamel signs would cost at that time, but it filled me with great regret.

I must admit, I spent quite a long time thinking about what those signs should look like. I had an idea of what should be shown, but I was not at all clear of how to combine the heterogonous issues of the Stedelijk Museum and the names of the artists in a sensible way. Until I was on an excursion with the staff in the Eifel. We were in a bus and the women were also with us. On the way, I saw the timber framing. It was a construction such as you would currently build with steel girders or T-joists. Then people used wooden beams and the space in between was simply filled up with straw and chalk. It was a black, dark construction against a white background. That's what I

saw. Those constructions are often quite pleasing and
they actually inspired me to create those signs, in
which I reversed things. I made the dark beams white
and showed the white background in primary colours.
    If you followed the official path for putting up
arrows for an exhibition, it would get you nowhere.
It took so many months that the exhibition was over by
the time you were given the o.k. So generally I sent off
people in our service van and wearing a service hat
and said: *That's where the arrows should hang.* They
hung them up and later I would receive the bill. But I
always got on well with my municipal colleagues, the
members of the Institute of Directors. That was a very
useful institute with thirty, forty people: the director of
gas, of electricity, of waste incineration, the water
board, the Bank of Loans, the City Theatre, the Municipal Museums and the like. Well, they knew me
a little. The Chief Commissioner of Police was also a
member of the club. I often explained my ideas to
them. They probably thought me something of an odd
man out, but they let me do as I pleased. It was also at
one of those occasions that I criticised the Amsterdam
municipal tram. I said that I thought those dark blue
trams that had a nineteenth century homely feel about
them were old-fashioned and that I thought they
should be given a new design, more in line with the
present times. With the aid of Ben Merkelbach and
others, we were able to involve some designers: Friso
Kramer and Jaap Penaat, who designed the current
yellow and grey trams. I would have liked them to do
the buses as well, but by then I had left. They are a
purplish red. If you were to combine that with yellow/

green, it would be attractive and hip. But I think it
awful the way it is, that purplish red colossus. They
probably also weigh a ton, but to accentuate that
weight with that colour, I think that's completely
wrong. But then, I had already left.

In this way, you're active of course in a whole lot
of areas. I felt that my job was not restricted to the
museum, but that I also had a little to do with other
matters and buildings in the city. I threw myself into
that. I remember that I also always went on about that
and wrote many letters to the Mayor and Aldermen
of the city. Sometimes serious letters, and then I tried
to give them a humorous touch so that — at least I
imagined — they fell about laughing. It was about the
new districts around the city, and the desolation of the
flats filled with families piled on top of each other
which were rising out of the barren sand that had
been sprayed there. Virtually the whole area had been
built up before anybody thought of making an entertainment centre, a community centre. I was then able
to force through the decision to appoint a municipal
committee to take a look at those district centres.
Paul Cronheim was on the committee, if I remember
rightly, and several people from Urban Development.
We held a few meetings but the people from Urban
Development were never able to attend. They would
send a neat little man who would patiently write down
everything we thought up, and that was the end of it.
It disappeared into a drawer and nothing was ever
done about it. I think: if you are going to build such an
area, you must start with a centre. A place where
people can meet each other and where they can find

some entertainment and relaxation — things other than the run-of-the-mill day-to-day things. And then you develop your district from that.

But people think here purely in economic terms. If enough land has been purchased, then a community centre can be built, instead of first building the centre and letting the neighbourhood grow around it. Then you achieve normal growth, and that's the way Amsterdam has grown, isn't it? First there was the dam in the Amstel and buildings arose on either side. From there, from that single point, it has developed fantastically. Vingboons, who gave the semi-circular shape to the city, was naturally inspired by the medieval city, but he did it in a way that still astonishes us. We must preserve that, notwithstanding the fact that we mustn't go down on our knees to the past, but rather let the past be of service to the present. Each period, after all, has its own language and the great art works of all periods are in harmony with each other, do not damage each other through their proximity. If we erect a façade by one of our best architects between all those canal houses, then it makes sense. I am thinking about the front of Metz & Co. designed by Gerrit Rietveld, the book shop of Schröder and Dupont by Bodon, and more things like that. Unfortunately, this is obstructed by the planning authority, but on the other hand, they allow such abominations as the University Library next to the beautiful Royal Stables. I think those stables are one of the finest buildings in Amsterdam and if you see the soulless University Library next to it — which was built by the council itself — then you see exactly what planning committees are worth. They obstruct the development of the city.

The same applies, for example, to the height of the buildings. I believe that people here in the inner city may not build higher than 22 metres. But if you come from the Central Station and walk along Damrak, then you have to be impressed. It really is beautiful: first the water to your left, then the Beurs van Berlage and, on the right, a row of fronts from very different periods, yet still characteristic. Especially the volume, the space of the street is good. When you come to the Dam you have to go farther into the city via Rokin. Rokin has gradually become a sort of shapeless worm, a trunk without any character. It could be because the water was drained there, but that is also the case with the Nieuwezijds Voorburgwal and that looks a lot better than Rokin. Rokin has much less shape and character, although there are a few magnificent small fronts. I think that if Amsterdam really wants to remain a world city, it will have to solve things differently. They will have to build high buildings on both sides of Rokin. I could well imagine there large transparent constructions with a lot of glass.
I am thinking, for example, of Park Avenue in New York where there are very tall structures of steel and glass, the glass fronts reflecting the clouds, so that you always obtain a very lively effect, except on a really sunny day. I could imagine that if Rokin were to be approached with this in mind — perhaps on a somewhat smaller scale and with more freedom — it could become the real artery for Amsterdam, for it is actually the central traffic artery of the city. You would

get a completely different impression when entering
the city. I think that, particularly with regard to Rokin,
a wrong policy is being applied. Okay, I can imagine
that you impose height restrictions within the ring of
canals. But in the centre, you should tackle things
differently. Incidentally, there is little remaining of the
seventeenth-century city there — with the exception
of the City Hall on the Dam — but they could have
been a little more careful there[12]. The fronts opposite
the Palace and next to it are not particularly attractive.
I am pleased that the Nieuwe Kerk [New Church] has
been somewhat stripped of later additions.

For Rokin, Mart Stam envisaged a new scale. He
was one of the most important Dutch architects.
He fully understood the radical change of scale in the
twentieth century and tried to give expression to that.
Unfortunately, because of his political convictions, he
was granted very few commissions. These only really
came about when he was no longer at the peak of his
abilities. It was over, because he was ground down
between the political movements. Because of this, a
very talented architect, perhaps one of the most
talented ever in Holland, was lost to us.

With regard to the city, I would like to tackle one
thing again and that is the suburbs. You saw it happen
again in the Bijlmermeer. First of all, huge residential
towers were built on the sprayed sandy deserts, and
then, when everything was finished, they started
looking for a neighbourhood centre. Sometimes there

12. The City Hall has since been restored and is now
    known as the Palace on the Dam.

is hardly any room for one anymore. As was the case,
for example, in the drama of Osdorp. Twenty–five or
thirty years ago, we made every effort to provide, first
of all, a centre to those districts and from there allow
them to grow outwards; first a sort of square, with
perhaps a few cultural buildings, a cinema, a library, a
few pubs and cafes. If the suburb develops from there,
people feel like members of that centre. Now you
have the feeling that people in the suburbs do not
belong together. They all have to go to the city centre
for entertainment or to find other people. You have no
opportunity there and it is very difficult to bring a
centre added retrospectively to life. I thought that
people had learned something from this, but they did
precisely the same in the Bijlmermeer. It was far
enough away from Amsterdam to have its own centre,
but people forgot about it. Perhaps it was on some
piece of paper or other at the architect's, but nothing
was ever built. It was quite simply impossible to do
anything about it, because people thought purely in
economic terms. Such a centre, which is built first and
precedes the houses, is, of course, economically
untenable, doesn't pay for itself, and is therefore neglected. There should be a subsidy for it. It is a basic
requisite for life, absolutely essential for the life of the
suburb. He who seeks for gain, must be at some ex-
pense, as we read on that old house on Damrak.
I believe that it's simply not possible in another way
and that all the protests we now hear about new suburbs are derived from this.
   There are many protests about high-rise, things
with ten or fifteen storeys, but I think that once you

have accepted the idea of a flat, you can better live on the tenth or fifteenth floor than on the third. Once you're inside, it's exactly the same, but the view and the air is much better. The air is cleaner and you are actually part of a larger community. I believe that this also makes gallery flats so useful. If you walk now, for example, along the Churchill-laan, you see six doors next to each other. Every apartment has its own door. All the staircases run parallel to each other, yet you could make do with just one decent staircase. The Dutch staircases are what the Germans call 'Hühner-leiter', even though you could have very decent stair-cases if more people made use of them. It is first and foremost uneconomical and second, it is a peculiarity of the Dutch from times gone by. In most countries people have always had flats and here people arrived at that only late on.

I have never felt — I must be honest — the need for my own little house. I grew up in the provinces with a large garden and I remember all the trouble we had with that garden. I am so glad that I do not have a garden. My house inside is something of a garden. I have no paintings on the wall — with the exception of one or two — I have nothing but plants. I have spent too much time with paintings to become attached to a specific painting. It would, I would almost say, exert too much influence on me personally and my ficus, my philodendrons and my African hemp don't do that at all. What's more, they grow and you have to prune them and replant them. You can put up with that be-cause they react well to such treatment. I noticed how my plants suffered during the years that I was away.

It is, of course, not as bad as when you have a dog.
A dog will die if his master goes away, but a plant
sometimes imitates the dog a little. It really does need
its master's green fingers to survive. Shortly before I
returned here from Jerusalem, I wanted to repot a
very large philodendron, because I thought it was
doing poorly after those four years. It was a thing we
had had for thirty years. When I took hold of it to put it
into a new pot, the whole thing turned to dust in my
hand. The whole stem was pulverized. But the nice
thing about this plant is that you can simply cut off all
the branches and put them into the ground again.
Now I have five philodendrons. Those are the plants
with the big leaves that Matisse so eagerly liked to
draw and which, because they belong in the jungle,
develop holes. The holes in the leaves get more and
bigger as they grow. That is to allow the scarce light in
the jungle to penetrate to the lower leaves. It is an
experience simply to notice that. The first leaves do
not have any holes, just some notches. They are just
like hands and get more and more holes. I have once
counted seventy holes in one leaf. In this way, you see
how nature is creating things before your very eyes
and adapting itself to circumstances.

    Back to typography. It was only during my time in
hiding, in the years 1943–1945, that I had enough
time to submerse myself in it. That was with my Typographic Experiments which were published in part
and which for the rest still exist somewhere in manu-
script form. In it, I found my own style. That style was
naturally influenced by the innovator of Dutch typography Piet Zwart, and by the visionary, in any case

the artist in Dutch typography: Hendrik Nicolaas Werkman. I got to know his work at the end of 1938, the beginning of 1939. This is how it happened: I was acquainted with the painter Jan Wiegers. He was from Groningen. He had worked extensively in Germany and Switzerland and was a friend of Kirchner. He helped to bring expressionism to Groningen. I hadn't been at the museum for long when he came to me with a large portfolio under his arm and said: *Look, I have some things here and I don't know exactly what to do with them. You dabble in typography and design, you may like them.* Then he pulled out those large sheets by Werkman.

I was enormously enthusiastic about them and said: *Leave the portfolio here; I'll see if we can buy something from it.* Then I asked Regnault about it. He was at the time the most modern collector, but he saw nothing in them. I asked Röell whether we could buy something for the museum and he didn't see anything in them either. Finally, Heleen Spoor who had an art gallery on one of the canals put them in an exhibition.

I was so curious about and intrigued by those large sheets of Werkman that I wanted to see the man and wanted to know what else he did. So shortly afterwards, I got on the train to Groningen and visited him in his small house there. I encountered a very reticent Groninger with whom it proved difficult to strike up a conversation. He was so typically taciturn. I understand the Groningen dialect very well, after all I grew up in Assen which is just a stone's throw from Groningen. After a first cigarette, things improved and I believe we became friends that day. He later took me to his business; it was already dark. Since then, we have kept in close contact with each other.

I was fascinated by his personality and his work. And to think that this man was, at a certain moment, a wealthy director of a book-printing company. At a given moment, the company went bankrupt because of difficulties in the family. And then he chose not to become the director of another company, but decided to withdraw to an attic on the Lage der A and, with an assistant, to print envelopes, headed paper and show-cards for shops. It was a very impoverished existence and he chose poverty in order to do as he pleased.

Between 1923 and 1945 (he actually stopped in 1944), this man made fantastic things, that not only broke free of the Dutch frame work, but are also as-tonishing internationally in the field of typography because of the way he freed letters from their tradi-tional context. He used them as independent entities and later also elaborated this idea further in large prints. In those, he actually laid bare his whole life. In the beginning he worked with letter compositions, later mainly with the ink roll and finally with templates and with the side of the ink roll. You could draw with it, make lines. He created an unbelievable body of work. At the time I visited him — early 1939 and there was as yet no talk of war or anything like that — he already had a magnificent oeuvre that, practically speaking, was unknown to everybody. Nobody had ever heard of it or seen it. He didn't exhibit it either. In the begin-ning — after 1923 — he published a small magazine at irregular intervals: 'The Next Call'. He printed fifty copies of it and sent it to people and artists throughout the world: in Japan, Russia, Turkey, Yugoslavia, Paris. They were people he thought might be interested in it.

It had no commercial basis at all. He sent those fifty copies free-of-charge. I have no idea what they're worth today. They are eagerly sought after by collectors. He thought and worked without any economic idea in mind. Whether he spent an hour, a day or a month on a piece of printing, it made no difference to him. It was all about the result. He really hated the idea of duplicating things. One copy was enough for him, wasn't it? He wasn't going to sell them anyway. He had absolutely no market. Fortunately, that changed with the years. I then regularly received portfolios from Werkman; he would bring them himself or he would have other people bring them or he sent them by post. I got friends together in my home and they loved them; architects, designers, painters and others who bought prints. The large prints cost forty guilders, the smaller twenty–five guilders and then there was a series that cost twenty–five guilders for ten items. Relatively speaking, this was cheap. But it made a hole in our income at the time, but in this way, we helped him build up a circle of Werkman believers.

Werkman himself was completely paralysed by the war between 1939 and May 1941. He made practically nothing other than his commercial printing jobs with his assistant. Then we invited him to spend a weekend with us in Amsterdam. He spent an evening with us in our home. He stayed with Jan Wiegers. On Sunday, I took him to the safe in Castricum where the Rembrandts and Van Goghs and all sorts of other things were stored. Later he produced a series of prints about it called: 'Amsterdam-Castricum'. There were ten large prints. On them he showed the safe in a fantastic way: some bird or other came out of the safe, something like inspiration. You also see the gramophone we had at home, on which we played jazz records, a bridge over an Amsterdam canal and things like that. All this came out of that visit and it actually helped him to get back to work. In the coming three and a half years, he made at least four hundred prints. It is impossible to state the exact number, because the Germans confiscated a lot of them when they took him prisoner. They all went up in flames in the Scholtenshuis, the headquarters of the German Security Service in Groningen. We don't know how much has been lost.

In the same period, he started to print and publish in collaboration with Pastor Henkels and Ate Zuithoff the series the 'Blauwe Schuit' [Blue Barge][13]. These were books with between four and fifty pages, small and large, in all sorts of sizes. They were mainly intended to boost the protesting morale of the Dutch during the oppression. I think the people who got these things were very grateful to Werkman. What's more, it cost virtually nothing, it was a trifle. Werkman also painted, mainly during the last year of the war,

13. Originally a medieval society-critical company, the jesters developed a car-ship that was pulled through the city with citizens dressed as their superiors and thereby mocking them.

147

during the winter of starvation of 1944–45. There was
no heating then in the print shop and the printing ink
was no longer fluid. His ink roll had become hard. He
simply couldn't work any more with his old process.
Then he returned to painting. As painter, he belonged
to the Groningen artists association De Ploeg [The
Plough] [14]. He also printed a lot of catalogues and
posters for them. But the texts that he wrote — dada-
like, I would almost call them surrealistic hippie texts
— are sometimes in a language he invented himself.
It does bear some relationship to other languages, so
you could understand what he was saying as you
read. It completely matched his printed work and his
whole creation.

Not that I ever became a disciple of Werkman or
Piet Zwart, but I was certainly influenced by their
work. I don't think I contributed anything new, but the
fact that I was able to make the large series of publications for the Stedelijk Museum and the like, gave
me the chance to develop a certain oeuvre that,
viewed from the outside, apparently forms a whole.
You naturally can't see that yourself, because you are
in the middle of things and actually work on diversity.
The typography, the way the page was divided, helped
me enormously when laying out an exhibition hall
and setting up a museum. I did that more or less as a
typographer. You connect planes and rectangles,
balancing or unbalancing them. It proved a highly
intriguing activity for me to set up an exhibition, where

14. Artist's collective founded in 1918 in Groningen to
promote the arts.

you didn't use the classic method of hanging everything at the same height and at the same distance
from each other, but where, for example, you hang
three paintings that belong together as a group. And if
they are small, you hang them at eye level and other
things that you should see separate from the rest you
hang much higher and free of everything else, so that
you end up with paintings being hung in a functional
way. I really enjoyed that work.

After I returned from Jerusalem, I gave a seminar
as 'Erasmus lecturer' at the University of Harvard in
America in the Carpenter Center for the Visual Arts.
That was in 1969–1970. I have given presentations
there about Cobra, Mondrian and Werkman and also
about myself, as introduction. The reaction of the
students to the lecture about myself was very positive.
I selected around fifteen people after the lecture and
we had tutorials of two hours, once or twice a week,
very serious and 'tüchtig'. We did practical and experimental things, for example how you could simplify the
address on an envelope by first giving the country,
then the town and then the street, and only finally the
person to whom the letter is addressed. We do the
exact reverse: first the man, then the street, town and
country. What we did was a lot easier for delivery. But
I don't do it myself, you understand. We also spoke
about what they were studying and what they expected.

How I did that was to set them a problem and then
to let them discuss it among themselves. For example,
before my departure in January 1970, I said: *We are
going to make a small exhibition, here at one of the
crossroads on campus, opposite the museum.* It was

covered in snow. I first asked: *What will we choose as subject?* Everybody could submit a note with their proposal. I submitted a note myself 'Heart for Harvard'. That was chosen. They didn't know it came from me.

There were also architecture students in the group and I let them work this out and present it. It was conceived in two circles. We had about twenty signs painted on both sides, each one metre twenty by two metres forty. These were used partly horizontally and partly vertically and they could also submit all sorts of designs for them. There were a lot of good ones. We selected together the ones that would appear on the boards. During later discussions, some things were changed. Then we bought a number of large pots of fluorescent paint and that colour was great, there in the snow. When you have six colours available (light and dark red, blue and purple, green and yellow) you are forced to combine and mix them yourselves. It all went together so beautifully.

In this way, each lesson had more or less its own subject or problem. We also made book covers. We chose a book of poetry by Edgar Allen Poe for this and everybody had to make their own design. We again discussed the designs together and chose the best one. Sometimes I came home and said to my wife: *Today, I didn't need to say a single word.* That was my glory, that they discussed and did the whole thing together. I got the discussion started, nothing more.

ARTISTS ORGANISATION AND RESISTANCE

It wasn't until 1932 that I stuck my head in the life of the Dutch artists organisation. I received a request at that time to become a member of the VANK, the Vereeniging voor Ambachts- en Nijverheidskunst [the Association for Trade and Industry Art]. I had never heard of the VANK, but I became a member. At a certain moment, I was even an active member and held administrative offices, including a seat in the Committee for Non-Permanent Exhibitions in the Stedelijk Museum — for VANK members and others — and in the Exhibition Committee for the Dutch department at the World Exhibition in Paris.

The Chairman of the VANK was Jean-François van Royen, a master typographer himself and, as we always said, in his spare time secretary-general of the PTT. He was owner of the Cunera Press and that was his real work. This man had, between the two great wars, a tremendous influence on the whole artist community, the life of the artist association and the position of the artist. First, he had a lot of work to award via the Postal services: for designing postcards or stamps, fitting out post-offices, designing letter boxes and so on. But he extended his influence far beyond this. He had, together with his friend, the architect De Bie Leuvelink Tjeenk, a great influence on the artist association life in this country. Tjeenk was, at the time that I knew him, Chairman of the BNA, the Bond van Nederlandse Architecten [Association of Dutch Architects]. The buildings he designed included the Jaarbeurs Building in Utrecht, that was pulled down about ten years ago — but his best work was perhaps the De Zwijger warehouse on the harbour of Amsterdam. He and Van Royen founded the Exhibition Board for Construction and Allied Arts. This included the architect associations BNA and Architectura et Amicitiae, plus the Circle of Sculptors, the VANK and perhaps something else. The Exhibition Board developed many initiatives and had a firm hand in all sorts of matters undertaken by the government. I remember that the Dutch entry for the World Exhibition in 1925 in Paris was mounted completely by the Board. And so too was the Dutch participation at the World Exhibition of 1937 in Paris. In 1925, Van Royen was secretary-general of the Dutch department and in 1937, Tjeenk held that position. I was one of Tjeenk's close associates and experienced first hand what took place and how you put such a pavilion together. That was, naturally enough, not simple. You had all sorts of committees that interfered. I remember that one of those had, for some inexplicable reason, commissioned an artist to make a mosaic. It was an awful thing and I didn't want to exhibit it. But it was commissioned nonetheless. Well, I dropped it and it broke. I have always been rather radical. I forget the name, but that thing wasn't exhibited.

I'd like to delve a bit deeper into my association with the organisation of the Dutch entry, because that is the one and only time that I ever became a strike leader.

In 1937–38, preparations were under way for the Dutch Pavilion at the World Exhibition in New York in 1939. Mr. De Graeff, former governor-general of Indonesia, was appointed Commissioner and he had a friend. That was professor Slothouwer, who built the

Grote Club near the Dam, but was largely recommended because he had made such a good job of the
restoration of the Dom in Utrecht. De Graeff wanted
to grant him the commission to build the Dutch Pavilion. Then we all said: *Hey, hold your horses, this is not
how things are done in the Netherlands; in Indonesia,
perhaps, but not here. We will have to take a careful
look at whether we are really getting the best architect
for such a Dutch calling card in New York.* And then
we finally agreed that a multiple commission would be
granted to seven architects. The names I remember
are: Wijdeveld, Dudok, Van Ravesteyn and Stam.
Others were of course involved, but I don't remember
them anymore. A board of architects judged the submitted plans. The first prize was for the design by
Mart Stam. It was, indeed, a fantastic pavilion, but it
was never built. The commissioner-general put great
store on granting the commission to the one that
came in seventh — namely Slothouwer. It turned into a
pretty heated meeting. In the meantime, De Graeff
had appointed a number of former Indonesian civil
servants to the committee and they listened to their
former boss. So in the meeting, he gained the majority for Slothouwer. I stood up and left. Then, in the
Board for Construction and Allied Arts, we deliberated
on what we should do and we organised a strike
among Dutch artists against this pavilion. The artists
who had already received a commission were allowed
to carry it out, but all the others were not allowed to
accept any assignment for this pavilion. The strike was
a fantastic success. I believe there was only one
blackleg. Later, during the war, it turned out he

belonged to the NSB[15]. Otherwise, everybody kept their word.

The Dutch Pavilion was really awful and the interior was little better. But the strike involved a whole lot of preparation and organisation. Chairman Van Royen was on holiday at the time. I was vice-chairman, so I had to lead the strike. That was very enjoyable, what with the press conferences and so on. The commissioner-general also gave press conferences with his side of the story. It caused a whole lot of work. I am very pleased that we were able for the very first time to test the solidarity of the Dutch artists. That must have been in 1938–1939. The exhibition was held in 1939. Very soon after that, the occupation took place, and other issues arose that were also about artist solidarity. Van Royen — who had an enormous talent for organisation and a special love for artists — had, in addition to the Exhibition Board for Architecture and Allied Arts, also tried to involve the painters in one general organisation for Dutch artists, the Central Committee. And that, naturally enough, was difficult. There were a lot of associations for painters but he got them together in that organisation and already had gone a long way by getting the painters together because of their profession and not because of the direction of their art. The associations were specially based on the various directions in painting. I believe that most of the meetings took

15. The National Socialist Movement — the Dutch party that supported the Nazis before and during the Second World War.

place in Pulchri Studio. It was a nice organisation and there was a pleasant mood among the people who participated. I think there were around thirty representatives.

The Central Committee worked very well until the invasion took place. Then Van Royen reached the conclusion that it was time to make a far more solid organisation of all Dutch artists. Actually against the Germans, but he couldn't say that out loud. That would be the Nederlandse Organisatie van Kunstenaars [the Dutch Organisation of Artists], the NOK. There was a lot of resistance from many sides to the NOK, including from me. The Germans were already threatening to set up a Culture Chamber here and we thought that, if we set up such an organisation, they would get their hands on everything in one go. So there were two sides: one to bring everything together in the spirit of resistance to the occupier and one not to play into the Germans' hands with one organisation so that they could more easily set up their Culture Chamber. The majority of Dutch artists were opposed to it.

I remember that in December 1940, there was a meeting in Pulchri of those thirty representatives. At the time, people had just received a brochure through their letter-boxes from Hein von Essen. He was a dance critic and I believe his wife was a dancer. The brochure that he had written was all 'Blut und Boden'. It was a real Nazi brochure and it was sent to us by our own organisations. I got mine from the VANK, in a VANK envelope. At that particular meeting, we protested virulently that we received such trash from our organisations. Van Royen tried to defend that by saying that he also had to let the other side have their say.

We were not at all happy about that and at a given moment in the debate I said that I felt more for the race of Christ than for Christians of the Race. Huib Luns, who was sitting next to me, patted me on the shoulder and said: *Chum, let's get out of here.* And so we stood up and left. That was the last meeting I attended of this organisation. It certainly caused a certain distancing between Van Royen and me, until a year later — the end of 1941 — he came to me and said: *I've come to the conclusion that it would still be better to disband everything. I'm travelling around the country now in order to disband all the organisations so as not to play into the hands of the Germans.* The Germans had set up the Culture Chamber in November 1941, and had made it obligatory for the artists who wanted to exhibit their work, for writers who wanted to publish something or for musicians who wanted to perform something in public and for the actors etcetera.

The whole action actually lumped all the artists who wanted to resist together and from that the artists' resistance was born. Then a document was handed to Seyss-Inquart[16] with I believe 2700 signatures protesting against the creation of the Culture Chamber. Seyss-Inquart then had anybody he thought was

16. Arthur Seyss-Inquart (1892–1946) was the Reichskommissar for the Occupied Netherlands. He was tried at Nuremburg for crimes against humanity and subsequently executed.

responsible for drawing up the document arrested. Jean-François van Royen was among them. He ended up in a concentration camp in Amersfoort, where he died in 1942.

That was an enormous loss for the Dutch artists and particularly for the unity of the artists.

After the Culture Chamber was inaugurated, many artists discovered that they had lost their livelihood. They were unable to handle any government commissions and could no longer perform. Then the artists' resistance, which had already been prepared, came into operation. This was already the case for the sculptors. The Dutch Circle of Sculptors then had around sixty members — and they had decided that, since their Jewish colleagues were no longer allowed to work on government commissions, they would not accept any either. They had organised themselves a year earlier. One of the organisers of the sculptors' resistance was Gerrit van der Veen, together with Frits van Hall. They also had a sort of support fund for the sculptors who got into difficulties by not accepting commissions. We then expanded that support fund because now, practically speaking, all artists were getting into difficulties. There was also a fund for the architects and visual artists and in addition, the writers also belonged to it. The actors also had one, and Hans van Meerten was largely responsible for that.

The visual artists and the writers were looked after by a group that included: Gerrit van der Veen, Willem Arondeus, Johan Brouwer, Koen Limperg and the architect Roosenburg was also involved for some time. I also remember meeting Antoon Coolen and

Han Hoekstra in these circumstances. We met together each month and looked at what was needed. There
was always somebody from The Hague who supplied
the money. How those people in The Hague got that
money is something I don't know. But in any case,
there was always money when we needed it. Each
time we had discussions with the representative who
supplied the money. For some time this was Leen
van Dijk, who at the time was Tax Inspector in Leiden.
Roel van Heusden was also involved. In this way we
became a sort of club and that club was, in some way
or another, involved in the resistance. I was, I believe,
the only person from the museum world.

And this is how we became involved in distributing
false identity papers. They were printed by Frans
Duwaer and there was a whole group involved who
carried out other things. Mart Stam was also involved.
The reason was the deportation of Jews, which was
just getting under way. Especially in the beginning, it
was very difficult to forge the watermark in the identity papers. I remember Gerrit van der Veen trying to
do this simply in the way you always make a watermark: by pouring the paper slurry onto a surface with
a relief, so that you got thicker and thinner paper. But
the paper itself didn't resemble in any way the original
paper. It was absorbent, so you couldn't write on it. We
simply didn't know how to do it. Later we tried cutting
out the watermark — we had a whole team for this —
but that wasn't satisfactory either. Until we — I think
together — had the idea of making a plate in negative,
which is in the paper when you look through it to see
the watermark. The light parts in that plate were light

The indictment for the attack on the municipal registry
in Amsterdam — 21 people were charged, 12 of them
were executed on 1.7.1943. Quotes from the indictment:

    Waffen SS
    SS-und Polizei-gericht X Den Haag

    St.L.IV. 54 / 43

Am 27.3.1943 drangen gegen 21.15 9 Täter in das Bevol-
kungsregister in Amsterdam, Plantage Kerklaan/Ecke
Plantage Middenlaan, ein. Von diesen 9 Tätern trug der
Leiter des Unternehmens die Uniform eines Polizeikapi-
täns, ein zweiter die eines Oberleutnants und 4 weitere
Polizeiagentenuniformen, während die restlichen
Teilnehmer in bürgerlicher Kleidung waren. Die zuerst
Genannten trugen für diesen Zweck notdürftig besondere
angefertigte Uniformmäntel und hatten aus Wachstuch
gefertigte Koppel und Pistolen-taschen umgeschnallt.
Die Pseudo-Polizeioffiziere trugen Mützen während die
Pseudo-Polizeiagenten mit Stahlhelmen erscheinen. Auch
der 10. Täter war in bürgerlicher Kleidung und hatte
lediglich einen Korb mit 26 Benzolflaschen bis vor das
Bevolkungsregister geschafft, worauf er sofort kehrt
machte. Der als Polizei-hauptmann verkleidete Täter
trat an die dort postierten zwei Polizeiagenten heran
und sagte, daß er das Bevolkungsregister kontrollieren
müsse, da der Verdacht bestehe, daß sich dort
verdächtige Personen aufhielten. Als die beiden Polizeiagenten den Leiter des Unternehmens in Polizeihaupt-
mannsuniform sahen nahmen sie stramme Haltung an,
grüßten mit erhobenem rechten Arm und sagten: "Jawohl,
Herr Kapitän". Mit diesem gingen sie dann zusammen an
den Eingang zum Bevolkungsregister und schellten,
worauf einer von den beiden im Inneren des Gebäudes
befindlichen Zivilwächtern an die Tür kam und fragte,
wer dort sei. Der Leiter des Sabotageunternehmens
nannte seinen angenommen Dienstgrad und einen falschen
Namen und erklärte, daß er Kontrollieren müsse. Als der
Zivilwächter noch zögerte, die Tur zu öffnen, sagte
einer von den Beiden Polizeiagenten, daß es in Ordnung
sei, er sollte öffnen. Nachdem nun der Zivilwächter
die Tür geöffnet hatte, gingen die beiden Polizeiagenten
zusammen mit dem Pseudo-Polizeibeamten in das Gebäude.
Nachdem der Pseudo-Polizeihauptmann festgestellt hatte,
daß außer den beiden Zivilwächtern und den zwei mit
anwesenden Polizeiagenten kein weiteres Bewachungsper-

sonal zur Stelle war, zogen die Pseudo-Polizeibeamten
ihre Pistolen und riefen dem Überwachungspersonal "Hände
hoch" zu. Dieser Aufforderung wurde Folge geleistet.
Nachdem den beiden Polizeiagenten die Koppel mit Pistolen (die Zivilwächter waren unbewaffnet) sowie die
Polizeimäntel und Feldmützen abgenommen worden waren,
wurde das Überwachungspersonal an Händen und Füssen
gefesselt (Hände auf dem Rücken). Außerdem wurde ihnen
ein Leinenlappen in den Mund gesteckt und Mund und
Augen mit einem 5-6 cm breiten Leukoplaststreifen zuge-
klebt. Alsdann bekamen die Gefesselten je eine Spritze
Luminal-Natrium-Lösung. Die so Überwältigten wurden
darauf auf den Fußboden gelegt. Zwei von den Pseudo-
Polizeiagenten zogen ihre Mäntel aus und legten die
Stahlhelme ab. Nachdem sie die Uniformmäntel der
Polizeiagenten angezogen hatten sowie deren Koppel umgeschnallt und ihre Feldmützen aufgesetzt hatten, gingen
sie auf die Straße und verrichteten dort den Posten-
dienst. Als gegen 23 Uhr die Ablösung (2 Zivilwächter
und 2 Polizeiagenten) einzeln erschienen, wurden sie
von den beiden in das Gebäude gebracht, wo sie ebenfalls
überwältigt und gefesselt wurden wie ihre Vorgänger. Der
zuletzt Gekommene erhielt keine Einspritzung, da Luminal-Natrium-Lösung nicht mehr zur Verfügung stand. Die
übrigen Täter hatten in 1 1/2 stündiger, mühsamer Arbeit
die Schubladen aus den Karteischränken gezogen und die
Karteikarten auf den Fußboden geschüttet und zum Teil
mit Benzol begossen. Es handelte sich insgesamt um etwa
den zehnten Teil der Einwohner der Niederlande und außerdem um die Karten der Familienkartei, die in dem
Bodemraum untergebracht waren. Der Einwohnermelderaum
ist 53 x 17 m groß. In diesem wurden 5 Sprengstoffherde
angelegt, ebenso geschah das auf dem Innenbalkon,
auf dem sich ein Projektionsapparat befand und im Boden-
raum. Es handelte sich um Trotyl-Sprengkörper mit
Sprengkapseln, an denen sich Schnellzündschnüre aus den
Beständen des früheren niederländischen Heeres befanden.
    Nachdem die 8 Gefesselten von den Tätern in den
hinter dem Gebäude gelegenen Garten "Artis" getragen
worden waren, wobei ein Weg von etwa 80 m Länge zurück-
zulegen war, wurden Brandsätze (Schachteln mit einem
Gemisch von Kaliumchlorat und Zucker sowie Glasröhrchen
mit Schwefelsäure, an deren Oeffnungen Cellphan gebunden
war) als Zeitzünder gelegt.
    Gegen 23 Uhr erfolgten die Detonationen. Es brach
ein Brand aus, der mit 18 Schlauchleitungen in mehrstün-
diger Arbeit gelöscht wurde. Der Dachstuhl und der Kar-

teiraum in der 1. Etage brannten vollständig aus, während in dem unteren großen Karteiraum vorwiegend durch die Sprengungen große Verwüstungen angerichtet wurden. Die Familienkartei (1893 bis 1940) ist nahezu restlos verbrannt, während von der Einwohnerkartei der größte Teil der Karten (ca. 85%) erhalten geblieben ist. Von der Familienkartei sind doppelte Karten, bzw. Filme vorhanden was bei der Einwohnermeldekartei nicht der Fall ist. Der gesamte Schaden wird auf 200 bis 250.000 Gulden geschätzt.

Die in den Garten "Artis" niedergelegten Männer konnten sich kurz nach 23 Uhr selbst von ihren Fesseln befreien. Nur bei einzelnen war eine leichte einschläfernde Wirkung von den Einspritzungen eingetreten. Bemerkenswert ist, daß den Überwältigten sämtliche Papiere (Persoonsbewijs, Polizeiausweise usw. sowie auch Geld entwendet wurden.)

Bei diesem Anschlag wurden 11 kg. Trotyl, oa. 35 Flaschen mit Benzol (einzelne mit Petroleum und Aceton) 2 Rollen Leukoplast, 5-6 cm breit, 3 Spritzen Luminal-Natrium-Lösung, ca. 10 Sprengkapseln, Leinenlappen, Stricke und einzige selbstgefertigte Zeitzünder verwendet.

Sämtliche 10 an diesem Anschlag aktiv beteiligten Personen konnten ermittelt und bisher 9 von ihnen festgenommen werden. Außerdem wurden 12 Personen festgenommen, die der Beihilfe oder Begünstigung beschuldigt werden.

Sandberg stand in Verbindung mit dem Amsterdamer Kunstmaler und Schriftsteller Willem J.G. Arondeus und dem Amsterdamer Bildhauer Gerrit van der Veen. Diese drei haben dann zusammen beraten, welche Künstler zu unterstützen sind. Es kamen nur Kunstmaler und Bildhauer in Frage, die in Not geraten waren und sich nicht der Kulturkammer angeschlossen hatten. Die Unterstützung wurde dann auch ab 1. Mai 1942 gezahlt und zwar übernahmen Arondeus und van der Veen die Verteilung. Im Sommer 1942 wurden dann von den Genannten fälschlich hergestellte Persoonsbewijzen an in der Illegalität lebende Künstler, besonders auch an jüdische Künstler und Intellektuelle, später als die Studentenrazzien erfolgten, an Studenten verteilt. In besonders großen Massen wurden die Legimationskarten an Juden abgegeben, wodurch dieselben in der Öffentlichtkeit als Arier auftreten konnten. Die Zahl der ausgegebenen Ausweise läßt sich schwerlich angeben, sie muß aber wohl auf ein paar Tausend geschätzt werden. An minderbemittelte Personen

wurden die Ausweise kostenlos abgegeben, während andere
bis zu 500 Gulden pro Stück an die Genannten zahlten.
Die Zwischenpersonen sollten jedoch schon mal bis zu
1.500 Gulden für einen Ausweis genommen haben. Das Geld,
das nicht zur Deckung der Unkosten Verwendung fand, kam
in die Künstlerunterstützungskasse. Es konnte bisher
nicht festgestellt werden, wo die falschen Persoonsbewijzen gedruckt wurden.

Arondeus und van der Veen hatten von Sandberg je einen
Stempel von der Gemeinde Amsterdam und von der Gemeinde
's-Gravenhage erhalten, ferner laufend Blanko-Persoons-
bewijzen, sowie die ebenfalls fälschlich hergestellten
Gebührenmarken, wodurch sie in der Lage waren, ständig
falsche Persoonsbewijzen auszustellen. Während der er-
sten Auflagen der falschen Persoonsbewijzen nicht besonders gut aufgefallen waren, so stellten die Ausweise der
letzten Ausgabe eine sehr geschickte Nachahmung der
echten dar, sodaß dieselben von einem Spezialbeamten
der Reichsrecherchenzentrale in Den Haag nicht so ohne
weiteres als Fälschung erkannt werden konnten, da diese
Fälschung bisher noch nicht erfaßt worden war.
     Als nun von deutscher Seite der totale Kriegsein-
satz gefordert wurde, was eine erhöhten Arbeitseinsatz
niederländischer Staatsangehöriger in Deutschland zur
Folge haben sollte, faßten Arondeus, Sandberg und van
der Veen im Februar 1943 den Plan, das Bevolkungsregister in Amsterdam, in dem der zehnte Teil des niederländischen Volkes erfaßt ist, zu vernichten, um so der
Besatzungsmacht die Einrichtung zu nehmen, die der Ent-
sendung der Arbeiter nach Deutschland dient. Arondeus
wurde der geistige Leiter und Organisator dieses Sabotageunternehmens.

Die zuletzt Genannten (Honig, v. Musschenbroek und
Reitsma) sind wohl, vom charakterlichen Standpunkt aus
gesehen, die besten von denen, die sich an diesem Sabo-
tageunternehmen beteiligt haben. Auch bei der Vernehmung
waren sie, ebenso wie Arondeus, soldatisch in ihrer
Haltung.

... wer die Stahlhelme und Mützen geliefert hat. Der
noch flüchtige Sandberg soll dafür Sorge getragen haben.

and whatever was dark, so the whole background,
was grey. We then printed the identity papers on
double paper and on the inside of one of those papers
came the pseudo watermark. I am still proud that
the 'Anklageverfügung' [indictment] for the attack on
the municipal registry stated that the identity cards
'von einem Spezialbeamten der Reichsrechercenzent-
rale in Den Haag nicht so ohne weiteres als Fälschung
erkannt werden konnten' [a specialist from the
German investigation centre in The Hague could not
easily recognise the forgery]. In any case, it was the
best piece of typography I ever worked on.

At least we were able to help a lot of people with
it. We were first able to provide Jews with different
identity papers and later also people who were sent to
Germany for labour service, and for illegals. That was,
in my opinion, very important.

Now there was a hole in this identity paper history.
The forgery couldn't be detected, because it was done
really well. But they could always verify them in the
municipal registry. So the logical consequence was:
the attack on the municipal registry in Amsterdam.
First, in the middle of March, a test was made but
then the weather wasn't right and there was too much
moon etc. Then the attack was carried out on 27
March 1943, with the known success. The German
report about this is magnificent, particularly the beginning. It starts like a police novel. Later it becomes
more business-like, especially when the punishment
is being considered.

The leader of our enterprise was Willem Arondeus,
painter, poet and also writer. He wrote a book about

Matthijs Maris and about monumental art and the like.
He was a — yes, how should I describe Tikkie — Tikkie
was his illegal name. He was an exceptionally courageous man who was able to express his courage with
a certain demonstrative 'grand seigneur' attitude. I
won't say it was acting, I believe this was essentially
his true nature. He was the police captain and Gerrit
van der Veen was the police lieutenant. There were
several other people who were dressed as police
constables. The rest of the story is known to us all or
can be found in books. In any case, the whole thing
went up totally in flames. The fire brigade lent a hand,
by doing as little as possible to put out the fire. Only
the Amsterdam police did their very best to find the
perpetrators. The perpetrators were, I won't say be-
trayed, but in any case found.
One of the people who participated and who was our
courier was caught and — I do not know under what
pressure — sang. Nobody can say whether, under
exceptional circumstances, when tortured or so, he
could keep his mouth shut — I would never blame
anybody for that — but he did give up all the addresses
and on the night of the first of April , virtually the
whole group was captured.
     I was somewhat in charge of the organisation.
I wanted to go along with the others, but they thought
my face was too recognisable. My friends said: *No,
you'll be caught. They don't know us, but your face is
well known.* Often during the war years, I had to show
police officers round the museum and was therefore
perhaps less suited for the job. But I did collect the
explosives in my home. The meetings were always at

my house. Arondeus had the police uniforms made.
I took care of the helmets, with some help from the
designer Berkovich. I mention the names of living
people as little as possible, but I want to involve those
who died. Of those, there was a relatively large group
who contributed. Some of them, such as Johan
Brouwer, had borrowed a revolver and Koen Limperg
too, I think. He sheltered Arondeus and his courier
after the attack. The majority of all these people were
shot on 1 July 1943 after a mock trial. These included
Koen Limperg, because he had sheltered people,
and also Johan Brouwer, because he had borrowed
that pistol or that revolver. I believe that twelve of our
group were shot at that time.

About a year later, Gerrit van der Veen was also
shot, together with, I think, Walter Brandligt and
Frans Duwaer. Frans Duwaer had stated that he was
prepared to print the identity documents on the condition that he would only have to deal with one person
and that was me. I had to go into hiding immediately
after the first of April. They came to my house, but
they didn't find me, because I was in the vaults for the
art treasures, in Zandvoort. I first visited Frans who
was lying in the Diakonessen Hospital on Overtoom
and said: *Frans, I have to leave now. Do you mind if I
put you in touch with Gerrit van der Veen?* And that is
what happened and Gerrit became the liaison with
Frans Duwaer. They worked very closely together.
I usually got together with Gerrit van der Veen and
Frans Duwaer once every month in Berg en Dal near
Nijmegen to discuss things with them. Gerrit was
taken prisoner in May 1944. Then Frans came on his

own and said: *Wil, I'm so grateful that you put me in touch with Gerrit. It was the experience of my life.*

On the second day of April, the Germans visited Röell in the museum and said: *Bitte einsteigen, we have to pick up Sandberg in the art vault. Come with us, you must show us the way.* I know that he almost wet his pants from fear that they would find me there. But I had already had a telephone call from my wife that they had been to my house and were coming to get me. I immediately went into hiding. When Röell arrived at the vault, I had already fled. I had an address in Amsterdam where I could hide. I even had a room in Amsterdam, where I would occasionally disappear if I was in danger. But I didn't really want to go there, particularly with that face of mine. I then went into hiding with Van Gogh, whom I did not know.

We had the large V.W. van Gogh collection in the museum, but it was one of those typical peculiarities of Röell that he kept all collectors and important people to himself. That was his domain and nobody was allowed entry. We had the whole Van Gogh collection hanging in the museum and Van Gogh and his wife at the time — his first — would regularly visit, but I was not allowed to meet them. Now I had heard via Berkovich — who knew Van Gogh — that Nel (the wife of Vincent Willem) had previously said: *Gosh, Sandberg could come and stay with us.* I had taken note of that. And so I went to Van Gogh's office on the Herengracht and said: *Could I stay with you for a little while?* He said: *Yes, of course.* Then I got on my bike and rode to the Gooi. Jan Romein was also in hiding there in Huizen, and he said: *What on earth are*

 I said: *Yes, but I
haven't got a hat. I can't find a hat in my size anywhere.
I've got size 53 and they don't usually sell them in that
size.* But his hat fitted me and I then spent my time in
hiding wearing his small green hat. I made a neat
business-man's crease in it. Romein had a long pointed head, but its circumference was the same as mine.
I also wore a pair of golden spectacles, with plain
glass in them. That is how I hid — and it worked. I was
hardly recognised there, not at all really. But since
people could easily recognise me by the way I walked,
I always stayed seated on my bicycle. I spent the time
mainly in Limburg and Brabant, and the last nine
months in the Betuwe.

The most important work that we did in the war
was the preparations for the post-war Artists Organisation. We started on it in 1941. We set up a committee, together with Reinink, who had already left the
department of Education, Arts and Sciences. Each of
the arts was represented by one person. Jo Voskuyl
was the representative for the painters. At a given
moment, he went into hiding with Bart van der Leck.
The sculptors had Frits van Hall, the architects
Wegerif, the writers Jan Engelman and the musicians
Bertus van Lier. There were other people on the committee, including myself. Reinink was the chairman of
the group and his assistant was Jan van Gelder, who
later became a professor in Utrecht. I may have forgotten a name. We met regularly and we reached the
conclusion that we should set up a federation of professional associations of artists and that a Council for

the Arts should be formed as a link between the federation and the government. That whole plan was at, I think, the beginning of 1943 already in the form in which it now continues.

I always discussed all these things with Gerrit van der Veen, but he was very annoyed at me for not having asked him to take a seat on this committee but had asked his good friend Frits van Hall instead. I don't know if that was the reason, but soon afterwards he set up a new committee. That committee had two representatives for each type of art, just like Noah's ark, although they weren't all male and female. This committee was under the chairmanship of Jaap Bot. I was also a member of this committee and something of a liaison between the two committees. I could therefore make sure that the plans were developed somewhat in parallel to each other. In the second committee — the one with two people for each type of art — nobody knew of the existence of the first committee, with the exception of Gerrit van der Veen. The reverse was not true — the first committee knew of the existence of the second committee. The two committees finally found each other in, I think, December 1944 and this formed the basis of the Federation, which came into being in May 1945. I think it took until 1948 before the Council for the Arts was organised. In this way, the principles of both committees were followed. I wouldn't stick my neck out for the way they were put into practice, but that's a matter for the history books. This was one of the issues I was involved with the Dutch art organisation. I had, among other things, completely worked out that plan of the first committee, so that everybody had it down in black and white if I were forced to go into hiding. Some people on the committee were very annoyed when they heard that I was also active in the artists' resistance and thus brought their work into danger. They thought that because I had come under scrutiny in the artists resistance, they would also be in danger. Nothing like that ever occurred, but I remember that they were very upset about it.

Gerrit van der Veen was probably one of the most courageous men I ever met. Willem Arondeus was also courageous. He was a sort of knight. He had a great disdain for danger, while Gerrit van der Veen was, I felt, fearful by nature. Gerrit had to make an enormous effort to defeat his fear and I call him courageous because he completely overcame that fear. That is a very important factor. You can be courageous by nature and you can be completely uncourageous and yet, driven by necessity, become courageous. I remember that he often said: *I put greater value on my children saying later: we had a courageous father than saying: we still have a father, but he's a coward.* Frits van Hall was an exceptionally talented sculptor, perhaps rather classical, but that is a characteristic of the style at the time. He had Indonesian blood in him and I think that can be seen in his work. That gave it a certain elegance and perhaps also a touch of the exotic. He died too young, perishing on the way back from the concentration camp in Germany. And thus he was unable to develop further.

There was a very convivial atmosphere in this group of people. Actually, we really loved each other, but naturally characters clash from time to time. At a given moment, Tikkie — that was Willem Arondeus — came to me in the museum and said: *I'm bloody finished. I can't work with Gerrit anymore. He arrives at every meeting one or two hours late, and I won't stand it anymore. He can get to things on time. When he made that bust of Juliana, he always arrived at Het Loo Palace on time. Why can't he be on time for me? It is pure discrimination.* Tikkie would explode like this on occasions. He was really offended and I said: *Let's discuss it together, the three of us.* We did that shortly afterwards in the office of the Stedelijk Museum and Tikkie really went to town on Gerrit: *I sat waiting then and then in the Americain for two hours, and I won't stand it. You're always too late. That's not of any use in the attack either.* He repeated the story about Juliana, about the bust he made of her and said: *That's not right.* Anyway, the argument got very heated and Gerrit improved, in any case with regard to Arondeus. He understood that it was a type of discrimination if he treated him differently than the princess. That was a typical example of a heartfelt argument.

There was also another group that discussed future plans a lot. That group was mainly made up of Johan Brouwer, Arondeus, myself and sometimes also Koen Limperg. We discussed setting up a magazine together or a newspaper and all sorts of fantastic ideals.

I think that the artists' resistance and the role that the artists played in the whole Dutch resistance plus the foundation of the Federation, gave the artists in the Netherlands a different forum than they had before.

The attitude is no longer one of: *Here come the actors, wife, go bring in the washing.* Naturally not enough has happened but I have the idea that today artists play a different role in our society than they did in the 'twenties and 'thirties. We didn't really speak much about that in this group. On the one hand, Arondeus was totally convinced that he would be able to realise his ideals of publication and similar things after the war. On the other hand, he also had that feeling he shared with so many other members of the resistance of: I'm now risking everything and I will probably meet my end. And he did meet his end. In the 'Anklageverfügung' by the Germans, they say of Arondeus that they had an enormous appreciation for his personality; that he was a typical military figure. That was remarkable praise from that side, but I can well imagine that he made an impression on his interrogators by the way he answered them.

Many people, after they had spent a whole year in hiding and had taken all necessary precautions, stopped being careful. They lost their control and were exposed. That happened to Frans Duwaer, who had printed the identity papers. Gerrit van der Veen had said to him: *Frans, if I am ever taken prisoner, I promise you that I will keep my mouth shut for a week. But then I will assume that you have all got away and I will tell them anything they can get out of me.* When Gerrit was taken prisoner, Frans Duwaer first came to me and we made plans together for possibly freeing Gerrit. But Gerrit had been shot in the back and could hardly walk. He was then executed, standing between two comrades who helped him stay

173

on his feet. He was indeed unable to stand unaided.

Gerrit was in prison and Frans was planning to go into hiding on the sixth day after his arrest. On the sixth, or seventh day, he left the house with his suitcase, but then suddenly realised that he was deserting the family printing works. He went back to his house, unpacked his suitcase, went downstairs, and came face to face with the Gestapo. That was on 8 June 1944. On the 10th, he was executed by firing squad together with Gerrit.

The liberation had hardly taken place when we got together again. Then the two committees were merged. We met somewhere on the Herengracht and that was where we established the Federation. The first chairman was, if I remember rightly, Nico Donkersloot. He was succeeded, for a short time, by Kees van der Leeuw, the former director of the Van Nelle factories. I became chairman in 1947 and held the position for four years. In the city council, people felt that the chairmanship of the Federation could not be combined with the job of city civil servant, but I always ignored them. I felt that a civil servant was free to spend his spare time as he wished.

The Federation was the first Federation of professional associations for artists. Before and during the war, the painters in particular had not had any professional association. There were exhibition associations, where people who thought and worked in the same direction, met together and organised exhibitions together. This was the same in different areas. Nor did the musicians have a professional association, and so the Federation first insisted that all artists should organise themselves in professional associations. This had already happened with the architects and the applied artists, designers and so on were already organised in the VANK. We actually left that VANK for what it was and we set up a new foundation, the GKF, Gebonden Kunstenaars behorende bij de Federatie [the Bond of Artists belonging to the Federation]. That has now partly become the forefather of the GVN, Grafische Vormgevers in Nederland [Graphic Designers in the Netherlands]. And so all those artists' associations were formed relatively quickly and the Federation as a whole began functioning very speedily. Eduard Veterman was the first Secretary. He died rather quickly, but he had had a cell mate while in prison: Jan Kassies. Kassies spent much of the war behind bars. He had learned a lot from Veterman and when Veterman needed a deputy secretary, that was automatically Jan Kassies. He was at the time in his early twenties. After Veterman died, Kassies took over, and we all know his further career. He became sufficiently well known as director of the school of acting in Amsterdam.

The Federation had a difficult existence financially. In the beginning there was a great mutual unity, with one exception. We had always thought that the architects, as creative artists, should be part of the Federation. A number of the architects thought differently. I led endless discussions with representatives of the architects and they always made a whole range of demands. When those demands were granted, new ones were added. Ultimately, it came to nothing because the architects in Zeeland did not want to participate in a Federation which also included dancers. That was, in their Christian conviction, unacceptable.

I remember that we held difficult negotiations for years on end with these people and that particularly in the provinces there were people who said: *no, we belong more to the group of notaries, lawyers and doctors than to the artists.*

DUTCH SOCIETY AFTER THE WAR

During the occupation, were the Dutch more preoccu-
pied with the future or with the resistance? In my
view, in my discussions with Jan Romein and Jef Suys
— a study colleague of Romein — and with Baert and
Valkhoff who were present, we were just concentrating on the future. The many afternoons and evenings I
spent with Johan Brouwer, Willem Arondeus and
Koen Limperg were also dedicated purely to the future. We were only brought together by the resistance, but we all thought that after the liberation our
society would change radically.

Perhaps if we had held elections immediately
after the war — as we should have done — something
would have arisen and there would have been a shift.
There were all sorts of attempts at breakthrough,
both from the socialist and the Catholic sides and
perhaps that breakthrough would then have been
possible.

But the military authorities obstructed everything.
Through the totally undemocratic behaviour of the
military that we were presented with after the war, the
liberation could hardly be called a legal liberation.
Military rule is the worst thing that a person can imagine. That is what we see in various South American
republics and what we saw in Greece, that mentality
of the military who have authority over the citizens.
We suffered profoundly under it. We resisted it, but
we still got that first ministry. What's more, you could
clearly see how it was composed — who was there
for the electric light bulbs, who for the oil, the marga-
rine and who was there for the artificial fibres. The
major corporations all had their own minister in that

first cabinet. Later they became more sensible and appointed different puppets. They were given seats on the board and the like. That all took place more covertly. But immediately after the liberation, it was all out in the open.

Everybody had their own representative except the people. And the liberation we envisaged thirty–five years ago has come to nothing. National recovery was the order of the day. The name alone was enough to turn my stomach. Recovery instead of renewal. At a time when old connections had been proven worthless, there had been a chance for renewal everywhere. But no, people sought refuge in the social society as we knew it before 1940, that anxious society under the rule of vested interests. I have written myself that renewal is ultimately a question of generations. The older generations were actually lost for renewal and so we had to build on the new ones if we wanted to make this society liveable, make it a human community. The word 'community' brings me to another area. Community in Latin is commune, and the awareness of community is communism. The fear of communism has radically coloured politics and also the health of many people during the first twenty years and certainly after the liberation. I can understand the fear for Soviet Russia. We saw it occupy Hungary, Czechoslovakia and parts of Germany and Poland in 1948. The fear for communism thus began to live.

I would like to make a sharp distinction between communism as I see it: in which the community precedes the individual, and our so-called democracy where profit is the main theme, the economic motive. With the fear of communism, people tried to nip all progress in the bud. Man is, after all, a predator who lives in herds or the only carnivorous mammal — all other herding animals are herbivore mammals and this gives rise to the constant tension in the human society.

The herd is naturally a relative term. Man likes so much to exclude certain groups of people that he doesn't like from the herd, make them outsiders and thus outlaws. They did that with the Jews and they tried to do it after the war with the communists. Once you were marked as communist, people could do anything they liked with you. Then they would write whatever they liked about you and you could be treated in any way they liked. Then everything was permitted and you really were an outlaw. I repeatedly experienced personally this sort of hate for communists. I remember that we were telephoned for months on end during the day and night. Then 'murderers' came on the phone and we were cursed in every way possible. Our telephone was disconnected. All sorts of things that were totally illegal were done to you, because you were known as a communist. I have personally never been a member of any political party. I would have felt completely out of place there.

One thing for which I have always reproached the Communist Party in the Netherlands is that they completely neglected to pursue communism but blindly followed all the regulations issued by Moscow, which were totally meaningless here in the Netherlands. I still remember the first elections immediately after the war. Then a third of the city council in Amsterdam were communists. Well, little of that has remained and they have themselves to blame for that. Later, they no longer followed Moscow but Peking, but they followed in exactly the same way. I only have to think of the time when Stalin threw all the Jewish doctors into prison, and here they immediately threw all the Jewish doctors out of the party. I think of Ben Polak who was at one time a member of the Senate and alderman of Amsterdam. What is completely incomprehensible is that Polak later returned when Stalin rehabilitated the Jews.

How, for example, can the Russian ideology and the Eastern Bloc anti-Semitism be in any way equated with communism? I see it as a sort of Russian imperialist politics in the Middle East, where Russia for the first time — the Tsar had always tried — managed to secure a foothold with major weapon deliveries etcetera. I understand its place in their general politics, but why on earth should it have a place in their domestic politics that all Jews should again be thrown out everywhere? They could have taken Hitler as an example and could have seen how spiritually and culturally Germany was impoverished by ejecting all the Jews and important people. In my opinion, Germany is still suffering considerably because of that. Then you would say: they should think about it. I would almost say that, because of the exceptional position in which the Jews found themselves everywhere, they have concentrated so much on the humanities, physics, chemistry and the like, that they have developed a special affinity with them. Such an enormous affinity

that we simply couldn't imagine that, on their return to
Israel, they would start tilling the land and doing all
sorts of manual labour that they hadn't done for centuries; and that they would be so courageous in the
army. Whether you should applaud that or not, in any
case you would have to agree that nobody had ever
expected that of the Jews, wouldn't you? After all, we
all knew the type of "geduckte Jude", the fearful Jew
and he no longer exists in Israel. We notice that our
idea – I talk of our idea, although it was not always
mine – about the Jews no longer reflects what we see
in Israel. In my opinion that is because the Jews have
always lived as a minority everywhere and have always adopted the habits of a minority. But as soon as
they are in different circumstances, they develop
totally different qualities. This attitude of the minority
towards the majority can be seen everywhere. You
see it with the Copts in Egypt, where the Christians
form a tiny minority. Everywhere that you encounter a
minority, you find characteristics that we consider
so-called typically Jewish.

I have always believed that the community should
precede the right of the individual and that that ultimately should be the driving force of our society. I am,
in addition, a fierce democrat. I absolutely do not
believe in a dictatorship, whether of the right or the
left. They are both as bad as each other and at odds
with human dignity. On the other hand I must say
that, at the moment, I see our democratic system with
all that voting as the only possibility, but I am not at all
happy with it. I do not know a better system, so I am a
democrat, but I am absolutely convinced that the

majority is always wrong. Except, perhaps, in times of
crisis.

How is it possible that during the last twenty years
so much has happened in this country? I think in
particular about the whole Catholic rejuvenation. The
Catholics, who still form an important part of the
population, have changed completely. At least when
I read the papers and see how the cardinals, the
bishops and the pastors treat young people; how they
currently exert their authority and how they speak.
When I came back here after many years abroad,
I couldn't believe my ears when I heard how people
spoke of the Pope: no longer was he His Holiness
who could do no wrong. He could even be criticised
in Catholic newspapers.

The whole hierarchy slowly began to shake and
our society has profited considerably from this. When,
in the post-war years, I sat on committees, boards and
in many associations, at least forty percent, and if
possible sixty percent, of all the board or committee
members had to be Catholic. Education and Culture
were always in the hands of Catholics. That was how it
was. There always had to be a majority of Catholics
everywhere and they always had to provide the chairman, of the Council for the Arts, of this and that. That
has now completely disappeared. I really don't know
anymore what has come over me when I compare this
to the pressure under which we lived for all those
years, particularly in the field of culture.

But when I read in the papers how minds in all
sorts of areas are moving and then I look at the elec-
tion results, I have the feeling: something isn't right.

Either the newspaper has given me false information or the people have simply got out the voting papers they filled in many years ago and filled in the new one in exactly the same way, with the same habits and without giving it any thought. There are small shifts, but you really cannot talk of any landslide in public opinion that you find in the newspapers, on the radio, on the television and everywhere around you. You find nothing of this in politics. Politics, which should really be a reflection of what is happening in our nation. Isn't that happening in our nation? Are the newspapers writing or the television broadcasting from a tiny minority? Where is the younger generation that hasn't been through so much — fortunately, or perhaps un-fortunately for them? I can really imagine that those five years of occupation and the heroism of the resist-ance means nothing to them. That wasn't heroism, but bitter necessity. Everybody who had even the slight-est feeling of responsibility had to take part. It was a natural consequence of your thinking.

That doesn't mean that for me personally those five years during which everything was turned upside down was not an exceptional experience. Just take those last two years, when I was outlawed, but then in a different way. You were in all the wanted reports, with a picture, and you knew you could be picked up at any time and be done for. For me, that proved a very positive experience because you prepared your-self for the fact that every hour could be your last. Every time you do something or look at something, you think: *probably this is the last time I do this.* I remember cycling from Nijmegen to Gennep in April

1943 and seeing all the fields of yellow coleseed and thinking: well, probably you have seen this for the last time, but it is okay. That thought is still linked to the colour yellow. When I made it through to 1945, it first of all gave a feeling of relief. You were amazed that you hadn't been done in. Every day that you subsequently live is actually a gift, and that is a rich experience.

The youth cannot imagine what liberation was for us. That is actually very positive and very good, but now I expect the youth to get together and try to build up a society on a different basis. Not only in their own interests, on the profit motive, or chasing profit as I prefer to call it, but in the interests of society. It doesn't matter whether you call that communism or something else. I think communism is a wonderful word and that I am called names and my reputation blackened because of that is something I consider an honour. Just as that group of Dutch who called themselves Geuzen [Beggars] [17]. 'Beggars' naturally had a negative meaning, but they turned it into something positive. I have never felt ashamed of being called a communist and I have never tried to defend myself against it. It is all nonsense, because I never denied it, even though Stalin for me was the greatest traitor to

17. "Geuzen" literally means "tramps, vagrants". In the 16th century, a large group of Dutch nobles presented a petition to the Spanish regent, Margaret, Duchess of Parma. One of her councillors referred to the group as "ces gueux", a name that was then proudly adopted by the freedom fighters in the battle against the Spanish rule over the Netherlands.

the communist philosophy.

Socialism is also a sense of society, a feeling of togetherness. The word socius means communal, connected. But that too, like communism, has gradually become a worn-out word. Socialism, after achieving so many socialist ideals, such as prosperity, has, in my opinion, never achieved equality for all. It's not something I see high on the agenda of the socialists either. The socialism of my youth was totally different. That was something really progressive. Those socialists were also people who dared to take over the stage. But Troelstra was ridiculed in his own circle, and Wibaut and so many more. But slowly socialism has become fashionable. You can quite easily be a factory owner or a bank director and still vote for the socialists. That says nothing derogatory about the director, but about socialism. That is why socialism has now acquired something of a negative overtone for me. I regret this, because the principles are, naturally, excellent. But currently you have the feeling that it means compromise and leaving everything to committees. And with this I would like to return to that democracy. It has been my experience that for every problem the government faced, a committee was formed and sent away to solve it. When it had all become less current, they produced some report or other, and extra desks had to be built with drawers large enough to store all those reports.

But I believe that when one is faced with a problem, one has to distinguish clearly whether it is a problem of assessment or a creative problem. Assessments of matters, issues or people can best be left to committees. But you shouldn't leave creative matters to committees. Creativity is the task of the individual. Then you have to search for that one individual in whom you can have full trust. But you must also hold fast to that trust until he abuses it. And you must leave that man alone, because creating something together isn't possible.

When I see the letterhead of a firm of architects with a whole list of names, I know that there is one person who creates and the rest follows. They implement the project and perhaps hold meetings. But creatively there is only one person in that team. You can work well in a team as long as you carefully allocate the roles. I think it would rectify our current democratic habits if people did not depend for everything on committees but that far more commissions were given to creative individuals to solve problems with a creative nature. This would allow the individual in society to come into his own better than in a committee.

To return to the situation after the war: then the youth of the day was in general far too restricted by what had happened and which they probably had not understood to expect much renewal. But things were different for the artists. I personally do not find that strange, because I have after all the feeling that artists have longer antennae than other people and can better sense what is really taking place below the surface.

Immediately after the liberation, I looked in all directions to see how the artists would react to the years behind us and to what lay ahead. I must honestly admit that I was somewhat impatient, because I saw little movement among those with established reputations. People simply returned to their easels, tried to mould something with dried out paint and continued with that little still life they had been working on a few years before. But shortly after the liberation there were a number of groups primarily among the young artists and, in 1948, the Reflex group emerged from these. I am thinking mainly of Constant, about Appel, Corneille, Eugène Brands and a few others. And I believe that those in the Reflex group — which later became internationally the Cobra group — gave expression to that which was actually taking place. That feeling of defiance, that revolutionary feeling, not only in their subjects but in their whole attitude and way of painting. They had of course their examples. They went back to expressionism and had certainly looked at Miró and Picasso, but they were able to express that in a very exceptional way.

The Reflex group, which had links especially with Scandinavia, in particular Copenhagen and its surroundings, and with Belgium, was for a long time at the forefront. Various members of the group were inspired by what I would call this mentality. But we also see similar movements outside the group, which sometimes were actually a one-man movement. I am thinking of Jean Dubuffet in France, Willem de Kooning in New York and Bram van Velde, also in France. It is probably not at all peculiar that both Bram van Velde *and* Willem de Kooning are of Dutch origin. There is a considerable kinship between these two individuals and the Dutch Cobra group, such as exists between these and the whole Cobra group. Then I think primarily of the Dane Asger Jorn and the Belgian Alechinsky. I would also like to mention the writer Hugo Claus, for it was a group of painters and mainly writers. And then I think of Jan Elburg, Gerrit Kouwenaar and Lucebert. Lucebert was, at the time, a member of the Cobra group as poet and only became a painter member at a later date.

That spirit was so typical for our collective post-war experience, I recognised myself immediately in it. I also believe that that was the expression that was appropriate for the times. It was also self-evident that, after being oppressed by the occupation for so long, something would erupt. When I think of the un-Dutch way in which the Canadian liberators were welcomed here on 5 May 1945 — we all went completely wild — then it really is self-evident that this period should be characterised by an eruption of colour and shape. But in the Cobra movement, there was also an eruption of monsters. All those monsters we had seen and experienced around us came to life there. Expression was also given to that.

Moreover, if we remember this time properly, we naturally moved towards peace in full expectation. We thought that the world would now change. We had all — at least, the people of my generation — worked together in committees or groups for the future. I was in the group with Jan Romein, Suys and a few other people. We were often in that little hut near the art vault in Castricum and really tried to imagine what that time after the war should look like. A booklet by Jan Romein, called, I think, "Nieuw Nederland" [New

Netherlands] came out of this and it was published soon after the liberation. In it, he also writes about the collaboration between those people.

We thought that everybody, after all those experiences of the war, the occupation and the concentration camps, would have been touched so deeply in their souls that new people would emerge from it. That was the great disappointment of the liberation. Nothing of that was visible. Everybody rushed back to the job, profession or company they had before 1940. While we thought that 1940 was completely gone and a new era would start. Holland was then, particularly in those first years after the liberation, an exceptionally boring country and probably the same was true of Denmark. That is why, I believe, we must also see the Cobra movement as a protest against the tedium, against the parochial small-mindedness that reigned everywhere. Fortunately, since then the provos[18] have contributed something to making life here a bit more bearable. And also the hippies, the Beatles, the youth protest that arose in the 'sixties. That was actually prefigured, predicted by the Cobra movement that dated from 1949.

The movement of hippies, provos and of nozems — to go back even further — actually started here in Holland. Holland can count it an honour that it has

18. "Provo" derived from the Latin "provoco", to provoke. This youthful protest movement in the 'sixties operated mainly in Amsterdam. Through fun action and civil disobedience, established authorities were challenged and social issues denounced. "Nozems" were also part of this movement.

now spread throughout the world. That youth protest
is, in my opinion, something enormously important,
because the youth is not connected to a society based
on profit. They turn themselves away from it. That
may make them apathetic to work, but they'll get over
that. What shall remain and what, I think, is a factor in
the history we are writing at this moment is that magnificent protest by the youth against the society in
which we have placed them and for which we older
people are responsible. I think that our society can be
proud that it is a democracy here in the Netherlands,
that your personal freedom remains guaranteed and
they you don't have groups of gangsters and the like,
such as you encounter in larger countries. That is
perhaps one of the reasons why I always feel at home
here when I return here from abroad.

Our hope is pinned on a new generation that will
distance itself from society with all its faults that we
bequeath to them, and that will go off in search of
something new.

They are genuinely searching. They have, as far
as I can see, not yet found anything, but any renewal
always begins with dissatisfaction and they are
demonstrating that dissatisfaction. Sometimes with
positive plans, I think, for example, of the white bike
plan[19] and of all sorts of other things. They are also
concerned about the housing shortage, the elderly,
and all sort of useful matters, but not about reforming

19. The white bike plan: one of the well-known Provo-
initiatives, white bikes would be available in Amsterdam as
collective property, free for all to use.

society. Perhaps the white bike plan goes further. For that is not some sort of social action, but very typically an action that goes beyond our capitalist society. Besides that I would like to ride a white bike myself at some time or other, I believe this plan would lead in the direction of a solution to a tiny problem in our society. And when one problem is solved, others will follow.

The fact of the matter is that we live in a community where the economy rules over welfare. Whenever I read something here in Amsterdam about the metro that they wanted to build, I thought: a metro is ultimately an inhuman means of transport. We are not moles and why should we crawl under the ground through this muddy, swampy land that causes so many problems for something like a metro? Why not build a monorail high above everything in the fresh air and with a wonderful view of this old city, instead of crawling underground? A monorail is a fast tram that travels high above the houses and which nowadays doesn't need to make any noise, because it travels on rubber tires. Why must that only be an economic problem? I think we are doing things wrong. I believe we should take into account the human factor of travelling either high in the air or crawling under the ground. We should include that somewhere in our calculations.

I believe that we would then reach different conclusions in the area of public transport, which is, of course, enormously important. Often it takes me three quarters of an hour to an hour to get home by tram or bus, if Rokin is jammed solid. This makes

everybody take their car. If I found a white bike,
I would ride on that white bike. That problem of the
car in the inner city has gradually become a car
mania. In large cities such as New York, it's not like
that any more. There you have taxis for everything.
Here, they are not yet used to that. The economic
relationships are not there either, but I do think we
should look at this in a different way. Not from financial calculations but from a more human viewpoint.

THE TASK OF
THE ARTIST

I am always very careful with the word art. I would actually prefer to reserve it for those things, those objects that have really opened people's eyes and have brought the development of art a step further; so only use it in connection with the development of art in main lines. I would not want to call everybody who plasters oil paint onto a canvas an artist. Preferably painter, just as I would prefer to call somebody who sculpts images, but in a traditional way without any personal contribution, a sculptor and not an artist. I would like to be extremely frugal with the words art and artist, use them as little as possible. You can always translate it with creativity or creative possibilities.

We have to take into account, in this context, that artists can also go into decline and become painters and sculptors. For, just like most people, they have ups and downs in their lives and more downs than ups. For many, it is an expression of youth, a sort of 'Sturm und Drang', an early blossoming, which contains promises that are never fulfilled. There are many, many people who have done very important work, who have helped art move forward enormously and then, often when they approach thirty or forty, fail, go into decline, repeat themselves or even make no further contribution at all.

To produce art, you need a tool or two. In the first place perhaps: vitality, in the second place: character, perseverance — they are very close together — and a sense of order. Ordering of the environment and sometimes even — if the artist is really committed — of society itself. When I see many of today's youth

197

rise in rebellion, I ask myself how long this will last.
Hopefully a new generation will arise to take over
from them but I would like to know where many of the
young people I see on the streets today will be in five
or ten years' time. I hope they will still be taking to the
streets, but I fear the worst. Our society and our whole
upbringing and education are all aimed at forming
young characters — perhaps I may say deforming, in
any case to make them suitable for a place in society.
To do that, they must adapt or, as the French say,
"ranger"; to find the way back to clean-shavenness,
to haircuts, to collar and tie and all the rest. I fear that
for most people that is still what's in store for them.
For the majority of artists, things actually take place in
much the same way. In their youth they are rebellious,
highly sensitive. They allow themselves to be swept
along by the undercurrent of our society, they are
committed. They become inspired by this and achieve
performances that are higher than normal, possibilities for renewal. But all too soon they conform to
society and they become painters and sculptors. In a
highly respectable way they try to achieve success,
to be granted commissions and get people interested
in their work. They start a family and have to pay for
the car and so on. Just as at the end of the nineteenth
century poverty was the greatest test for the true
artist or the most severe examination that had to be
passed — irrespective of whether his work was appreciated and whether it was sold or not — at the moment
the greatest test is success. And only the very strongest characters can endure success. Most of them are
destroyed by success.

So art is closely connected with character. There are but a few people who have sufficient character to keep going until the end. Let me name a few from the last hundred years. First Edouard Manet, who kept going until the end. He didn't live to a very old age. He died when he was fifty-nine. Then Claude Monet. He was the first to introduce impressionism into painting, I could say discovered it. He dedicated his life to it. He reached the age of 84 and in his old age, when he was almost blind, he actually freed himself from the impressions of the outer world. He only used them as a pretext. He was able to express that which lived inside him. I am now thinking in particular of his very late landscapes and of his water lilies. His last paintings are actually precursors of what we would come to know after the war as formless art. He did that when he was in his eighties. I consider it a very important quality that you are able at that age to see so far ahead, that these things would only be discovered twenty years later.

Another such figure was Cézanne. A completely different character, more a hermit who wanted to do everything in compliance with his roots, the bourgeois environment to which he belonged. He dressed accordingly, he lived accordingly, but when it came to his art, he knew no compromise whatsoever. He had it in his head that he could represent what he saw around him with geometric shapes and that colour would be the modelling clay. Cézanne was certainly one of the true greats and his immediate successors became the cubists: Picasso, Braque, Juan Gris, and the abstract Mondrian. I wouldn't go as far as saying — after all, I am no seer — that these people wouldn't have discovered it without Cézanne, but Cézanne was certainly a very important pioneer. He made it possible for the later generation to cover that stage more rapidly and to find a new point of departure for the art of painting. A new point of view on the world outside, just as Einstein in the same period discovered a new point of view in the sciences about the universe, and Freud found one that explained the human soul and gave us a new picture of it.

Immediately after Cézanne I would then mention Van Gogh. Van Gogh also continued to develop until his very last breath. He died young, he was 37 years old, but he completed all the stages at a lightening pace and in a period of just eight years developed into an artist who, even today, can still shock us, inspire us and bring us to new ideas. Monet, Manet and Cézanne were not at all integrated, I would almost say, in the political and social development of their time, but Van Gogh was exceptionally integrated.

Van Gogh was the son of a Dutch vicar and grew up in a very orthodox Christian family. He was able to free himself from that and was, in my opinion, the first socialist artist. He understood what human equality means. He lifted his simple models to his level or he descended to theirs. In any case, he felt one with them. He dressed the same as them, because he no longer wanted to be a gentleman. We can think of his early self portraits, from around 1886, when he was still a highly cultivated gentleman, with a hat and a beard and a pipe. When we look at his last self portraits, all we see is a human being. We cannot place him in any social class. He is nothing more than a human being. Everything that was around him has been absorbed into that same human drama. His landscapes and his still lifes have also become carriers of that human tragedy that was his own tragedy.

He also always tried to form a community with his friends, his art brethren. That never succeeded. He tried it, for example, with Gauguin. He was certainly not an easy man to get on with and they very soon split up, but he always tried to live according to that community idea. He did not, like Jozef Israëls or Max Liebermann, try to portray the poverty or the labourer — those were synonymous at the time, but thankfully no longer so — and to show the aesthetic aspect. That was foreign to Van Gogh. Van Gogh plunged into poverty. He lived the life of the labourer and highlighted it.

Then I turn from Van Gogh to a complete opposite, also a Dutchman and also from an orthodox Christian environment: Piet Mondrian. I spoke about him earlier, but would like to talk about him further. Mondrian's evolution took place very slowly. Perhaps that is also the guarantee that this evolution would continue. He had placed the aim he had set for himself so far in the distant future that he would have needed more than a lifetime to reach it. It is also a very important thing for an artist who wishes to continue to grow right to the end to have an aim in his mind that is actually beyond his reach. Mondrian only really became more or less himself when he was around 38. He was already in his forties when he became abstract and he was one of those people who tried in a magnificent way to illustrate a new space. To purify the space, I would almost say to make it intellectual. I think that's a nasty word, intellectual — just like spiritual, which I do not like either — but in any case he tried to approach space from a scientific angle. He first followed a naturalist path and then the expressionist path. At a given moment he became a symbolist under the influence of philosophy, because he was a seeker. But during the First World War he found himself. I think particularly of the moment in 1916–17, when he banned the object, so actually the external inspiration, from his work. He had been a cubist from 1910 until that time and there is always still in the work of the cubists an object that the artist has seen and tries to illustrate, albeit in a very special, personal way. Because the cubist artist as it were, went around the object he wanted to show and would try to represent it from different sides, the paintings were very centripetal, with forms assembling towards the centre. They compressed everything to the middle of the canvas. That is also the reason why various cubists made oval paintings, because they didn't know what to do with the corners of the canvas.

Then suddenly, in 1917, Mondrian's art became centrifugal, with forms diverging from the centre. For he was actually trying to impose an order in our environment that was not restricted to the extremes or the dimensions of the canvas, but which had to stretch much farther in order to influence the whole environment. I experienced that myself. I remember, just after the liberation, sitting in my freshly painted white room in the Stedelijk Museum, which we had managed to add during the war. That thing subsided later, because it didn't have any foundations. I had a nice old painted Bavarian cupboard there — I had it on loan from Kasper Niehaus — and characteristic old furniture stood around the table. The table was made of simple wood, but there were some other decorative touches in the room. At the time, we had a lot of paintings on loan from the Kröller-Müller Museum that had been bombed and badly in need of repair and was thus unable to hang its paintings. We couldn't do that either, because the glass in our roof had not yet been replaced and the rain came in. Then I found a painting by Mondrian in the depot dating from 1917 and I hung it in my room opposite me. Involuntarily that painting drove out all those things that didn't belong in the room, no matter how beautiful they were in themselves.

Those things just didn't suffer each other and I preferred the Mondrian to that beautifully painted Bavarian whorehouse cupboard. It was painted in green and red, a jewel so to speak, but it had to give way. And my chairs too had to make way for very simple chairs. Fortunately, the rest of the room was completely white, with large red flagstones on the floor. There was hardly a stick of furniture in the room, but that Mondrian convinced me by the mood that the painting then radiated on me. I had regularly read 'De Stijl' since 1925–1926, I always had been familiar with it, but I only really experienced it then. Now nobody can afford to have a Mondrian in his office. Then you could get hold of a Mondrian for a thousand guilders and then I'm talking about 1945–1950. Mondrian

continued to explore the purity from 1917 until 1944
— the year of his death — so for more than 25 years.
In addition he was also, to a certain degree, socially
committed. He was aware of the worker's class and all
those things. I think he would have called himself a
socialist if you had asked him, but on the other hand
he lived and worked like a monk. When you entered
his studio, you were first of all amazed by the abstract
colours red, yellow and blue, with the non-colours
black, grey and white. And he only knew straight lines.
No diagonal straight lines, but a horizontal and a verti-
cal, and as shape only the rectangle. He worked with
these elements for more than 25 years and revealed
for himself a sort of life conviction.

Then, in this connection, I return to Paul Klee.
Klee also started very hesitantly and only found himself very late. He was incredibly tense about what he
made, but I have the idea that earning money did not
play much of a role with him, even though he was very
poor. At the start he made things that nobody could
use. I am thinking particularly about the time before
the First World War. Klee was born in 1879 and was,
at the outbreak of war, about 35 years old. It was not
until 1919, in my opinion, that he found himself and
became the Paul Klee whom we really love. He was
forty at the time. A very late development. Paul Klee
is really somebody from the century of Freud. He was
occupied with making man's subconscious visible,
particularly his own subconscious. That made him a
very fascinating and unique figure. There is no possible comparison between Paul Klee and others. You
cannot indicate a master anywhere. The man abso-

lutely found it by himself. He was also something of a
hermit, but not in the degree of Mondrian. He was, as I
said, very poor, lived in an attic room and lived from
the money his wife earned with piano lessons.
Campendonk told me in one of his last conversations
shortly before his death about his first visit to Paul
Klee. He had travelled to Munich with the German
painter August Macke – his cousin – and the collector
Hermann Köhler to look at art there. They were all
from the Rhineland – Campendonk was from Kleve
– and came into contact with the artists in Munich
by chance. They discovered, I think, a charcoal drawing in an art gallery which they all found delightful and
it turned out to be by Franz Marc. This was how
Campendonk and Macke discovered Franz Marc, with
whom they became close friends.

I think that Marc in turn put them in touch with
Kandinsky. Kandinsky was much older than them.
This must have been around 1910, 1911. Kandinsky
was then in his mid-forties, whereas they were still
young men. Macke was something like 22, 23 and
Campendonk perhaps a little older. They therefore
very much looked up to Kandinsky. They met him in a
beautiful, rich apartment in Munich. He was then just
at the end of his expressionist period and had started
with his first abstract water colours. What is remarkable is the fact that Kandinsky and Klee had probably
lived in the same street for eleven years and had
never met each other. Later they became close
friends. They were teachers at the Bauhaus together.
It was strange that they lived so close to each other
for so long without knowing each other. Perhaps that

205

was because one was extremely wealthy and the other extremely poor. Perhaps that was a boundary they could not breach.

I shall now quote something I wrote in 1959 in "Nu, midden in de XXe eeuw" [Now, in the middle of the XXth century]. At the time it gave rise to a lot of controversy, but fits in perfectly with the theme we are discussing now:

Art can be a means of contact with the present. For what is the task of the artist? To beautify life and make it more pleasant, to help us with beautiful thoughts, to transport us from the wretchedness of the everyday to the sublime? Or to stand guard with all his senses as it were to taste what is going to come — long before we, normal people, have discovered it. To go where life is most intense. To grope for the society that is growing and to give it its form, its face.

But there are two breeds of what we call artists. The first builds faithfully on that which excellent pre-decessors have created. They form a school, they try to make art and manufacture paintings, sculptures. The second group borrows the technical resources of their predecessors, but renews them, tries to illustrate what is not yet apparent, to establish what is growing. They are the vanguard, they do not talk about art. They bring a message, their creations open eyes.

The first group of artists calms, uplifts, 'ennobles'. People immediately dub their work beautiful. The public is grateful to them and forgets them. The other shocks us. We are touched, impressed, inflamed or simply repelled. The next generations will talk of their work as 'beautiful' and 'wonderful'. The art history only knows this group, naturally after their death. Then they are called 'great artists'.

Great art is always an experiment. Great artists live now. They can usher us into the present, prepare us for the future. Where do we find them? In the museums?

The artists feel themselves attracted to the place where life is most intense. That was, in the nineteenth century and at the beginning of the twentieth, Paris. They all came together there. From there, people such as Picasso, Léger, Mondrian made great contributions to the renewal of art. The French came, of course, to Paris, but people from outside France also came there: Picasso, Mondrian, Jongkind of the earlier generation; Van Dongen and so many others; Gonzalez, Juan Gris, Arp. The artists who gathered in Paris are, in fact, countless. Kandinsky went there when he was older, when he had to flee from Hitler. Paris actually gave them all the stimulus they needed. And here again we see the antennae that the great artists have and from which they learn where they have to go.

Of course, many more people came to Paris and burned their wings in the City of Light, but on the other hand, going to Paris was a condition for coming to true development. We were able to see that in Jongkind, and Van Gogh is an excellent example. He would probably have got stuck in his dark brown style if he had continued to live here in the Netherlands. But it was exactly those last five years when he went to the south — first to Antwerp, then to Paris and finally to the South of France, Arles and Saint-Rémy — that made him into the colourful dramatic painter who we all hold in high esteem and who has penetrated to all levels of the population. It is remarkable that thirty, forty years ago, you would already find his sunflowers in the lodge of every caretaker in Paris. In reproduction, of course, but they appealed to all levels of the population, regardless of their social or intellectual standing. His work is reproduced more than that of almost any other artist. A very remarkable fact, that can again be traced back to the fact that he was, as I said before, the prophet of equality. That is something that fascinates people, even if they do not take it into account.

Then Mondrian. Mondrian was, when he lived here in Holland, occupied with expressionism. Then he suddenly came into contact with the first beginnings of cubism and found, via that cubism in Paris, his own development. Although the abstract art of Mondrian was actually born here, during the First World War when he couldn't leave Holland. He first came back to Holland in 1914 on holiday and couldn't return because of the war. He dedicated himself here totally to exploring the abstract and he returned to Paris in 1918 as a complete abstract artist and as one of the great leaders of abstract art.

We have seen it with so many other artists: they needed Paris to come to complete development. That was not the case at the time of Rembrandt. Then Amsterdam was the centre where everything happened, the economic centre of Europe. The people felt attracted to this city. At the time, life here was the most intense and that was why, in the middle of the seventeenth century, that magnificent Dutch art could develop with Rembrandt, Vermeer, Frans Hals and all the rest.

Naturally the question arises: has the capital of art moved? We can all agree that it is no longer Paris. It seems that in the 'sixties, New York became the art capital of the world. In New York, a number of artists made a special American contribution to the development of art during and especially after the Second World War.

One American artist does not come from New York and had, in fact, already made his contribution before that time: Alexander Calder. Calder introduced motion into art. Others had been working on the issue before him, I think of Gabo, of Marcel Duchamp and perhaps a few others. But the man who really turned it into his profession and concentrated completely on motion in art — in sculpture that is — is Calder. The others needed electricity or machines to bring that movement. Calder created mobiles, moving sculptures — I don't know whether you can call them sculptures or tangible creations — based on balance. The slightest draught or wind would disturb this balance and set them in motion. Calder did start with an electric motor, but he soon made this invention of motion in space. The mobiles did not require any mechanical means and I believe that that is a very important contribution to the development of the plastic arts — in order now to make no distinction between painting and sculpture.

Movement is something that has always interested me, which is why I organised several exhibitions of Calder and other artists. Together with Pontus Hultén, at the time director of the Moderna Museet in Stockholm, and Spoerri, who was originally a dancer and later concentrated on motion art, the art of movement, we organised the exhibition "Bewogen Beweging" [Moving Movement] in 1961. First, because we liked exhibiting moving things, but also because people were allowed to touch them. I understand that it is necessary to have signs saying 'Do not touch' or attendants who correct visitors who touch a Mondrian, but on the other hand, eyes are sometimes not enough for people. They must also be able to touch things, to feel them and if they can set them in motion, then that's perfect. "Bewogen Beweging" was primarily directed at involving the visitor in the exhibition. People could touch things, press buttons, they could make them produce a sound or start them rocking. The things by Nicolas Schöffer, which moved in rotating spotlights, could be shown in a dark room. With the work of Agam, people could make a composition themselves on a tableau and with Calder, they could also let things move, simply by blowing at them.

Calder came to Paris very early, I think it was in 1930 or 1929. He then fell under the influence of Mondrian. From this he has still retained his primary colours, red, blue, yellow and white and black. He has freed himself from Mondrian's way of painting and for that has fallen more under the influence of Miró. Yet there are several Mondrian-like paintings by Calder from that period. I think it was in Paris that he discovered the mobiles. And so Paris was an inspiration point for him, in the same way it was for many artists until 1940. But then it seems as if, with that whole exodus that Hitler put into motion, the spirit also left Europe, as if it moved to America and found accommodation in the pre-eminently international city of New York. First because of the immigration of important European artists. I think especially here of Léger, Chagall, Zadkine, Lipchitz — Miró also belongs to that period — André Masson and we mustn't forget Mondrian.

I assume that these immigrants had an important influence on the younger American artists. Then we get a transitional figure, Arshile Gorky and after that it explodes with the informal art of Pollock. There is actually a whole group at work then: Barnett Newman, Willem de Kooning, Franz Kline, Mark Rothko and that's about it. Of these personalities some I have known well. It was noticeable that the spirit apparently had left Europe. In my opinion, you can immediately distinguish an American painting from a European, although sometimes it is done in the same style. Naturally, the American style and the rapid changes in American painting soon came over to Europe, but you can clearly recognise the Americanism that those paintings radiate. On the one hand because of the manner of painting and the broader idea behind it, but also because they are so large.

I believe that size is a very important element here. I did not understand that for many years, until I once entered the living-room of an art dealer and there, directly opposite the door, hung an enormous painting by Pissarro. It was a landscape and when you came through that door it was as if you were right in the middle of the landscape. That is also the intention of that large size used by the American artists, that you actually seem to stand right in the middle of their painting. Later that was continued in environmental art, in which an attempt was made to turn the whole environment into a work of art.

That is something which Kurt Schwitters in Hanover began in the 'twenties. He created the 'Merzraum', the 'Merz Space'. In his house — of which he was the owner, fortunately — he had made a space that passed through several storeys; it was like a sculpture and you stood in the middle of it. That first 'Merzraum' was unfortunately destroyed during the bombing of Hanover. Before that happened, Schwitters had moved to Oslo in 1938, and he made a second 'Merzraum' in Norway. When Hitler invaded Norway, he went to England. He crossed from Narvik to England in, I believe, a rowing boat and was, as German, immediately confined to a concentration camp on the Isle of Man. He later emerged from the camp and then created his third 'Merzraum' on the border between England and Scotland in a sort of hut or shed. That must still exist, although I have never seen it and the photographs that I know of it are not very clear. But he actually gave the impulse to the principle of environmental art, what the French call the 'ambiance' and the Americans call the 'environ-ment'.

Kurt Schwitters, as independent artist, also cre-ated important art works. He was one of the pioneers, because he developed much further the collage that had been invented by Picasso and his group at the start of the cubist era. Whenever he was walking he must have gathered whatever scraps of paper he found and put them in his pockets. He also had a girlfriend, Hannah Höch, who always carried a large bag around and collected things for him. He created art works from all those pieces of paper, train tickets, postage stamps, pieces of print, pamphlets, advertisements, and possibly pieces of wood and balsa wood, which had their very own character and which inspired many young people, particularly in this time.

Probably that 'Merzbau' was in the back of our minds and inspired the exhibition "Dylaby", a dynamic labyrinth that we made in 1962. See, you walk around a piece of sculpture. Sometimes, if it is a gate, you can crawl through it, but that is about it. At the time, we thought more about an artwork which you could enter. That is, as I already said, something which the American painters who made those enormous canvases also thought a lot about. People often laughed about it and said: *If it is a red plane with a little blue and yellow stripe, why does it have to be so big? You could easily make do with a tenth of its actual size.* But the American artists wanted people to come into their work, that they were practically surrounded by their work. So if you stand at a certain distance from such a canvas — by Barnett Newman or Morris Louis or whoever — you really have the feeling that you are in the artwork.

That is exactly what we wanted to do with such sculptures or rather with three-dimensional things, and "Dylaby" was the result. It went like this: the artist could fit out his own space and the people could walk through it. I think about the labyrinth of Spoerri that

was largely pitch dark, but where you could hear and
smell and touch all sorts of things. You could also walk
up and down stairs and open doors. If you opened a
door, a pulley was attached to it and then something
or other, I think it was a chair, went upwards. When
you shut the door again, something would fall with a
crash to the ground. So the people controlled the
objects and found themselves in the middle of things.
I chose the people who made "Dylaby" — Martial
Raysse was one and Tinguely and Rauschenberg — in
the hope that they would install all this space together.
That unfortunately did not happen and so the upstart
was that everybody chose their own area and decorated it themselves. Niki de Saint Phalle made two
monsters. They were white plaster beasts and a bag
with coloured liquid was suspended above them. For
a guilder, you could use a shotgun and aim at the
various bags hanging there. If you hit the red bag, red
powder fell from it and the monsters would turn red
on the top, and otherwise yellow. I remember that
Councillor De Roos opened the exhibition at the time.
He naturally aimed at the red bag and the monsters
turned red. Another shot at the blue bag etcetera.
Thus, the visitors were also able to participate in all
those areas that the artists had installed themselves.

The "Dylaby" exhibition actually came about like
this: I sat drinking coffee with Rauschenberg and
Tinguely in New York and I said: *It is common practice
that museum people install the exhibitions, but I would
rather like it if the artists themselves were to do it. The
museum can provide carpenters, electricians and
material and you can do what you like, involve artist*

friends and if possible achieve one single design together. That latter didn't happen. Bob Rauschenberg
in particular was very disappointed about that.

215

THE WORLD OF THE EYE

What has particularly gripped me is architecture and
the visual arts, actually the world of the eye. Before I
had ever thought about museums, I spent much of
my time in the circle of architects, because I considered it a related area. When 'De Stijl' appeared, I regularly went to the library on the Herengracht and
I devoured every edition that appeared. Later I discovered there the books of Le Corbusier: 'Vers une Architecture' about architecture; 'L'Urbanisme' about town
planning; or 'L'Art Décoratif d'Aujourd'hui' about applied arts today. Le Corbusier in particular made a big
impression on me. Not only by what he said, but also
by the way in which he said it. Not long afterwards,
I met Rietveld. That was in the early 'thirties. Together
we visited several of his new buildings, including the
Rietveld-Schröder house on the Prins Hendriklaan in
Utrecht, buildings in Bilthoven and its vicinity.

A little later, I met Mart Stam. That was four years
before I came to the Stedelijk Museum. But I was
there then for the VANK, organising an exhibition
called "De Stoel" [The Chair]: the history of the chair
in the past forty years. It included the Berlage chair,
and the Rietveld chair, and then I also asked for a
chair by Stam. For he was the first man to design the
freely suspended steel chair. He delivered it himself.
He had just returned from Russia. He saw me working
there and said: *Sandberg, can I help you?* This is how
a very close cooperation and friendship arose between me and Stam. I profited enormously from this
contact with Mart Stam, in my work and especially in
my intellectual life. We spent a lot of time together,
founded many things together, I think of the magazine

"Open Oog, Avantgardecahier voor visuele vormgeving"
[Open Eye, Avantgarde Magazine for Visual Design],
in 1946. In addition, the "Stichting Goed Wonen"
[Good Living Foundation]. The magazine only appeared
twice. There were various other things, we actually
had a daily conversation about matters that interested
us. He frequently helped me with my exhibitions in the
Stedelijk Museum and he also thoroughly modernised
the entrance to the Fodor Museum, so that you could
finally mount the stairs properly, which had previously
proved very difficult.

Later, Stam became, at my instigation, director of
the Institute for Industrial Art Education — now called
the Rietveld Academie. He did that excellently for ten
years. I have always remained extraordinarily grateful
for all the collaboration, advice and ideas that he gave
me, not only in the years immediately before the war,
but also during and immediately after the war. In 1948
he left for Germany, because he wanted to build and
here he received, as communist, practically no commissions. He had two important commissions, neither
of which came to fruition. He had received first prize
for his design of the Dutch pavilion at the World Exhibition in New York in 1939. But Professor Slothouwer
was finally granted the commission. Subsequently, as
compensation, Stam was awarded a commission by
the government to make a pavilion for the International Water Exhibition in Liège. That exhibition was can-
celled because of the war which broke out at the time.
He never really got going here, even though he had
occupied a leading position in Dutch architecture
since 1927, when he worked on the Van Nelle factories

in Rotterdam. Although he did spend a lot of time abroad. He was a teacher at the Bauhaus in Dessau. He spent a long time in Russia and later in East Germany. I have always considered him one of the most important persons in the field. Alongside Gerrit Rietveld, who was perhaps more of a genius with all the simplicity of a genius and who had such a direct, almost primitive approach to design that everything he touched acquired a personal charm.

All at once I think of the Red-Blue Chair from 1918. That was the first work which made him well-known and even famous. That chair is in all the museums of modern art, the Museum of Modern Art in New York, the Museum des Zwanzigsten Jahrhunderts in Vienna. The chair is known everywhere. I also made a gift of one to the museum in Jerusalem. That chair is actually a three-dimensional Mondrian. There are coloured planes, blue, red, yellow connected with black bars. What is remarkable is that this chair dates from 1918 and Mondrian only started using his black lines, his bars in 1919. He went to Paris in 1919 and I don't know whether he ever saw the chair and was influenced by it, but whatever the case, the black lines appeared in Mondrian's paintings a year later. And those black lines of Mondrian are still very exceptional. Fernand Léger, the French painter, drew my attention to that. He said: *Now Mondrian, I don't really understand him very well. I see that he is an important painter, but I cannot follow him. But what I adopted from him is the black contour. That eliminates the way the different colours react to each other, what you call in scientific terms the simultaneous contrast. That is*

*what I learned from him. That is something I also want-
ed myself and that is why I always made my contours.*

And thus I come from Rietveld via Mondrian back
to architecture. Naturally, architecture has been considerably influenced by De Stijl group. Particularly in
De 8 en Opbouw [The 8 and Construction][20], that
became very important. One of the leaders in De 8 en
Opbouw, next to Stam, was Merkelbach, who did a lot
for Dutch architecture. He later became the City
Architect of Amsterdam. Not that he was such a creative architect. The creativity was mainly found among
his employees. But he was a man with a great vision
and a talent for organisation, somebody who knew
where it should lead and he based all his work on that.
In the short time that he was City Architect here in
Amsterdam, we worked a lot together. He didn't
design a lot himself and his own designs may not have
been all that innovative, but his influence was decisive
for the architecture and the urban development of
Amsterdam in that period. Merkelbach was a man
who saw everything with a grand vision. He wasn't
concerned with trifles, but he knew how to lift everything to a certain level, even a conversation.

I had a lot of dealings with Rietveld, Stam and
Merkelbach, and with Van Eesteren, of course, and
much later with Bakema as well. And I regularly went
with various architects to view their latest construc-

20. De 8 was an association of architects, founded in
1927 in Amsterdam with the emphasis on a functional
architecture with minimal means. De Opbouw was a
similar group, founded in 1920 in Rotterdam. They merged
in 1927.

tions. In the later years, I went on a trip with Rietveld every year or every other year — sometimes it took a day, then two days, then three — to view his new architecture. I did the same with Bakema and I often did it with J.J.P. Oud as well. Every time Oud completed a new building, he would write me a letter and draw the floor plan to indicate how I should view it. For Oud had the feeling that in the 'twenties, his architecture was the most important, not in volume, but very much in the spirit of what he had made. And later he would have liked — in my opinion — to return to that time again. He didn't succeed, but he really made an attempt to return to De Stijl architecture. He was farthest removed from that in the Shell building in The Hague. It had all sorts of decorations, even though De Stijl said that ornament was a falsification, covering up the mistakes in the architecture.

I was not only friends with Dutch architects, but also with many from abroad. I think here of Le Corbusier in particular. I got to know him in 1938 and immediately after the war, when so much of this country had been destroyed — particularly the centre of Rotterdam, but also Nijmegen and other places — I thought that we needed a new urban planning and that we now had the opportunity of rebuilding city centres in a new way. I thought then that Le Corbusier was somebody who had put forward the most innovative ideas for this. I visited him and said: *Look, so many cities have been destroyed and so much must be rebuilt and I find your urban development ideas so very important now. I would like to put them on show at our place and would like to start immediately with a*

Le Corbusier exhibition. Then he said: Yes, but you have to bear one thing in mind: I am first and foremost a painter. I paint every morning and if I still have time I do it in the afternoon as well. This is the source of all my architecture. So if you want to exhibit me, you must first show me as painter. Then you can also show me as architect and as urban planner.

And so we did indeed stage a Le Corbusier exhibition with his painting, his architecture and his urban redevelopment plans. That was in 1947 and he has never forgotten it. Whenever he saw me, he started with the words: *Sandberg, you were the first to exhibit my work in a museum, I am still grateful to you for that, what do you need?* I always really liked that very much about the relationship and one of my last contacts with him, just before his death, was when we presented him the Sikkens Prize in 1963.

I also got to know Ludwig Mies van der Rohe. That was here, shortly after the liberation. The German sculptor Ewald Mataré came to Amsterdam together with Mies van der Rohe. Mataré telephoned me and said: *Sandberg, we're sitting here on the terrace of the Schiller Hotel and we would like to see you.* So I went there and spent a very pleasant evening. We had dinner at Schiller's and afterwards we all went to visit Kees van der Leeuw, the director of Van Nelle. He had a flat at the top of the Carlton Hotel which had been designed by the architect Elling, with murals, or rather a wall division by the painter Bart van der Leck, a member of De Stijl. Since then, I have regularly been in touch with Mies van der Rohe and whenever I went to Chicago, I would visit him.

He had already spent perhaps thirty years in America, but he still felt somewhat lonely there. He was extremely pleased when such an old European friend visited him. Just before his death in 1969, I had a long conversation with him about the National-galerie, the museum in Berlin, which he had designed and in which I was involved from the very start. For at the start of the 'sixties, Arndt, the former senator for culture in Berlin, asked me whether I would come and look at the model and the drawings for the new museum produced by Mies van der Rohe. I looked at them and said to him: *I don't know whether this will be a good museum, I can't possibly comment on that, but I think it is a fantastic building. Build it here and we'll see later whether we can make it into a museum.*

That building offers enormous possibilities. It is a large steel square, which is completely filled with glass and standing, I think, on eight legs. It is of a purity and simplicity which only the architecture of Rietveld could sometimes have. For comparison, I think of the Arnhem School of Art, which Rietveld built there on the Rhine. I consider it one of the purest creations of contemporary architecture. But when I look at the Amsterdam Rietveld Academie and see the ugly white knots that they have placed above the windows for ventilation — Rietveld knew nothing about this, he was already dead — I fear that they have done the same in Arnhem and thus have, I wouldn't say destroyed but at least considerably damaged the purity of the architecture.

Rietveld was a particularly warm person and, like all geniuses, very simple, very direct , never beating about the bush. We have always enjoyed a very personal relationship. I corresponded a lot with Rietveld. We met each other often and worked together a lot, particularly in the post-war years, when he was still finding things difficult. Notwithstanding the fact that he was one of Holland's greatest architects, a true genius, he received few commissions. We tried to help him make a living at the time by giving him commissions for exhibitions. I think of the exhibition "Weerbare Democratie" [Resilient Democracy] in the New Church in Amsterdam at the beginning of 1946. That was in remembrance of the liberation and the war years. Rietveld also designed and built several other exhibitions, because he did not have enough architecture commissions. That improved in the 'fifties. Then he no longer needed this, thank God, and he built, for example, the Dutch pavilion for the Biennial in Venice. He had by then become an international celebrity. One of his first buildings, the Rietveld-Schröder House in Utrecht, has become an international place of pilgrimage for people interested in architecture, and not just for architects.

I also knew Walter Gropius. Fairly intimately, for we travelled to Brazil together. We were both there with our wives. We had received an invitation from the governor at the time of the state Minas Gerais, the general mines. That was Cubicek. Later he became president of Brazil. He asked us to visit him and look at the new architecture in his state, which was largely influenced and built by the architect Oscar Niemeyer. I also met him frequently. That trip through the red Brazilian dust together, which lasted four or five days, made an enormous impression on me. When you are with somebody from early morning to late evening, you get a good idea of people. Gropius may not have been a great architect, but he was a great human being.

Luis Sert is another architect I got to know. That was in 1937 when he built the pavilion for the Spanish Socialist Republic for the World Exhibition in Paris next to the Dutch pavilion for which I was commissioner. For that pavilion he had involved — an act of genius — the best artists from his country. Picasso painted 'Guernica' for it, Gonzalez made 'La Montserrat' for it, a metal sculpture, which I acquired immediately after the war for the Stedelijk Museum. In addition, Miró made a large mural for this pavilion. And the non-Spaniard Sandy Calder — the man with whom America in the 'thirties began to participate creatively in the development of the visual arts — made a 'mercury fountain' for it.

There were, you see, mercury mines in Spain and people wished to publicize this. Calder made a sort of fountain for this. The mercury came out of a sort of pipe at the top and fell into a large shovel. When the shovel was full, it tilted and allowed the mercury to run back into a larger basin. In this way, Calder used the mercury to set a whole sculpture in motion. This was one of the first moving sculptures that I had seen. He made this for Sert in 1937 and I also saw Sert a lot in 1969 in Harvard. He was head of the department of architecture there, the successor to Gropius. He was extremely interested in the visual arts as well and we had a lot of contact. I remember very enjoyable meals in his fantastic, simple, modern house.

In 1962, I received, together with Kenzo Tange, the well-known Japanese architect whose buildings include the Olympic Stadium in Tokyo, and Gordon Bunshaft, who is one of the best-known architects of the American steel and glass architecture, an honorary doctorate at the University of Buffalo. Such an honorary doctorate is in itself a boring ceremony, I have to say, but the company that received their honorary doctorates together there made it more attractive. That company included Tange from Japan, Bunshaft from America and then four other people who, in their opinion, had contributed something to the world of museums and modern art: Alfred Barr, the founder and director of the Museum of Modern Art in New York; Herbert Read, primarily writer and leader in the field of modern art; James Johnson Sweeney, who was, for some time director of the Museum of Modern Art, moved then to the Guggenheim Museum and finally to the Museum in Houston, Texas; and myself. The four of us really enjoyed ourselves. Each of us had to give a talk and I spoke about fake and real for private collectors. I was pleased that we were considered a group. That is what I appreciated so much about that honorary doctorate. It was to celebrate the hundredth anniversary of the museum in Buffalo.

Then, of course, I got to know a lot of other architects. I think of Richard Neutra who built especially in California and actually introduced the new building there. Then there was Louis Kahn and Bruno Zevi, with whom I sat on the Jerusalem Committee, an international committee of urban planners, writers, politicians and other people, who were to advise Teddy Kollek, the mayor of Jerusalem about the old city and how to integrate it into its surroundings.

Then there is also Hans Scharoun who, I would almost say, is not only an architect and a good human being, but also a sculptor. I consider the interior of his building for the Berlin Philharmonic of Von Karajan a sort of a sculpture without parallel. Scharoun is a man who, during the Hitler period, had a 'Bauverbot'. He was not allowed to build and suffered extreme difficulty. But he didn't go into exile. He stayed where he was and after the war he virtually emerged all by himself. I say 'by himself' because he was a man who didn't use his elbows. He was somebody who would never put in a good word for himself or wheedle his way in. But apparently somebody noticed him, understood him.

It was mainly in Berlin where he played a very important role, also in the world of art as such. He was for a long time director of the Akademie der Künste and was important because of his masterpiece, that building for the Philharmonic. I do not find the exterior at all attractive. It is, perhaps, curious. You have the feeling that it has not been completed. That is probably because he had very little money to build it. He had seventeen million, and when you consider that people thought you would need fifty million to build the opera house in Amsterdam, then we understand to some degree the proportion. But inside and especially in the concert hall — the orchestra podium is in the middle and the listeners sit around it — the building breathes such an atmosphere that you have the idea that you are sitting in a very large sculpture. In an immense modern structure which, as it were, engulfs you. With a normal sculpture, you walk around it and you look at it from the outside, but here it is as if you have been absorbed into it. I became very aware of the space when I sat down there once. In my opinion, it has become one of the great masterpieces of modern architecture. I consider the form, as well as the use of materials and the function an expression of genius.

I believe that simplicity, normality is the characteristic of genius, and Scharoun certainly has that. He is not an interesting figure, not a man with whom you would hold an important conversation, but he is a human being. He was also a friend of Hugo Häring, another architect, more from the school of anthroposophy. Häring was a prominent German architect. He played an important role in the years before 1933 and after the Second World War, primarily as, I would say, inseminator of the youth and his contemporaries. In the 'twenties, he did this as editor of magazines. Particularly in 1925. We must also recognise the enormous significance German architecture had at that time. Peter Behrens was actually the grandfather of German architecture, as Berlage was for us. The important architects all came to learn from Behrens. Le Corbusier attended, Mies van der Rohe and Gropius too, the later founder of the Bauhaus. That studio had an enormous influence on German architecture. On the school too, that concentrated more on the decorative aspects. I think of Hans Poelzig and Bruno and Max Taut. But it also influenced people, who were more driven by expressionist architecture, such as Ludwig Hilberseimer and Erich Mendelsohn. Hugo Häring also worked in this atmosphere and he saw a building more as something organic than as an intellectual construction. He was — and that is, of course, typical for the time after Jugendstil — strongly influenced by the growth of plants and such like. I assume that he was at the time already a member of the anthroposophic community, under the leadership of Rudolf Steiner. Anthroposophy is a branch of philosophy, you could say, which also and primarily concentrated on the arts. The last important man from this whole circle was Hans Scharoun and he was awarded the Rotterdam Erasmus Prize in 1970. It was a highly active circle, and still shines through in German and European architecture.

Hugo Häring showed me several single-person homes, which he built in the vicinity of Biberach, where he lived himself, at a time when he was still relatively healthy. You noticed immediately that there were very few rectangles. Everything was oblique. The pentagon was frequently the basis for his plans, but not in an intrusive way. He believed, I think, that a five-sided space better encapsulated the human being. I got to know Häring when I was trying to acquire the Malevich collection for the Stedelijk Museum. And so we come full circle. I believe that we have now said enough about my interest for architecture to explain why I became so involved at the time in the rebuilding and expansion of Dutch cities.

BAUHAUS

As all will know, Gropius founded the Bauhaus in Weimar immediately after the First World War in 1919. Henry van de Velde, the Belgian architect who had previously been director of the industrial arts school had recommended Gropius as his successor. Gropius accepted and combined the school with the school of architecture and the academy. In this way he created a completely new system for art education, in which he linked everything together in a creative way: architecture, painting, sculpture and the design of utility items. Partly under the influence of Johannes Itten, the preliminary course arose from this; this proved the start or rather the foundation of art education. That happened straightaway in 1919–1920. Later, after 1923 when Moholy-Nagy came there as successor to Itten, the functionalism arose from the 'clash', when the Bauhaus and De Stijl movement coincided — Van Doesburg had lived for some time in Weimar. Functionalism was championed mainly by Moholy and quickly became a commonplace term. It implied that the function should impose the form on the objects. I knew Moholy-Nagy well, particularly in the period when he fled from Hitler to the Netherlands in the early 'thirties. Although I didn't have any official position at the Stedelijk Museum, I still organised an exhibition of his work there and we remained friends.

I came into contact with the Bauhaus fairly early in its existence. That was in 1923 and at the time it was still in Weimar. In 1924, it closed down there and moved to Dessau, where it was given its own building. The Bauhaus is based on the unity of the arts, especially the visual arts and architecture. The idea behind

the construction of a cathedral in the Middle Ages
also played a role. The Bauhaus was the 'Bauhütte',
the building shed of the cathedrals where all the
artists, architects and everybody who had anything
at all to do with building gathered together. They built
the cathedral together, as a community of artists,
a team. This concept inspired Gropius to set up the
Bauhaus in the same way and to create a unity of
the arts.

Gropius, who himself was an architect, initially
based his thinking on architecture. He was, I believe,
not at home so well in visual arts. If I am not mis-
taken, the first teacher he appointed was Lyonel
Feininger, an expressionist. I have the impression that
in the early years he vacillated, not knowing whether
to follow the expressionist path or some other that he
did not yet know. His wife, Alma Mahler, who was the
widow of the composer Gustav Mahler, probably also
influenced him. She had been close friends with
Kokoschka and had allowed him to introduce her into
the world of visual arts. I think that Kokoschka was
also a candidate for teacher at the Bauhaus, but that
probably didn't come about because of personal
reasons.

Another friend of Alma Mahler, Johannes Itten
— who was Swiss and worked in Vienna in 1918–
1919 — was appointed second 'Meister', as it was
called, at the Bauhaus. Itten exercised considerable
influence on the development of the Bauhaus by
setting up that preliminary course. All prospective
students had to take it. It dealt with the basic principles of shape, colour, balance and so on. It also

included the principles of materials: the effect of material, rough, soft, smooth and so on. He developed the preliminary course and later he wrote a book about it. He was the founder of this and I believe that there is not a single art school at the moment in the world that has escaped this influence. One may apply it more strictly than the next. Perhaps there are new tendencies at the moment, in which people no longer start with the material but with a certain idea or exercise and only then explore the material and the principles. Perhaps this is also a purer approach to creative problems, but in any case Johannes Itten had a great influence on the development of art schools and academies.

As I already said, each pupil had to follow the elementary or preliminary course and then they could split into all directions: applied arts, painting, sculpture or architecture. The preliminary course was the basis of the whole education. I knew Johannes Itten extremely well, from 1922 until his death in 1967. He was 78 when he died. After leaving the Bauhaus he worked in Berlin and in Krefeld. That was made impossible for him at the end of 1937, the beginning of 1938. He then came to Holland and gave a lot of courses here. He also designed the fabulous awning for the Stedelijk Museum, which unfortunately was destroyed during the war when the windows were broken.

Johannes Itten was a pupil of Adolf Hölzel who taught at the academy in Salzburg. Hölzel is the man who started to research the theory of colour. Many current books about colour all have their origins in the theory of Hölzel. He had various pupils who later came to the Bauhaus; I am thinking here especially of Oskar Schlemmer and of Gropius. I assume that the theory of colour by Josef Albers — he later went to America — was passed down via Itten to Hölzel. As far as I know, Hölzel never wrote anything about it, he simply used it.

Itten was a figure who, on the one hand, was strongly influenced by Eastern mysticism, by all sorts of mystical movements, health care and the like. For example, he had his pupils do breathing exercises in the morning before he started with his lessons. I believe that relaxing exercises were done every hour. They would also sing in class. He made a very deep impression on his pupils and they found it difficult to shrug it off. One of his Dutch pupils was Paul Citroen. He remained friends with Itten until the very end. One of his Israeli pupils was Mordechai Ardon, who later worked in Jerusalem and Paris. Itten's successor at the Bauhaus was Moholy-Nagy. But perhaps I should first mention another story from the history of the Bauhaus.

I explained that at first the Bauhaus was not certain about which direction it should take; expressionism or constructivism. Two very strong, opposing directions. Our countryman Theo van Doesburg played a role in this. Van Doesburg was very attracted to the Bauhaus, to the Bauhaus philosophy and he had hoped to become a teacher there. For that reason, he travelled to Weimar in 1921 and settled there. He rented a studio and worked and also gathered a number of Bauhaus students around him. And he fiercely attacked people, particularly Johannes Itten. At one meal where both were present, things almost developed into a fight. In any case, it was a mess. The students were then forbidden to attend the courses given by Van Doesburg, but I believe that from the shock between these two ideas — the constructivism, the abstract art on the one hand and the direction adopted by the Bauhaus under the leadership of Itten and Feininger on the other — functionalism arose. And functionalism has become the ideological foundation for the Bauhaus.

Gropius was, as I have said, perhaps no great architect, but he was a great man. He supervised the Bauhaus as chairman of the teachers' meeting and perhaps one of his greatest features was that he attracted men greater than himself to the Bauhaus. I think of Paul Klee and of Kandinsky, who arrived in 1921 and 1922 respectively. When Itten left and his place became vacant — I think they quarrelled, but that is irrelevant — Moholy-Nagy was summoned to the Bauhaus. He actually continued the functionalist trend and developed it further, both for architecture and for typographic designs and all applied arts. Moholy-Nagy was an extremely inspirational figure; he spent 1933–1934 in Amsterdam, because he had to flee from Hitler. From here he went to London, from London to New York and then he founded the new Bauhaus in Chicago with Mies van der Rohe. That acquired a certain name as 'design pool', although after the death of Moholy-Nagy in 1946, it not longer maintained the standing that it had had at its original foundation.

I have never met Klee; but I did meet Kandinsky. I visited Kandinsky in Paris and a correspondence developed from this. I went to him to ask for his assistance for an exhibition of abstract art that I staged immediately after joining the Stedelijk Museum. Kandinsky was a remarkable figure. He was one of those intellectuals from a good background. I have already drawn attention to the fact that Klee and Kandinsky lived in the same street for many years and never met each other, because one had a very rich apartment and the other lived in an attic. I don't know whether that was the reason, but it is worth mentioning. But they were both invited to the Bauhaus shortly after each other and together they left their mark on it.

The mark of Klee was a more human attitude, which he tried to impart to his pupils. Kandinsky's mark was more analytical about art and the way in which a work of art should arise. Kandinsky was the first abstract artist, the first man to turn his back on the subject, in the years 1910–1911. To me, the years 1910–1911 are indeed his great years. In 1914, he had to leave Germany because of the war and he returned to Russia. He never really found his feet there.

Strangely enough, on the day that war broke out between Russia and Germany, two people stood on the platform of the station in Munich, both of whom would make an important contribution to the development of art in his own field. They were Kandinsky, by then a middle-aged man, and Gabo, a boy of 23, 24 years old. They stood on the same platform, but they were waiting for different trains. Kandinsky was heading for Switzerland and via that country he finally reached Russia; Gabo was heading for Norway, for otherwise he would be taken prisoner of war. He was allowed to leave Germany on the condition that he would not return to Russia and fight in the Russian army against Germany. And so he went to Oslo where, a year later, he was joined by his brothers Antoine Pevsner and Alexei Pevsner.

Returning to the Bauhaus: I visited it on several occasions, first in Weimar. I had many contacts with teachers and students, also later in Dessau, where I talked at length with Gropius. Gropius had designed a new building for Dessau, together with Adolf Meyer. What is remarkable is that you never see Gropius on his own as designer, but always together with somebody else or a team, like he did later in America. Gropius had the gift of being able to distinguish the greater from the great. So many people are scared of associating with people who are more important than themselves. That is, in my opinion, the cause of the decline of the Schule der Gestaltung in Ulm, which was founded in the early 'fifties as a sort of revival of the Bauhaus. It was founded by Max Bill, the Swiss artist, but he only engaged — as far as I can tell — second-rate teachers. People who were weaker than himself. That is what caused the decline of the school after a life of around fifteen years. It is remarkable that those weaker boys threw Bill out after three years and that in the Bauhaus, the stronger always worshipped Gropius. The bond that Gropius had with his employees and former employees always remained strong. Subsequently, in America, he also exercised considerable influence on the development of American architecture. Hitler helped America enormously in its further development in the area of design.

In this connection, I must again mention Mies van der Rohe. He and Gropius led American architecture towards new roads and took the first steps. It also became more of a European architectural style, notwithstanding the fact that there have been very important purely American architects;
I think of Frank Lloyd Wright, Sullivan and others. In my opinion, the German invasion suddenly elevated American architecture to a different level.

Mies van der Rohe was a totally different type than Gropius. Gropius was a large-scale intellectual and leader of men. Mies van der Rohe was, for a short time after Gropius, leader of the Bauhaus, when it moved to Berlin in the early 'thirties, but he started as a bricklayer. He therefore grew from a bricklayer into one of the greatest architects. Through this he always retained a great sense for detail and the way in which it is created. He settled in Chicago and built very important buildings there, but his purest creation is, perhaps, the museum in Berlin, which was opened in 1968. It is a construction of steel and glass and can be called fantastic in dimensions and proportions.

RUSSIAN
REVOLUTION
ARTISTS

Since the age of about twenty, I have always been enormously impressed by Mondrian. For me, art began with Mondrian. I have always had considerable difficulty getting used to the expressionists. Later I got to see it, but in the beginning it was a strange world for me. The world of Mondrian and the architects of De Stijl group was really more my world than that of the expressionists and the like.

When I came to the museum, I at once began to prepare an exhibition of abstract art. Before I took my position there, I had already mounted an exhibition of Moholy-Nagy and one of Van Doesburg. Initially I continued in that direction. At the Van Doesburg exhibition, I managed to persuade the old Mr. Baard — I would almost call him my grandfather in the field of museums — to purchase a Van Doesburg. There was one Mondrian in the museum on loan and nothing else in that field. After the war, I immediately tried to fill that gap. Then it was still very easy. I was able to purchase various Mondrians that were available and on offer here in the Netherlands.

Thus I felt very much at home in the Mondrian ambiance and slowly I discovered that, simultaneously with Mondrian's abstract period, there was a very strong movement in Russia which had developed completely independently of De Stijl movement. That was during the First World War, when communication was completely impossible. And so I stumbled upon Malevich. From two sides, I had heard about the existence of a Malevich collection in Germany.

Malevich had visited Western Europe for the last time in 1927. He visited the Bauhaus because his

245

book 'Die gegenstandlose Welt', the 'World without subject' was to appear in Dessau as a Bauhaus publication. He brought a whole lot of paintings with him and those were exhibited in Berlin. Then he said to his friends: *You keep the collection here, don't send them back to me, because in Russia this art is not 'persona grata'. Keep it for me.* He had actually asked the German architect Hugo Häring, whose wife was Russian. Since Malevich spoke other languages very poorly, the wife became his link with the outside world. And because of this he became friends with her husband. At that time, Häring was probably just an architect in an architect office and had no room there to store the crates belonging to Malevich. He then asked Dorner, the director of the Kestner Gesellschaft in Hanover, and someone who was very partial to this type of art, whether he could store the crates. Dorner did this and the crates remained in Hanover until around 1933, perhaps even longer. I will return later to why I think it was probably longer. But at a given moment, Dorner could no longer keep them and he sent them back to Hugo Häring.

In the meantime, the Bauhaus in Dessau had met its demise, for the country where Dessau was located was the first German country which had a Nazi majority. They erected a sloping roof on the Bauhaus and the Bauhaus had to vacate the premises. In 1931, it was transferred to Berlin. Gropius had already left in 1928, Hannes Meyer was director for a few years and at the time of the removal to Berlin, Mies van der Rohe was director. They were also unable to hold out there under the Nazi upsurge and the school in Berlin was disbanded. A lot of the Bauhaus students went to a related school. That was the Reimann-Schule.

The Reimann-Schule was actually somewhat based on the same principles, had, in any case, been set up in a similar way to the Bauhaus. Mister Reimann was a Jew, but because there were so many foreigners there, he was able to continue the school for quite some time under the Hitler regime. By then, Häring, just like the architect Scharoun, had been given a 'Bauverbot' and he had no income or employment. He then became the director of the Reimann-Schule and stored the crates there.

The reason I cannot give the exact moment at which they were taken from Hanover to Berlin is because I know that Dorner fled to America in 1938. At that time, he plunged into the crates — I do not know the exact reason, but it would appear that he wanted to arrive in America with some funds — and probably took eight, but it could have been six or twelve, canvases by Malevich, probably rolled up. In America, he gave them on loan to the Museum of Modern Art in New York. Dorner has since died, but what exactly the illegal position is with these canvases is unknown to me. They actually belonged to the collection of Hugo Häring. The collection must have had just under fifty paintings plus a number of drawings and a series of fifteen didactic panels. They were rather large panels, I think around one metre high and a metre and a half wide or the other way around. He had written the German text himself on them, with a lot of mistakes. And there were architectural drawings. They were very interesting, particularly because

Malevich's pupil El Lissitzky continued in this direction, actually towards spatial architecture or abstract art in space.

In the early 'fifties I was in Munich, together with deputy director Hans Jaffé. In Zurich, I had heard talk of the Malevich collection which was stored in a small place in Bayern and Jaffé, who had travelled a lot in Germany after the war as an officer in the recuperation service, had also heard of it. We were able to obtain the address in Biberach of the architect Hugo Häring via the director of the America Haus in Munich. We then went to Biberach, together with that director, to visit Häring. He was happy to receive us, was pleased that there were people who were interested in the collection, although I don't think he had much affinity with it himself. He was a very modern architect, but he was really an anthroposophist. And anthroposophists do not like squares, but prefer pentagons, and rather than rectangles prefer polygons. According to me, Malevich doesn't really fit in his own architecture. He showed us the collection. I think that one or two of the canvases were mounted in his house, but the rest were in a drawer. He had the canvases in it, without canvas stretcher and stored rather untidily. They were not in a very good condition. But for me, it was a completely new and wonderful discovery. We stayed there the whole day and examined everything through and through. A few months later, I went there again and said: *Would it be possible to let us exhibit these in the Stedelijk Museum and to allow them to circulate?* He was immediately interested in the idea. This took place in the early 'fifties, but I was in contact with Häring constantly until 1957. In 1957 the sale was finalised. We first spoke of a travelling exhibition that would start in Amsterdam and then travel throughout Europe. He was rather in favour of this, but he was frequently ill and easily fatigued. He would then, quite suddenly, begin to cry and say: *Ist die Welt so gut dass Sie zu mir kommen? Ich bin Ihnen so dankbar* [Is the world that good that you are coming to me? I am so grateful to you]. On another occasion, you couldn't get anywhere with him so it was very difficult to nail down the negotiations.

But around 1955 he agreed to letting us have the collection on loan. He was no longer able to build and I think he had received the German Architecture prize, but that was only ten thousand marks. He had very little money and wanted to earn something from them. So we reached an agreement by which we would receive the collection on loan for a fee of ten thousand German marks per year. We would restore them and allow them to circulate around other museums and we would have the option of purchasing them. When we actually made the purchase, the fees we had paid him each year would be deducted from the amount we owed him. We rounded everything off at thirty thousand dollars — that was one hundred and twenty thousand marks — because an American collector had offered this sum for the collection. That was his only point of reference. He said: *Right, one hundred and twenty thousand marks. That's it.* We didn't discuss it any further, didn't try to bargain; it seemed reasonable to me.

So we brought everything to Amsterdam.

We spent a whole year restoring the things, it was
very disappointing but they were really well restored
in the restoration studio in the Stedelijk Museum.
We set up the educational drawings, did everything
possible and then had the exhibition circulate. It went
to Brussels, to Basel and Zurich. It also travelled
around in Germany and I think it also went to London
and the Scandinavian countries. The museums that
mounted the exhibition contributed to the ten thousand guilders fee. We made an illustrated catalogue
which the museums could include in their own catalogue. Our catalogue consisted of reproductions of
the drawings, paintings and gouaches. I purposely did
not make a complete catalogue because I always had
some uncertainty about the dating of the items. The
following history is attached to them: there were two
leaders in the renewal of Russian painting. Those
were Malevich and Tatlin. Tatlin was, perhaps, ten or
twelve years younger than Malevich but he was a very
exuberant figure. They couldn't stand each other.
Tatlin had started producing abstract reliefs in metal
in 1914. Malevich had gone through a period of development. This can also be seen in the Stedelijk Museum collection. Around 1905, we have an impressionist painting, somewhat later a watercolour. Then
an expressionist period begins and that is relatively
extensive. Later it shows the influence of Matisse,
from the Matisses he had seen in the Stschukin Collection in Moscow. That is, let me say, around 1911.
Then there is a cubist period and then finally the abstract period which he called suprematism: the su-
premacy of the pure form.

It is extremely difficult to date the start here. The literature tells us that in 1913 he made a front curtain or something like that for a futurist opera, with a black square and that black square was, for him, the principle of suprematism. I think that has been confirmed. On the other hand, when looking through his development I was able to get all sorts of photographs of exhibitions in which he participated and those show that until the middle of 1915, he only submitted expressionist and cubist works for them. I even had, I believe, the proof in my hand that the cubist canvases that he submitted in February 1915 to the "Tramway W" exhibition were still wet when he sent them in. Now it has always been a mystery to me why, if Malevich was already concentrating on suprematist canvases and had thus made a magnificent discovery and was totally convinced that with suprematism he would change the world, he did not exhibit those canvases.

It is certain that he only showed them in December 1915, in the "0.10" [Zero–ten] exhibition. My suspicion is that the suprematist canvases do actually date from 1915, but that Malevich, in order to beat his enemy Tatlin, antedated them to 1913, when he already had suprematist ideas. That is a supposition. They were arch-enemies, perhaps they sometimes drank a glass of vodka together, I don't know, but in any case they were such enemies that they threw fists at each other, something which also occurred in other circles. It is not surprising that Malevich wanted to precede the younger Tatlin in the field of abstract art. Antedating of art works by artists themselves is done throughout the world and it would not be surprising if this also happened here. For me it is the only logical explanation of why he antedated them although only showing them at the end of 1915.

Whatever the truth, it isn't really important, except for the historians. What is important is that Malevich is the originator of this type of abstract art in Russia and exerted considerable influence in Western Europe, particularly through his pupils such as Lissitzky and others. He remained in Russia. He had a large family and he didn't want to leave them alone and couldn't take them with him over the border. He did go abroad on occasions; he spent a couple of months in Warsaw in 1924. I also traced his footsteps there, but after 1927, he virtually disappeared from the surface.

Here and there I was able to pick up something. Hans Richter told me that he met Malevich in his attic room in St. Petersburg in 1932, while he was painting plates with abstract patterns. He did indeed produce those. Whether he painted them himself or only designed them is something I do not know. He died in 1935 after painting a series of portraits at the end of his life. They are self portraits and portraits of others, which are interesting from an historic point of view, but certainly contributed nothing to the development of painting. His contribution ended in the early 'twenties when it slowly became impossible in Russia to make or exhibit, let us say, progressive art.

In the early days of abstract art, there was a whole group of younger painters who gathered around Malevich. Later, sculptors such as Gabo and Pevsner also joined. They had been in Norway during the First World War, but after the revolution they immediately went to Moscow and St. Petersburg. Antoine Pevsner became professor of painting at the academy in Moscow. Gabo was more an organiser of art and actually had little need, or even perhaps no talent for giving lessons. During the early years of the Russian Revolution, art had to be of service to it. Art by the new generation of Russian artists played a very important role at major celebrations, folk festivals, parades. I am thinking here especially about the art of Malevich and Tatlin, of Gabo and also what Chagall did in Vitebsk.

After the revolution, Chagall was appointed head of the academy of Vitebsk and mobilised everybody who painted there. Not only the artists, but also the house painters. He formed a new type of guild in which the house painters and the artists worked together to decorate the city, to give the city a new colour and a new form. It was an exceptionally nice idea and really caught on.

One of his most faithful pupils was El Lissitzky. He initially grew up totally in the school of Chagall. His first works are all very reminiscent of Chagall. Later, in 1918–1919 he fell strongly under the influence of Malevich. He then persuaded Chagall to appoint Malevich as professor at the school in Vitebsk. As a sort of guest professor, for Malevich visited regularly. At a given moment, Chagall travelled to Moscow to visit the heads of ministries there and to ask them for a subsidy for his academy. While he was away, Lissitzky and Malevich really set to work in Vitebsk and when Chagall returned from his trip — it would have lasted several weeks — he found that his academy had been completely transformed in the spirit of Malevich. It had changed from the friendly figurative art of Chagall into a fortress of abstract constructivism.

Lissitzky also became an abstract artist. Painter and architect. Only, his contemporaries were very annoyed at him that he did not call his art suprematist but gave it his own name, 'Proun', even though he was so close to what Malevich made. Chagall took his leave of Vitebsk, went to Moscow and shortly afterwards returned to Europe.

Gabo exerted considerable influence on the young Russian artists in that same period between 1917 and 1921. Certainly not least with his Realistic Manifesto, in which he laid out his ideas for the new direction for the development of Russian painting. He told me once that he wrote that Russian manifesto in one night. In the morning, his youngest brother Alexei said: *What were you up to all night long?* For they had been living, sleeping and working in just one room since the revolution. Then he said: *I have written a manifesto.* Alexei read it and then Antoine Pevsner, the older brother, read it and he asked: *May I also put my signature to it?* He was delighted with it and signed it as well.

Then Gabo took it to Tatlin, who was commissioner at the ministry. He asked him for funds to allow him to print it and post it on the city walls of Moscow. I don't know if a minister took part or not, in any case I do remember that Gabo told me that Tatlin took a bundle of roubles from his pocket and pushed them into Gabo's hand without counting them and said: *Have it printed in the state printing works.* He was also given a piece of paper with some signature or other and stamps and in this way the manifesto was approved without any intervention from the authorities. They had simply read the heading: 'Realistic Manifesto'. Realism began to crop up even then. It was still the time of Lenin, but already there were forces in the background who began to push social realism.

So it was printed and the next morning it could be read on every corner in Moscow. It caused endless discussions, particularly among artists and students, until in the years that followed Stalin closed his grip on the arts and made social realism supreme. Through this, virtually all the important artists — particularly the visual artists; the authors could stay for a while longer — left Russia. Kandinsky left, so did Gabo, Pevsner came to Europe a year later and Chagall to Berlin. The only important people, in my opinion, who stayed were Tatlin and Malevich. Tatlin never made anything further of importance and Malevich too was unable to do very much. He came to Europe for the last time in 1927 because the Bauhaus wanted to publish his book. Moholy-Nagy and Gropius did that together.

Back to Hugo Häring. In the beginning when I came into contact with him he said: *I can only hire out those works because they are not my property.* This led to the creation of the rental agreement. But around 1955 he told me that his brother-in-law — the brother of his second wife, who was a notary in Braunschweig — had said: *but old chap, you are the owner. You have had them in your possession for more than 25 years and after possessing them for 25 years, you become, under German law, the owner.* So he then changed and said: Now I can sell them. At that moment, we drew up the sales contract which included the rent, the option and the purchase price. We first rented it, partly because I thought that the Russian state may have made claims to it or Russian museums or his family. I immediately had photographs taken and sent them to Russian museums and other official institutions asking them whether they could give me more documentation about Malevich. One museum, I think the Tretyakov Gallery in Moscow did indeed answer. They sent me a series of photographs of the Malevich paintings they owned and all sorts of data and material. Including photographs of the last portraits that he had painted and which I did not know of before. In 1968 I was able to see a whole group of Maleviches in the cellars of the Russian museum in Leningrad. There I saw all sorts of paintings which in time and ideas matched those in our collection. But there were also paintings, perhaps of a later date, which had, I would almost say, something of Oskar Schlemmer about them, which had something of his style. It was, of course, long before Schlemmer himself, but they were in a different spirit than the ones we had.

Except for this period and naturally also the portraits from the last period, to which I would not attach much value, we had here the same periods as those in that Russian museum. I would say that the quality of both collections was about equal. I must have seen forty or fifty paintings there, all of them put out specially for me, otherwise they were in racks or standing against each other. I also saw a whole wall there, hung with paintings shoulder to shoulder, just like stamps in an album, with early Kandinskys and there were also very large Chagalls. All these paintings may not be exhibited in Russia. For three days, the director of the Majakowski museum held an exhibition of Tatlin and Malevich. I don't know whether it was planned for three days, but whatever the case it only lasted for three days. He also published a pamphlet that I was able to acquire, but that is the only time, I think, since 1921 that this art has been on show in Russia. And even now, the Russians know nothing about it.

I noticed that when I walked around in the Hermitage. There you have a magnificent collection of French painting from the start of this century until 1914: Matisse, Picasso, Braque, cubist Picassos, and an abstract Léger also hung there, Derain, anyway a whole lot of these artists together with Cézanne, Van Gogh, Gauguin etcetera. Virtually all of them are from the Morosow and Stschukin Collections that, after the revolution, were divided between the Pushkin Museum in Moscow and the Hermitage in Leningrad. When I strayed into an anteroom with German art — by Liebermann and so, those brown paintings from the end of the nineteenth century from the Munich school — I saw a canvas directly opposite a door and I though: gosh, that looks just like a Chagall. But Chagall may not be exhibited here, so I quickly walked up to it and it turned out to be a Campendonk. Campendonk, who was so inspired by Chagall, could hang there, but Chagall himself — and probably also because he was an exiled Russian — was not allowed to be exhibited in Russia.

The new art of Chagall, Tatlin and Malevich was the first original Russian art expression since icon painting. During all those centuries between the icons and, let's say, 1913–1914, Russia lived completely from the West. The Russian impressionism was, after all, inspired by Western impressionism. It was not until 1913 that a team of artists started on their own path. I believe that artists are frequently forerunners of major movements and this was apparently in the Russian air. Just as Bolshevism sat in the Russian air and the Russian mentality. People were working with great enthusiasm and perseverance on a completely new beginning. In all areas not just social but also spiritual. There were great Russian discoverers, particularly in the medical field. There was that team of Russian artists and we certainly shouldn't forget Russian literature, with Majakowski and so many others. Russian was then suddenly in the vanguard of the whole artistic movement in Europe. Earlier than other countries. It may have been inspired by what was happening in Paris, but the Russians processed that in their very own way and actually turned them into deeds much more than the French. It must have been an especially lively group of artists in Russia in the years from 1914 to 1920, particularly in Moscow. Perhaps to a lesser degree in Petersburg. It must have bubbled with creative efforts in all directions. In the field of literature, music, painting and stage design. Tatlin made many stage designs and so too did Chagall. I have already mentioned the front curtain by Malevich. Artists were engaged from all sides, just as later Diaghilev would do with the Ballet Russe. He started with Léon Bakst and later involved Picasso, Bonnard, Gabo, Pevsner and many others.

The interaction between Paris and Moscow was extraordinarily strong in the years prior to the war. First, Tatlin, I think, came to visit Picasso in 1912. It was then that he saw the first abstract constructions, or rather the assemblies, of Picasso, with which he would later continue. It is said that Malevich also visited Paris, but I seriously doubt that, for there is absolutely no evidence to support it.

But you could see the crème de la crème of Parisian painting in Moscow. Easier than in Paris. For there were two major collectors, Morosow and Stschukin who brought the Parisian school to Moscow. They were dealers who travelled to Paris regularly with well-filled purses and purchased Cézannes there, even during Cézanne's life and they-also bought Gauguins and Van Goghs. Among the paintings were the finest works of these artists. Later, Stschukin became friends with Matisse and invited him to visit Moscow. It was there that Matisse painted the great canvases 'The Music' and 'The Dance', which were shown in 1970 at the Matisse exhibition in Paris. Stschukin was in very close contact with Matisse. I think he had something like 25 or 30 canvases by him. Via Matisse he came into contact with Picasso; initially he was very dismissive of him. Subsequently, he acquired a very large collection of Picassos, until the outbreak of the First World War. Then it was all over and the revolution put an end to it all.

ABSTRACT
ART

In the period before I was at the Stedelijk Museum,
I mounted various exhibitions including one of Theo
van Doesburg, who had died in 1931. At the time, I had
many dealings with his widow, Nelly, and that friendship has remained throughout the years. When I was
later appointed to the museum, on 1 January 1938,
my first idea was to put on an exhibition of abstract art
and she helped me considerably with that. We drew
up the programme together and visited some artists.
Others I visited alone, but in any case she gave me a
lot of tips and brought me into contact with all sorts of
people. I would think initially of Hans Arp, who was
born in Strasbourg, then part of Germany. After the
First World War he took the French nationality. During
the war he lived, as far as I know, in Switzerland.

Arp is a typical Strasbourger. He was originally
called Hans Arp and after 1914, continued his life as
Jean Arp. He has taken from those two cultures, on
the intersection of which he was born, the best of
both. I actually only know his artistic development
from the years 1914–1918 in Zurich, where he was a
very active and productive member of the dada movement, together with Tristan Tzara, Hans Richter,
Marcel Janco, Richard Hülsenbeck and lots of others.
Those are all people who I have met during the course
of my life.

The dada group proved extremely fertile. Hans
Arp and also his wife Sophie Taeuber-Arp, who was
Swiss, participated very actively and productively in
it. Later other people joined, including Kurt Schwitters,
but the initial period in Zurich was very inspirational. I
have always had the feeling, but I do not know whether

it is right historically, that Marcel Duchamp, the Frenchman, also participated in it. In any case, he influenced
it with his ready-mades, the existing objects that he
elevated into art objects. Hans Arp later developed
this direction to a very high degree, especially in
sculpture and but also in graphic design, and certainly
made a contribution to it.

He created this special fluid form which you recognise everywhere in nature. When I flew over the
Sinai during the time I spent in Jerusalem, the shapes
of the dunes reminded me of the sculptures of Hans
Arp. In addition, Arp was also an important poet. Our
first meeting was very inspiring and we remained
friends in the thirty years that followed. He was a man
with a very peculiar combination of characteristics. He
could be extremely gentle and yet be fierce and sharp
as well. That is something that only occurs rarely.

When I was preparing the exhibition, I also got to
know Robert Delaunay and his wife Sonia, and
Otto Freundlich and Henry Moore. For this exhibition I
also visited Kandinsky, Kupka and Fernand Léger,
who had had a short abstract period in the years
1918–1920. Further I visited Alberto Magnelli,
Mondrian, Ben Nicholson, Kurt Schwitters, Georges
Vantongerloo and Friedrich Vordemberge-Gildewart.
Vordemberge-Gildewart came to the Netherlands in
response to the exhibition and lived here for some ten
years. He was very typically at home in the further
development of De Stijl movement.

If we were to select several of these people to say
something special about, then I think that would in the
first place be Fernand Léger. Fernand Léger was a

typical Frenchman from Normandy. His father had
been a stock-breeder and he was raised on a farm. He
looked like a sturdy sportsman and he was also someone who belonged on a bicycle and apparently not in
a car. He could not drive a car. He always needed his
wife for that. When he came to pick me up to go
somewhere together, his wife would always do the
driving, as that happens so often in artist and professor marriages, when the wife would turn on the
engine. Fernand Léger is perhaps the most extreme
opposite to Picasso. They were friends, frequently
worked together, particularly in the early days and
also later, and shared the same political ideas.
Fernand Léger was an enthusiastic communist and
Picasso also later became communist.

Léger was a man who had both feet firmly on the
ground. When he was in his studio and showed what
he had made recently, he was always relaxed and
would explain exactly how he had arrived at making
exactly this work; why he had done this and not done
that, with complete candour. You felt very much at
ease with Léger. He was just a strong, resolute man
and utterly dependable, without excuses or suspi-
cions, his word was his word. And the stance he
adopted, with his head erect and not quite challenging,
was very typical for him.

This was in contrast to Picasso. When he was in
his studio and showed you what he had made recently,
he supposedly looked at the painting. But if you
looked carefully, you saw that he was looking at your
face from the corners of his eye, trying to assess what
your impression was. I don't believe that distrust was

a characteristic of him, but he was somebody who was not as absolutely certain of his affairs as Léger. I am totally convinced that he was completely behind everything he produced, but he was interested in the judgment of others. Not that he wanted to ask you anything about it, but you nevertheless noticed that he was constantly alert, nervous, tense to know what you thought of his work and that's why he tried to read your thoughts from your face. That was a remarkable experience.

Picasso was very ordinary, very simple I would almost say. He was always very simply dressed and often liked to talk about clothes. I remember that we once happened to be in England together. Then he said: *Well, I wasn't able to do very much there, but I did buy an English jacket.* Some sort of chessboard-like black and white jacket, of very rough cloth. It did indeed look like a Scottish fabric, but later, when he looked into the inside pocket, there was a French label. So he could have bought it just as well in Paris. He enjoyed such conversations about very ordinary things. I never heard him talk about art. I believe that he didn't do it very much. He was a man who, right up to 1936, was not socially engaged. He lived purely for art for all that time and he tried to capture and record what was happening in the world. He had a fierce expression, but not a strong social engagement. As far as I can tell, it was the Spanish Civil War that shook him awake. Because of it he realised the fact that he had a function. The Spanish republican government immediately appointed him director of the Prado. I think it was more an honorary position than one in which he was expected every day to assess the condition of the paintings. But they wanted to express that they had enormous admiration for this man who was the greatest among Spanish visual artists, and not only admiration for the man but also for his art. That was rather unusual for a government, for I don't believe that the government of France, where he had resided by now for something approaching seventy years, ever concerned itself with him officially. Perhaps also because of his later political conviction.

In the beginning, he more or less made caricatures of Franco and they are highly amusing, very sharp. He recorded them in a number of etchings. Then, in January 1937, he was given the commission to produce a large painting for the entrance to the Spanish pavilion at the World Exhibition in Paris, which was due to open that same year. He was given complete freedom in his choice of subject and he apparently thought long and hard about it. As far as I know, there are no sketches from that period. He carried the commission around inside his head and apparently didn't know how he should approach it. Then suddenly, on 28 April, there was the bombing by the Italian and German air force, which Franco supported, of the open city of Guernica, a pilgrimage place in Northern Spain. And the report of the bombing and the colossal effect it had on man and animal, shook him awake.

He immediately set up the 'Guernica' and made five or six studies for it during one single week. Then he knew how he would do it. He ordered the canvas and started to paint. Dora Maar, his girlfriend at the

time and photographer, captured it all in photographs.
Picasso then painted 'aus einem Guß' [all at once] that
painting which is a great warning against the war. For
me it is the symbol of the artist who warns against
what people are doing and tries to call a halt to their
actions. The symbol of the horrors of a bombing from
the air and what it all means for man and animal. It
shows a horse that is mortally injured and a bull. That
inspired him to what we would call: the 'Night Watch'
of the twentieth century.

It is in my opinion the greatest masterpiece that
this century has produced thus far. From that moment
on, Picasso remained committed and he later became
a member of the Communist party. I don't think he
ever read Marx or concerned himself with the communist theories, yet he had considerable interest for
the anti-capitalist social attitude. I would prefer to call
it anti-capitalist rather than pro-Marxist. He went to
all peace conferences that were organised: to Stockholm, from where he sent me a postcard, to Warsaw,
to Sheffield. He wanted to make an 'acte de présence'
everywhere and wanted to support the case without
participating actively with anything other than his art.
I have the idea that this became a very important
stage in Picasso's life and work. This also inspired him
during the war to the portraits of Dora Maar — in
which all the horrors of war are reflected in her face
— and after the war to his great compositions of war
and peace. They are very large canvases that, in my
opinion, do not have the same conviction as the
'Guernica' but which still became fantastic paintings.
From that moment onward, Picasso grew from a, how

shall I say, purely aesthetic artist to an aware, committed artist and I believe that that is important in order to judge his art.

Now about Henry Moore. I also met him before the war, when I was running around for the "Abstracte Kunst" [Abstract Art] exhibition and that also became a friendship that has continued. We have always remained in contact with each other since then. In my opinion, Moore was a typical artist, in the sense that he was an exceptionally modest man. He never placed himself in the foreground and was rather shy. He didn't like to speak in public. He was very fond of children and people and he wasn't at all ashamed of revealing the source of his ideas. It is sometimes said that Moore discovered the hole in sculpture, drilling through the plane, in fact. If you were to ask him he would say: *That is completely untrue. I looked at Mexican statues, at pre-Columbian and Indian sculpture and all sorts of other primitive sculptures. I learned a lot from this and applied it in my work.*

I would also like to mention a human quality of Moore. We were once standing together by a large sculpture of an old, seated woman, which he had just started. He stroked the back of the sculpture with his hand and said: *Do you know how I found the shape of the back? My mother was stiff with rheumatism. My father was a miner and not at home very often, and then I had to rub her back with a particular oil. I can still feel my mother's shrivelled back in my hand and I've tried to capture it here in this sculpture. That is the back of my mother.* There is something movingly simple in that and it is typical for the nature of this

artist, who has contributed so much to the development of sculpture, particularly in the last forty years.

Then I would like to talk of another sculptor, who
also participated in the exhibition of 1938: Antoine
Pevsner. He is a typical sculptor. I would say a man
who is able to give a three-dimensional form to
material. But it then becomes a very material thing. It
is very strongly constructed in a geometrical way, but
he was able to imbue that geometry with a sort of
material strength. He was, in common with all great
artists, a very modest man and had a completely
unremarkable appearance. When I think of Antoine
Pevsner, I think of a grey mouse. Everything about
him was grey — his eyes, his skin colour, hair, everything was colourless.

Very curiously, he was fully aware that he produced
important work, but exactly where he should place it
he wouldn't have known himself. I put so much
emphasis on the material qualities. A sculpture by
Pevsner you can hold and touch. I say that because
this is in such contrast to the work of his younger
brother Gabo. For Gabo tried first to construct sculpture and then to dematerialise it. In his later work in
particular he solved the sculpture, the shape, in straight
lines and he again constructed his round shapes,
which always appeared, from the straight lines inter-
secting each other. It is a very unusual, mathematical
approach to sculpture. Gabo started with this in, I
think, the 'thirties, but he had already started producing
a sort of constructivist sculpture in 1915–1916 in Oslo.
At that time, his brother, Antoine Pevsner, who was six
years his senior, was still a painter.

I first met Gabo in 1927 in Berlin, while I was living there for a few months. We encountered each other there and from that moment onwards we were friends. That friendship stretched out through the years and whenever I was in America, I would always spend my first weekend with Gabo and we would talk about all of his work together. Gabo gave the first push for constructivism in the visual arts, then for a more geometric-abstract direction and he dematerialised sculpture. I remember once in 1930 visiting his studio and he had made everything from celluloid, from transparent material. Celluloid was, particularly at that time, not at all durable. They made films from it and they always broke. Little of that work has survived. Later he turned to nylon and plastic. His later work has been well preserved, although it is still very vulnerable. With his sculpture, he inspired his brother, who, in the early 'twenties, had got into a tangle with painting, to turn to sculpture. In 1923, Pevsner made his first sculpture and he turned out to be an extraordinarily gifted sculptor.

I believe these two brothers became great artists simultaneously. Pevsner died in 1962. Gabo lived into his eighties. He lived in America and visited Holland every year. It is a well-known fact that he made his most important, or in any case his largest statue, here. It is 26 metres high and stands in Rotterdam on the Coolsingel, in front of the Bijenkorf. It is one of the most important works of its kind in the world and I think Rotterdam should be exceptionally proud of it.

Through Nelly van Doesburg, I also came into contact with Constantin Brancusi. Since Brancusi,

I believe, was a member of De Stijl around 1920, Nelly had very special links with him. It was actually self-evident that he should receive us and what's more, we came to invite him to participate in the exhibition in Amsterdam. He lived in a shed on the Impasse Ronsin, a cul-de-sac where several artists had their studio. It was a large room, a large studio, where he slept, cooked and did everything. It was a space that the French call 'absolument dépouillé', completely empty, extremely ascetic, I would almost say, without any comfort.

Brancusi was a man who made little publicity for himself, but was absolutely withdrawn, like a hermit, and did his own thing, completely satisfied with himself, is the feeling he gave you. I assume there were women in his life, but there was nothing around to suggest them. He sculpted various women, but whether they meant anything more to him I do not know. In that large spacious, whitewashed studio, his sculptures stood there on plinths. Each sculpture was wrapped in a sheet, so that you saw nothing when you entered. Later he had a pulley in the attic and then he could raise the sheet with a rope. But in 1938, he hadn't organised that yet. He still worked at the time. What is remarkable is that he never made anything during at least the last ten years of his life. I believe that he made his last sculpture in about 1949, and then it was over.

In his whole life, he only handled a small number of themes. He constantly returned to the same theme, with an intervening period of ten or twenty years, and then improved on it. He actually searched for the simplification of forms in order to say only what was absolutely necessary. There are very few people who can do that. In that he was something of a monk, that he didn't want to decorate anything, not beautify anything. He really tried to reach the core and perhaps he finally did reach the core, and then found that his work was complete and left it for what it was.

He was something of a poetic figure, a small man, with in 1938 a relatively short beard. Later the beard grew longer. He was dark blond, always wore something on his head, some cap or other, and he always dressed in white in his studio. He wore a pair of white trousers and a long white shirt over them. If I remember correctly, it was a sort of Russian shirt, with a collar that was buttoned to the top, an upright collar.

If he trusted you, he would start unpacking his sculptures and then he would stand beside them. He would first have to clean them and make them presentable before you were allowed to see them. I also have the idea that he spent the last ten years of his life mainly on making his existing works presentable and perhaps reworking them with a file. I don't know how many things he made, it will certainly be less than a hundred and fifty, and that is not many in such a long life. You have people like Picasso who made several paintings a day and if you showed the yield from one year, there were hundreds of paintings, drawings, etchings and whatever else. I did not have the feeling that Brancusi was an industrious man. He was not someone who would work from early morning to late evening. I think that he would often sit on a chair, look at his work, think about it and then continue further.

That's the impression it made. I was never there when he was working, but I think he worked very slowly, assessed the thing from all sides and perhaps the next day he would change everything he had done the day before or chuck it in the bin. He was extremely critical of his own work, which few artists are, but because of this he was able to achieve that internalisation.

He was somebody who first built everything in his mind until he could see it in front of him. Then he made it, like a true 'artisan', a craftsman, even though he had won prizes at the academy in Bucharest, in his homeland Romania. So he actually came to the fore from the very beginning, but he went to Paris very early, in 1904. He returned a few times, went to America on a number of occasions, was in Holland and in Egypt. He travelled a lot. I found that quite remarkable. Many such artists would not, I believe, have travelled for their pleasure. Certainly not Mondrian. Good, when he had to flee France because of the war, he went to England and when he had to flee England because his house there had been bombed, he went to America. But he would never have taken a trip to get to know something or for the pleasure of it. He did visit Germany early in his life, but he actually had all he needed in himself.

I have the feeling that Brancusi wanted to see something of the world and let himself be inspired. His art after all had something to do with what the early Egyptians had done. They also searched for a very strong simplification. Details on a statue were not sculpted but, as it were, engraved, I mean an eye or a navel or the like. He may have got that from the Egyptians, but he could also have seen it in the Louvre.

Anyway, after all the sculptures were unveiled, he would make coffee in his kitchenette. He made extremely strong, devilishly tasty coffee. And then you sat down and just spoke about very simple things. I cannot remember ever talking about weighty matters. Perhaps that was just me and he did it with other people, but I have never found anything in all the literature about Brancusi about his stories or his fantasies. I don't know whether he had ever exhibited in a museum before 1938. Perhaps in America, but certainly not in Europe. So he was very keen on the exhibition. That's why he came to deliver his sculptures himself. He was so very particular about his sculpture that he wanted to deliver it himself and clean it up, but he was immediately full of confidence. I always retained that confidence and when I later visited him, it was always very pleasant and often the coffee was immediately put on the table before the sculptures were unveiled. The man and his work radiated an atmosphere that you never forget.

I can't remember anything about the reactions of the press to the exhibition. I also assume that there weren't very many. I can be wrong, after all it is a long time ago, but perhaps there was something in the odd magazine. Kasper Niehaus would certainly have written about it, and in a sensible way.

Kasper Niehaus was one of the Dutch critics who was always open and could discuss things from a certain perspective. He knew a lot himself and thus had the ability to compare, while most critics did not have that. I have always considered Kasper Niehaus and Jos de Gruyter, both before and partly after the war, as the leading Dutch critics. Otherwise there was nobody who could talk knowledgeably about things. Nor was there anybody who had his own opinion, independent of the person concerned. Most criticism was directed against the museum, against me and hardly ever about what was shown. Kasper Niehaus always defended the young artists. Even when he did not exactly understand it, he instinctively felt where talent lay. He defended, for example, Lucebert. Lucebert was a poet and as such a member of the Cobra group. One of my memories: at the start of the exhibition, he erected a sort of cage with black bars with all sorts of texts in it, anti-religious texts to which various people took exception. They may in fact have been partly responsible for the scandal. For people are less likely to rant about a painting than about a text that incites them. They can quote a text; they must first understand a painting before they can criticise it. Everybody thinks they can understand a text even if this is not the case. But in addition to his poetry, Lucebert always made drawings and watercolours, fantastic watercolours. I think that would have been at the end of the 'fifties. Then he also began to make oil paintings. Thanks to the "quid pro quo arrangement"[21], he was able to live from his watercol-

21. 'Quid pro quo arrangement', in Dutch Beeldende Kunstenaars Regeling or BKR. Founded in 1949 as a form of social welfare to support artists. Local councils received governmental budgets to purchase art as a way of supporting artists. In 1956 it became BKR.

ours and one of the people who devoted himself to this in a masterly fashion in the quid pro quo committee in Bergen was Kasper Niehaus. I frequently received one of those beautifully written notes from Kasper: *I see a lot in this artist but at the moment he does not have enough to live on. Please, come and take a look, let us go there together.* And so I visited, very frequently guided by Kasper Niehaus, young or old artists. He really prospected for me, scouted the territory and frequently discovered or helped me discover people. I not only appreciated Kasper Niehaus for the things he wrote, but also for the things he did. He really devoted himself to artists as human beings.

In general, a review arises like this. The critic begins to write in the vein of: *On such and such a date we had a previous exhibition by this man and this new exhibition is much poorer than the former one,* and that's about it. Then they can construct all sorts of literary stories around it and refer to just about anything but it's actually more about their judgements than providing background against which you could understand the artist. Making clear how you should look at it is something I see much too seldom. But Jos de Gruyter did that, and he later entered the museum business. That is, I believe, the proper approach.

There are now some among the young art critics — I must admit I don't read all that many — but there are people who approach things in a business-like way and explain things from that background. I believe that something has been released in the younger generation of art critics that is very promising. It has,

of course, become much more difficult and I believe
that because of this we have a different type of critic
to those of thirty years ago. Then, somebody was just
given the job. He had to report things and he did it,
for better or for worse. I remember one very well-
known art critic who wrote a short article in which he
treated the three Duchamp-Villon brothers as one
person. He didn't know there were three of them:
Marcel
Duchamp, Raymond Duchamp-Villon and Jacques
Villon. Things like that happened a lot back then.
I believe this no longer happens, I believe that people
now approach things from a different perspective.
I actually think that we should no longer call such a
person an art critic but instead come up with a different name. Kritein in Greek means to judge and I
don't believe that we are mainly there to judge art but
that our challenge is to understand art in the context
of today and particularly that of tomorrow. When we
look at art — I don't like the word art either — but
when we look at something creative, we should try to
ask ourselves: where can this lead, what does it express about the direction we are taking? I believe we
should approach creative expressions with a question
rather than a judgement. We really do not need the
judgement of Mr. X or Y, but we do ask for an explanation. If we look at things from this angle, there are still
enormous possibilities for those we now call art critics. Clarifying, explaining is the only thing that is
valuable. Frequently, authors or poets are excellent at
that. It is not always necessary to be one of those, but
I do think, for example, of people such as Baudelaire

and Apollinaire, who led the way. Here in Holland, too,
a writer such as Gerrit Kouwenaar has frequently
written excellent articles about art. Because he had
experienced it himself, in the literary field and therefore was right in the middle of it.

PHOTOGRAPHS OF SANDBERG

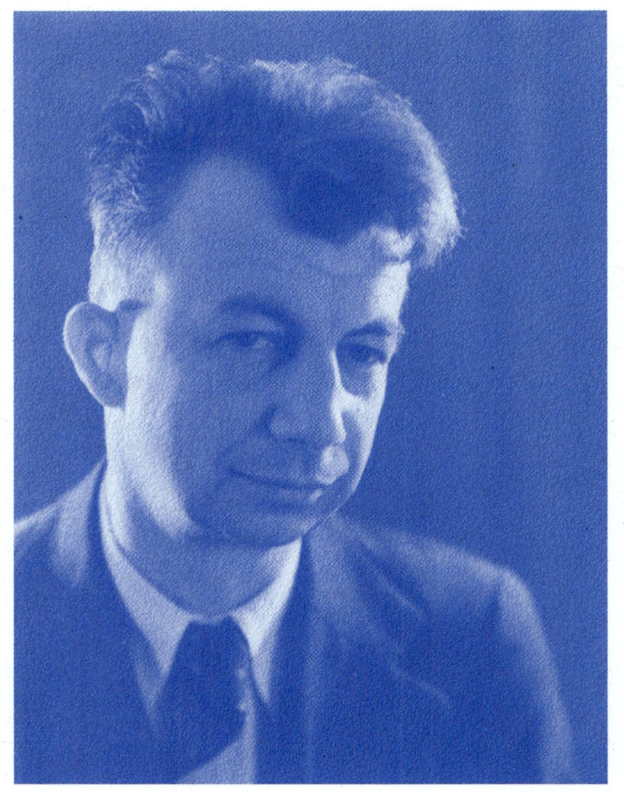

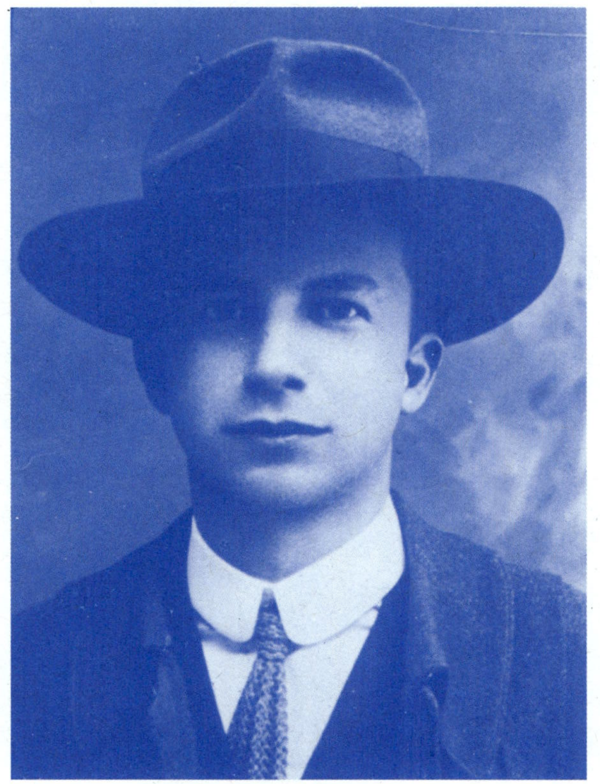

Willem Sandberg, Milan, 1920 and around 1938

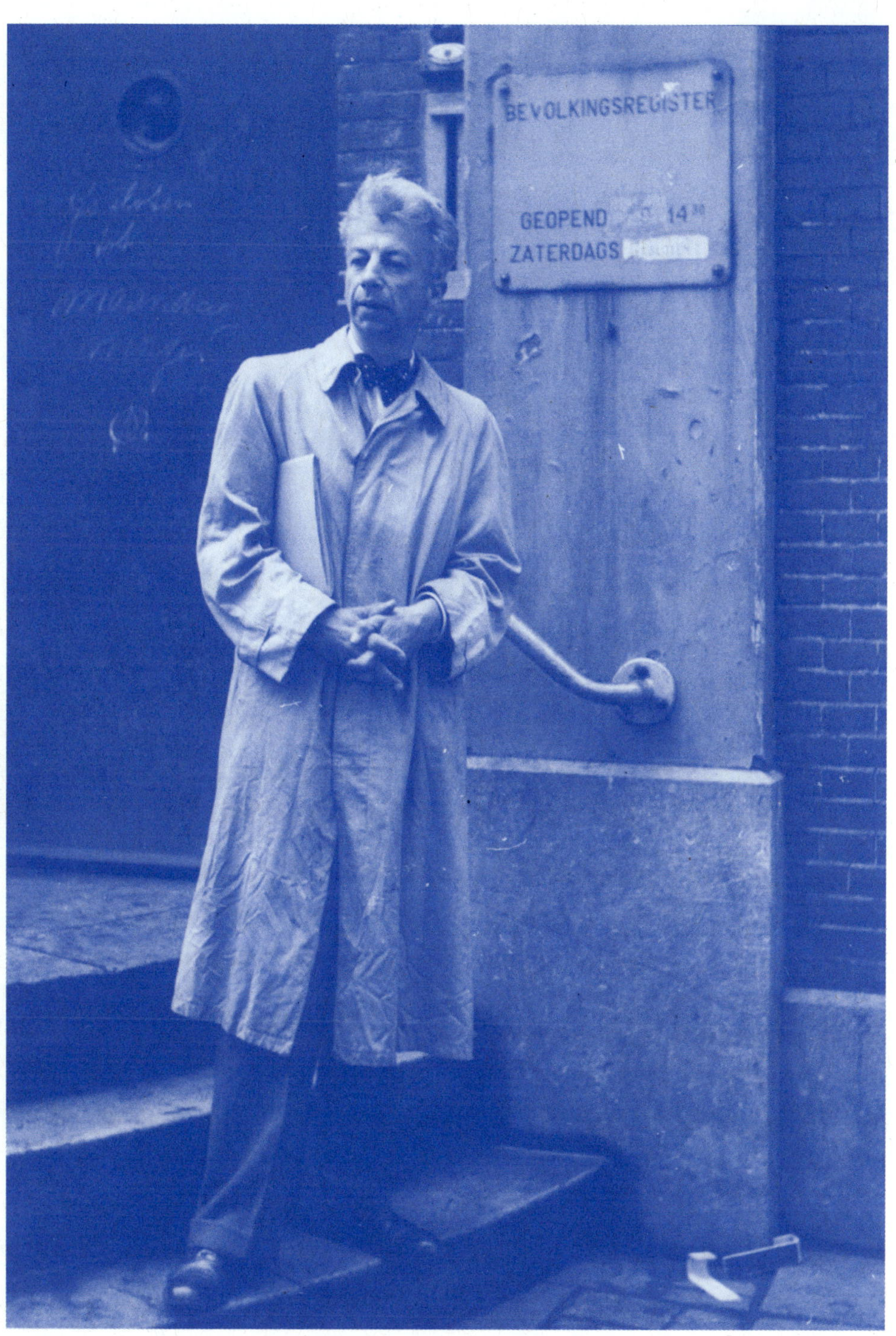

Willem Sandberg in front of the Amsterdam municipal registry,
shortly after the war

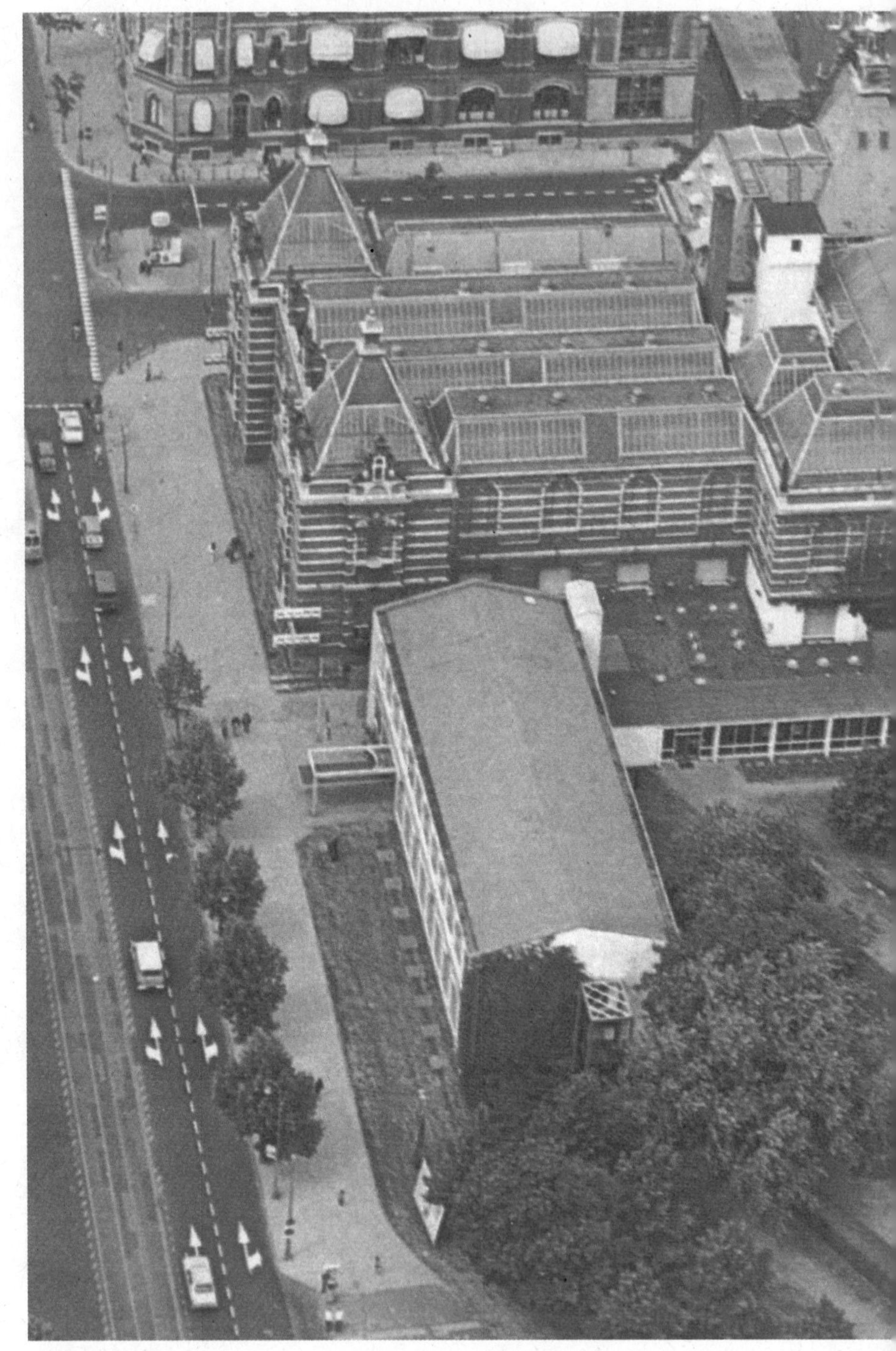

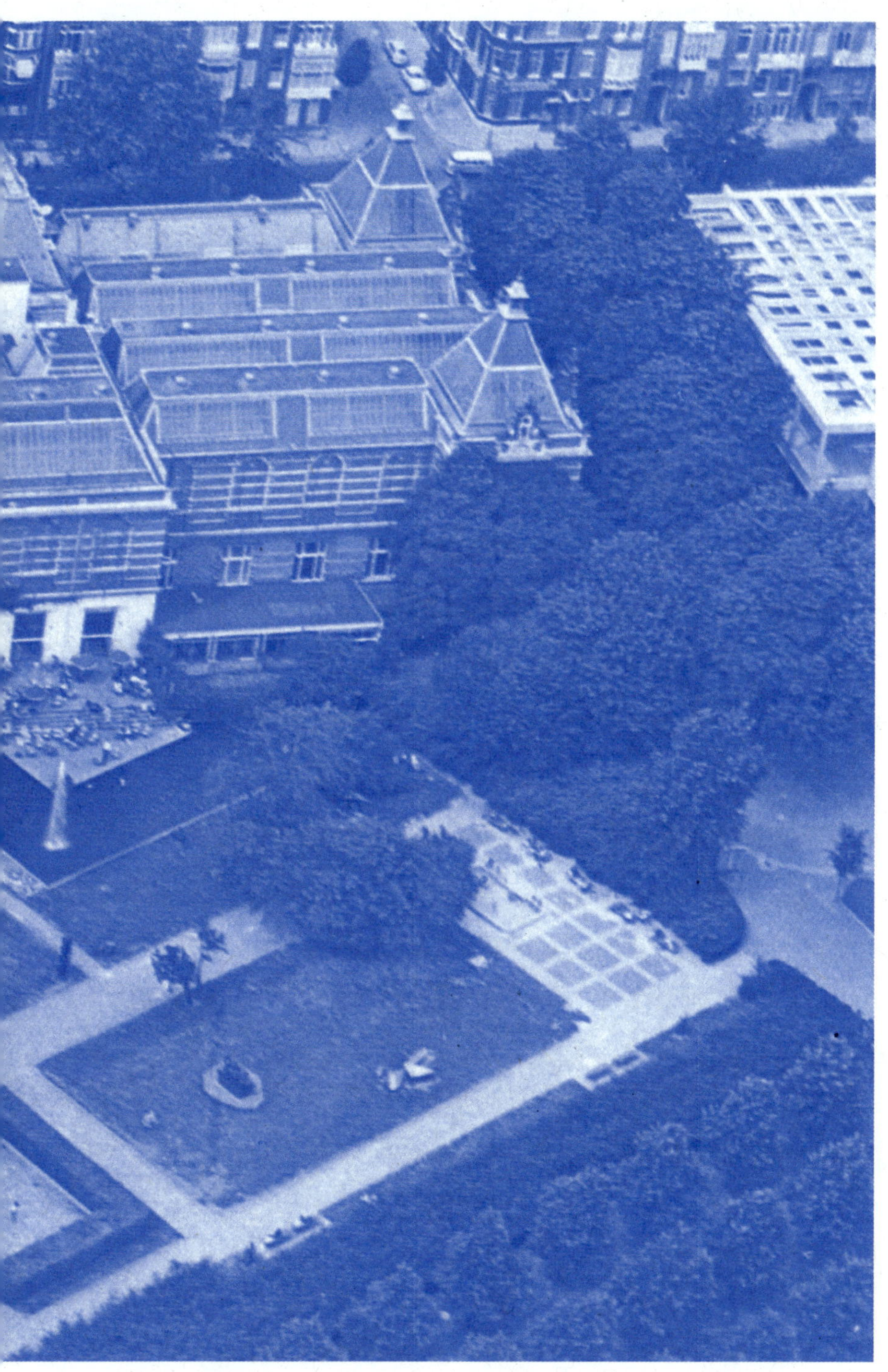

Stedelijk Museum, Amsterdam, around 1960

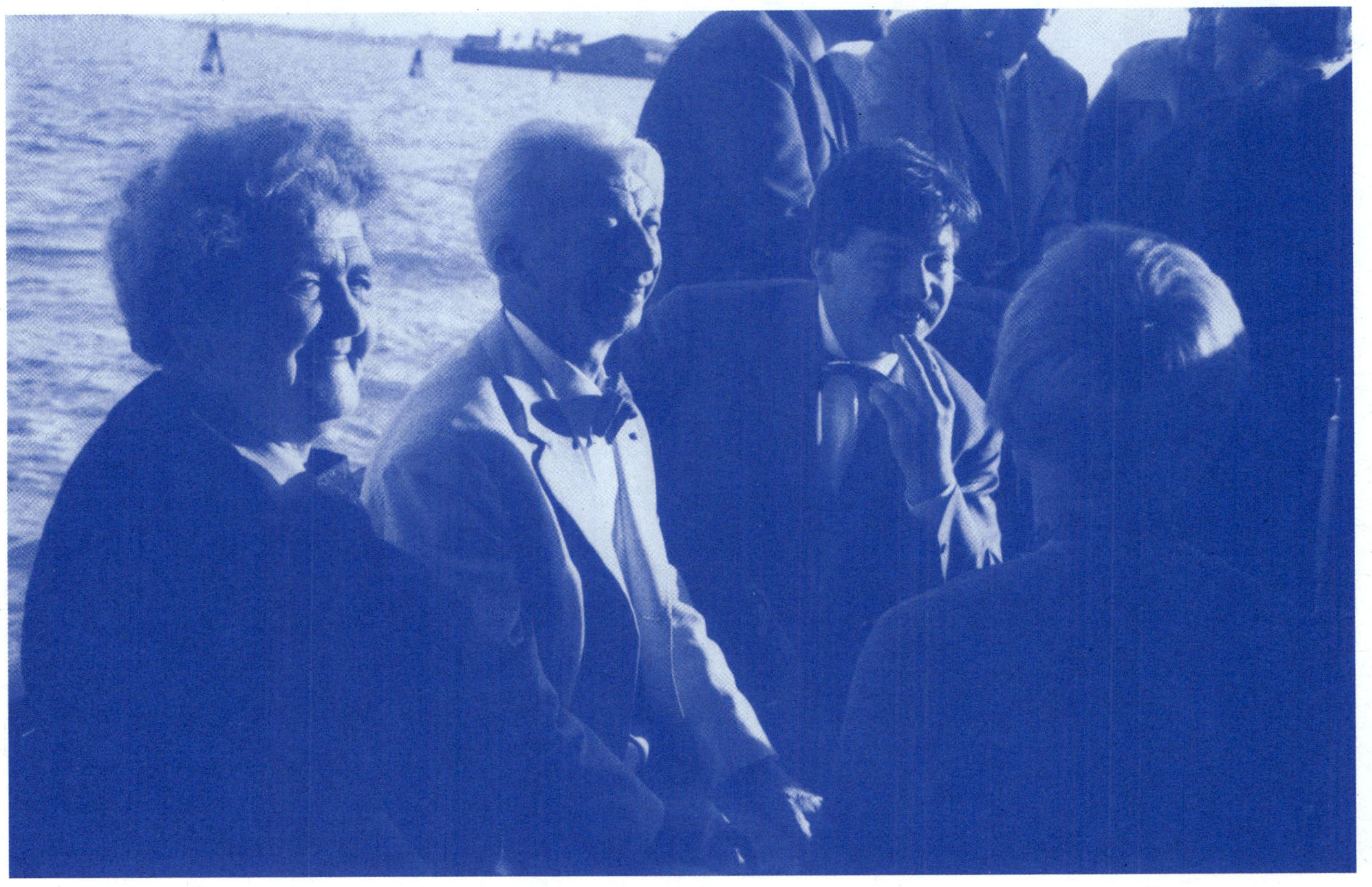

Lida and Willem Sandberg with Karel Appel, Venice, 1960

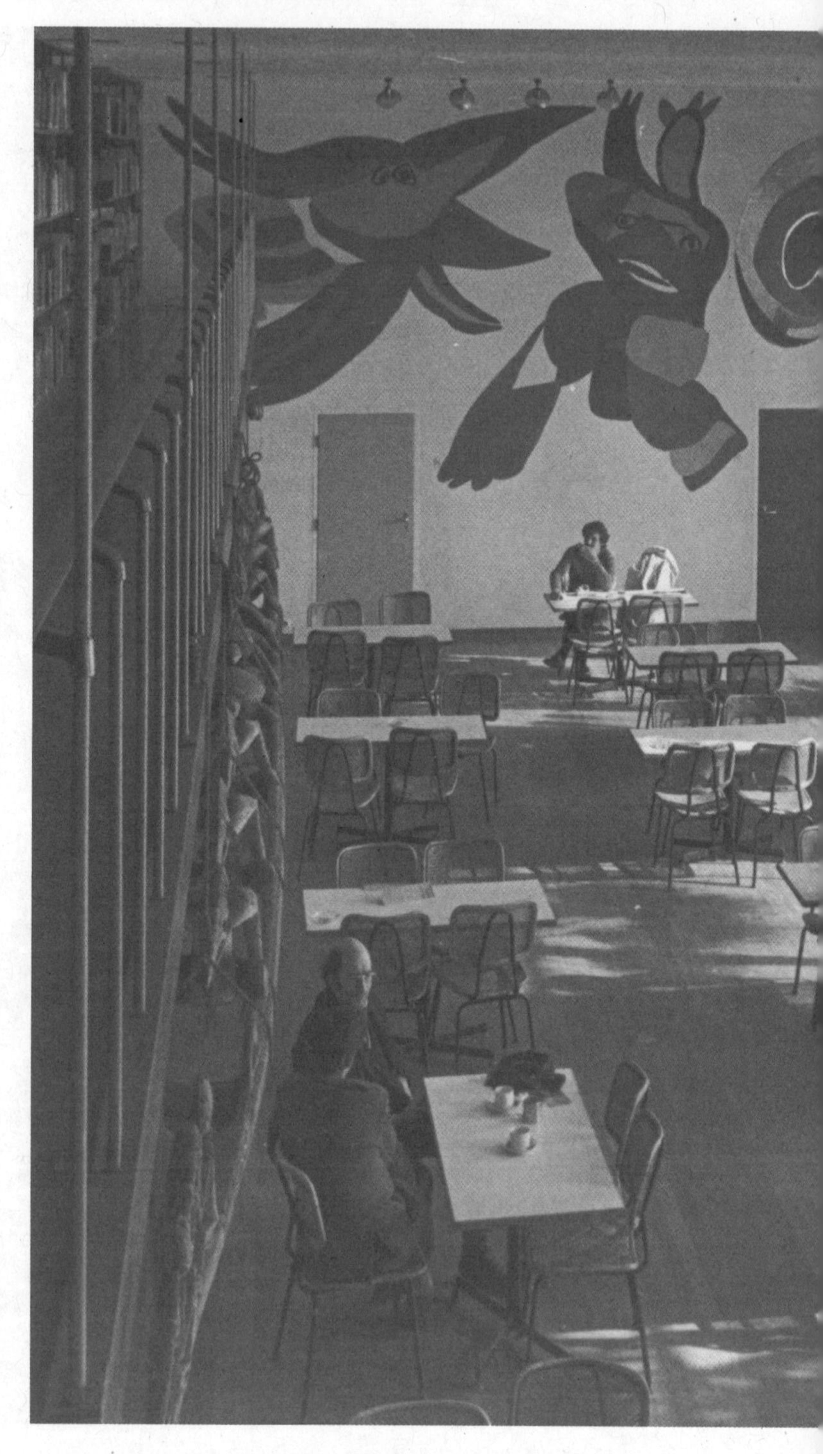

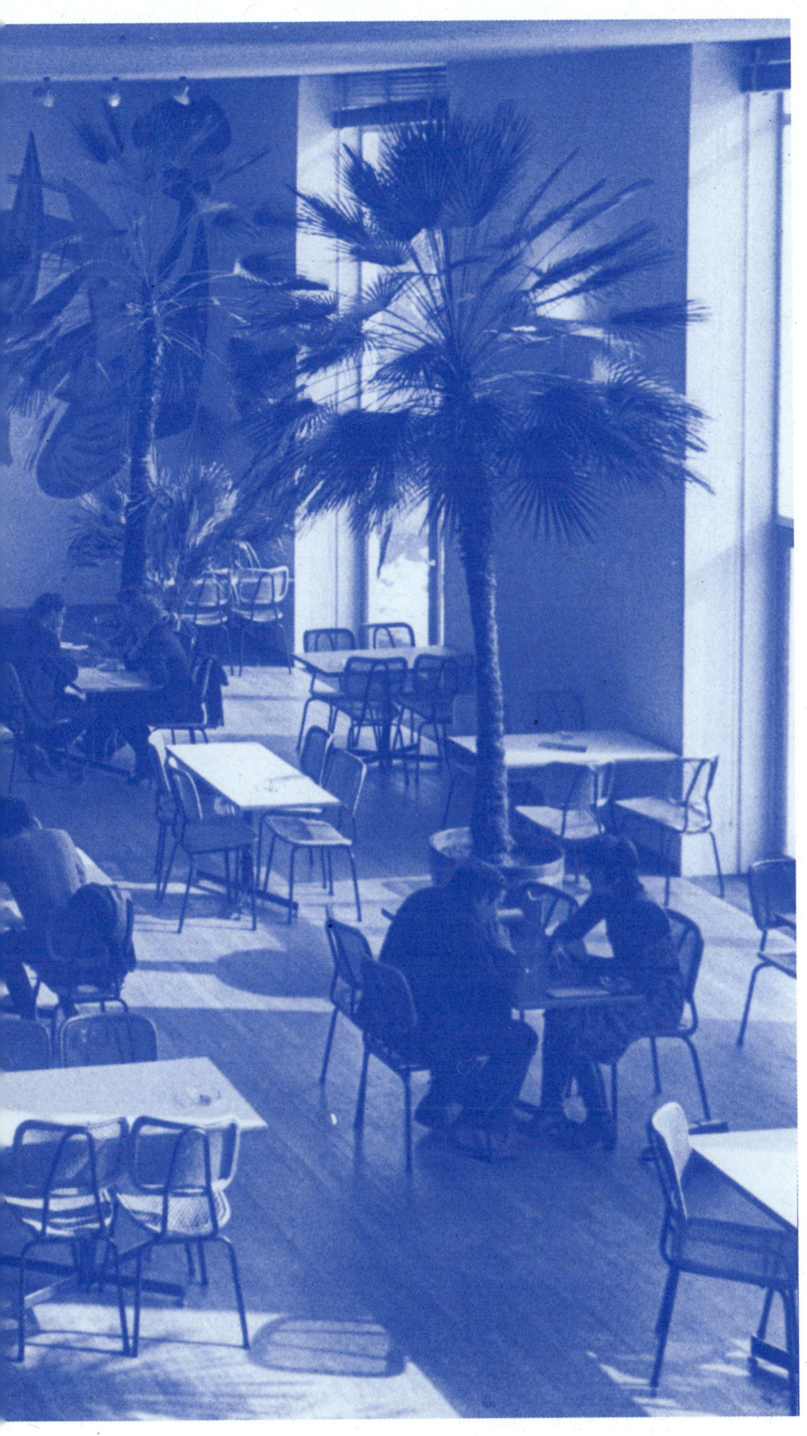

Restaurant Stedelijk Museum, Amsterdam, 1963

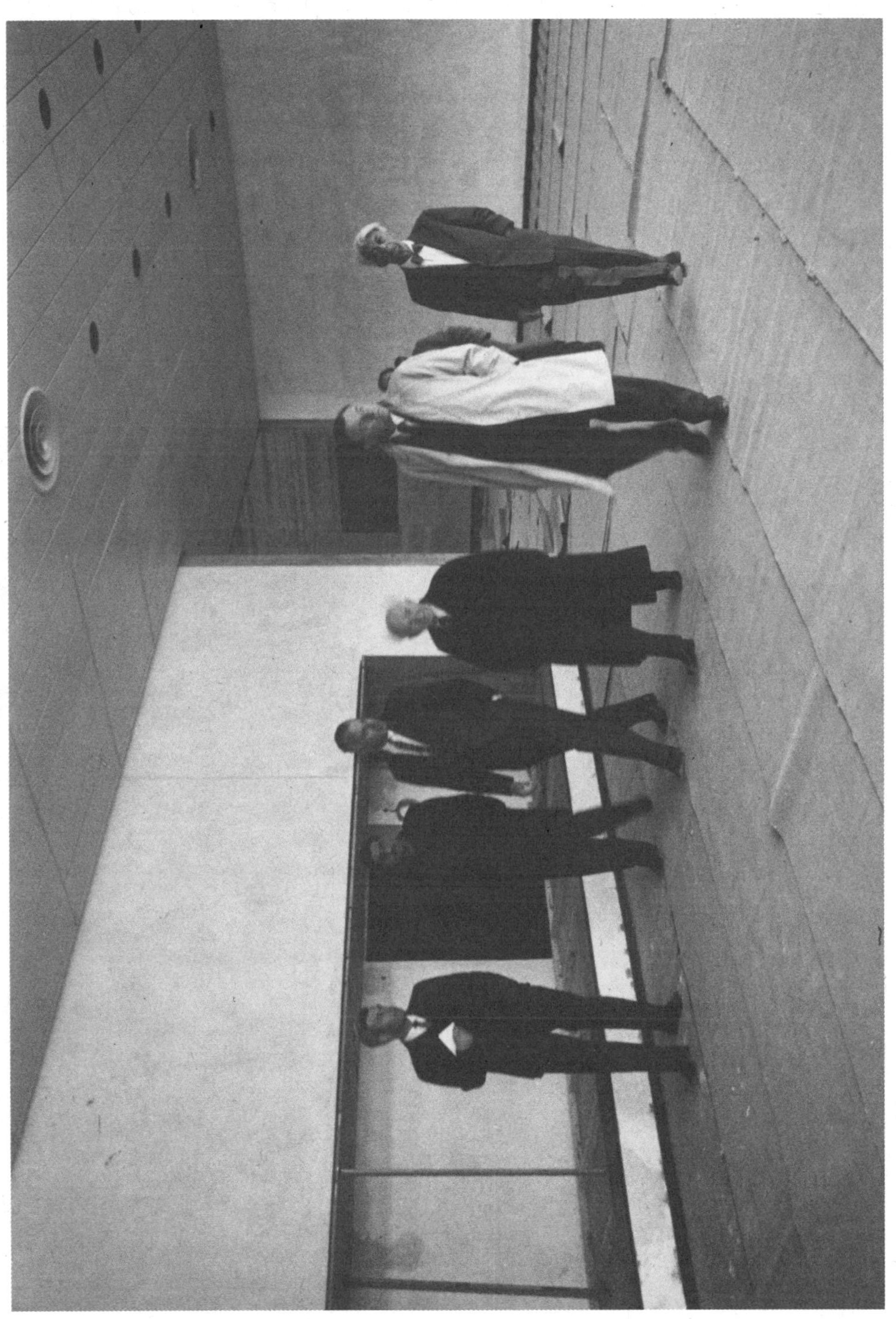

David Ben-Gurion, Teddy Kollek and Willem Sandberg at The Israel Museum
shortly before the opening, Jerusalem, 1965

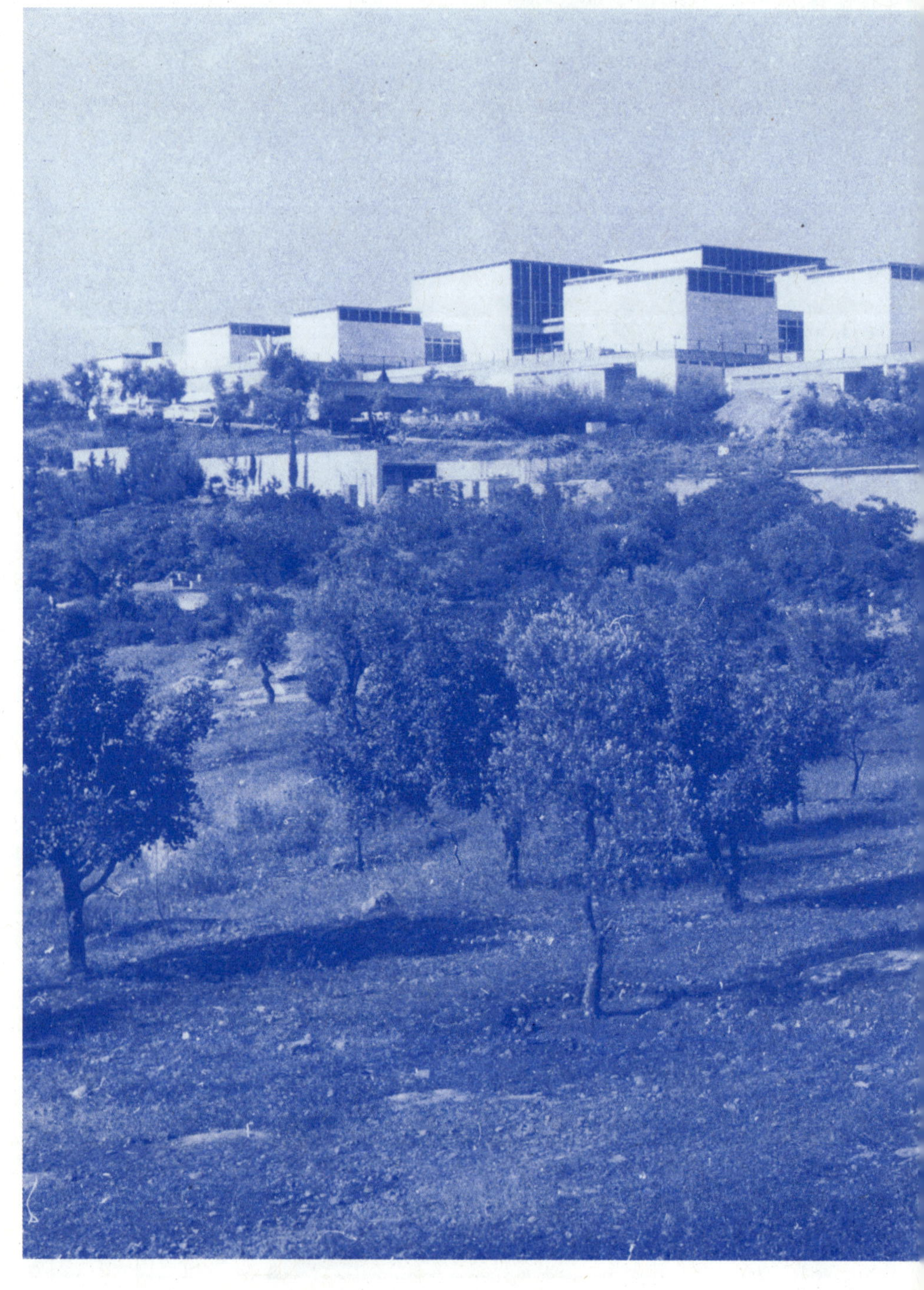

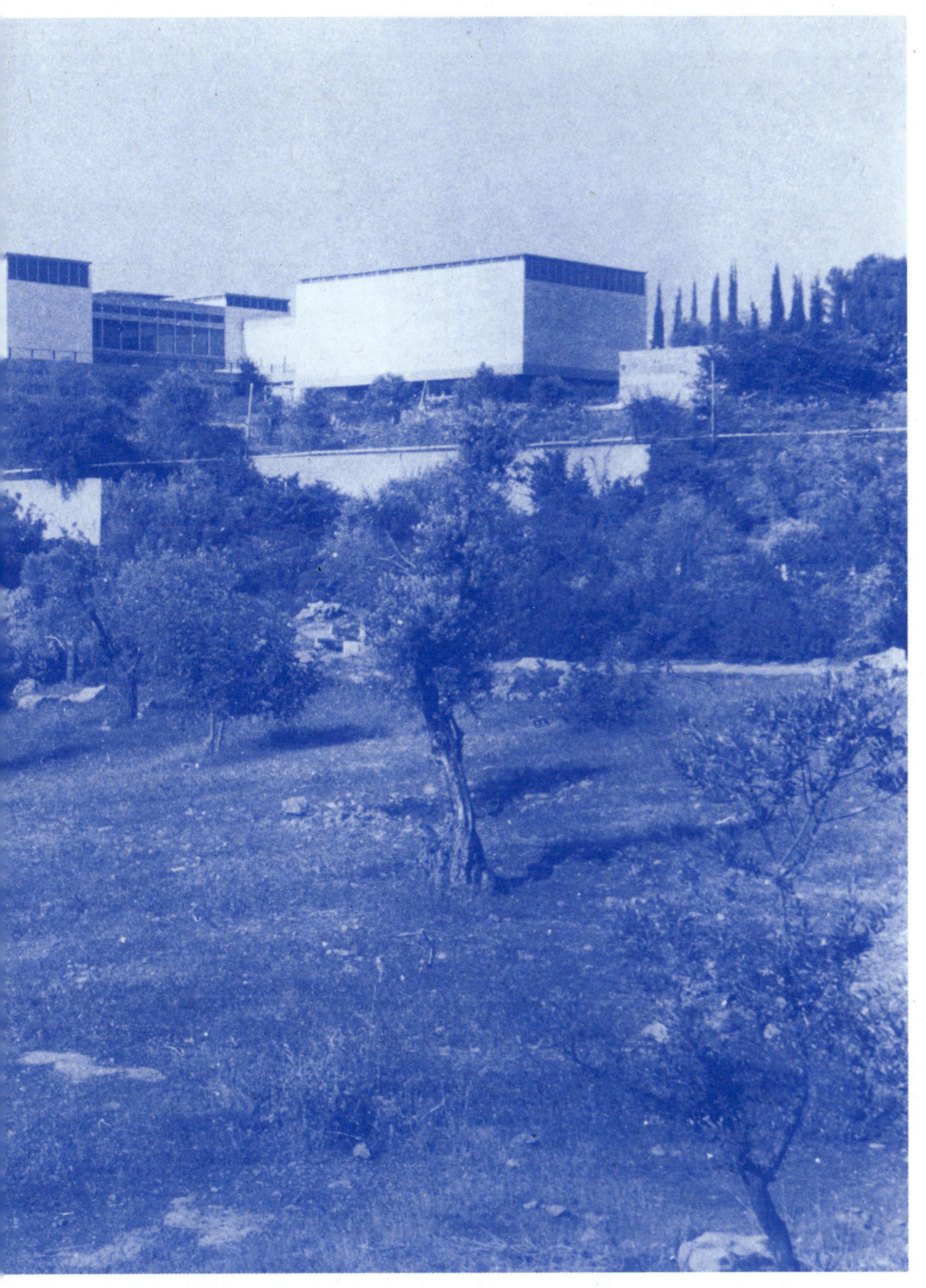

The Israel Museum, Jerusalem, 1965

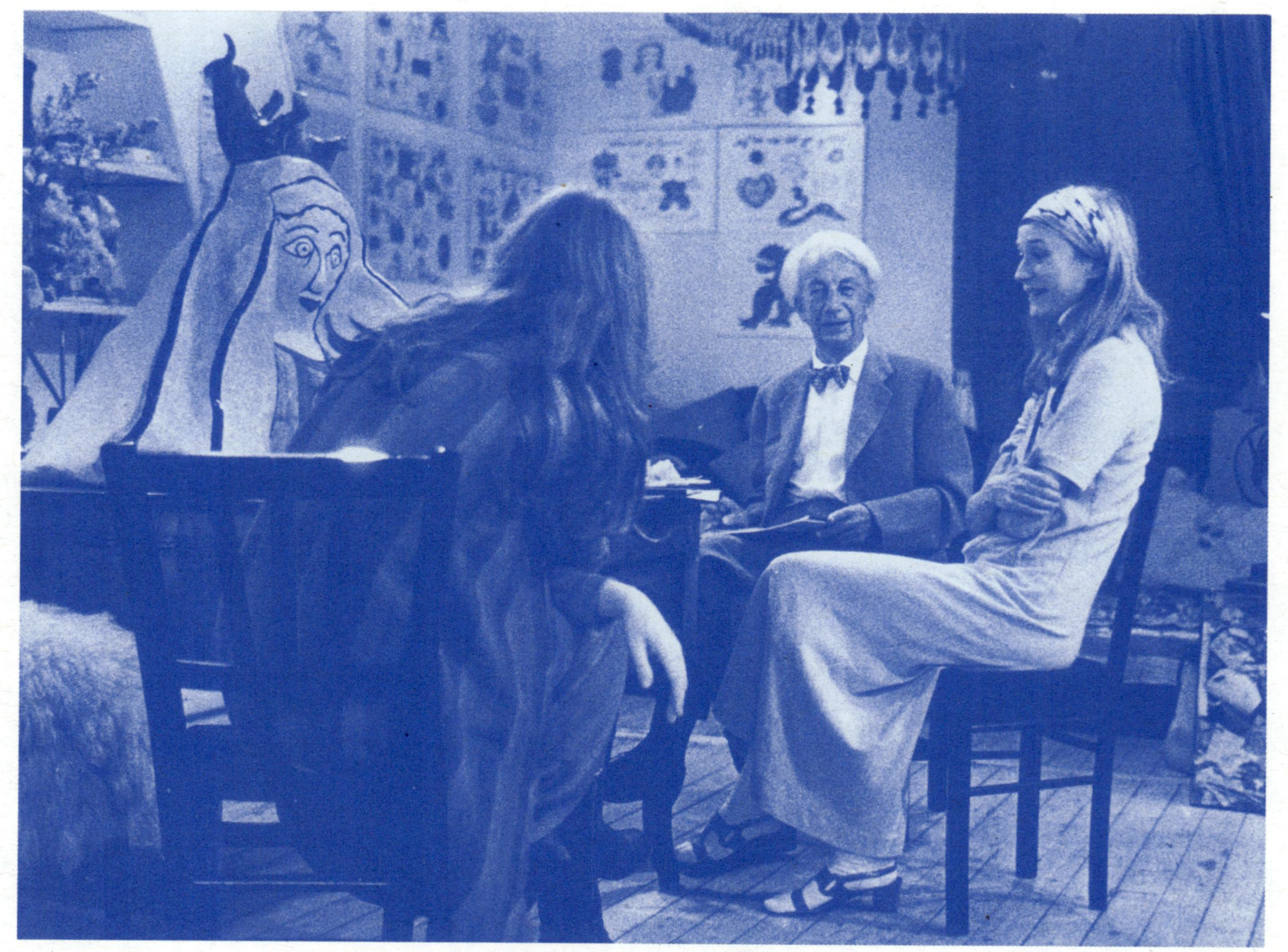

Marijke Conijn, Willem Sandberg and Niki de Saint Phalle, Soisy-sur-École around 1969

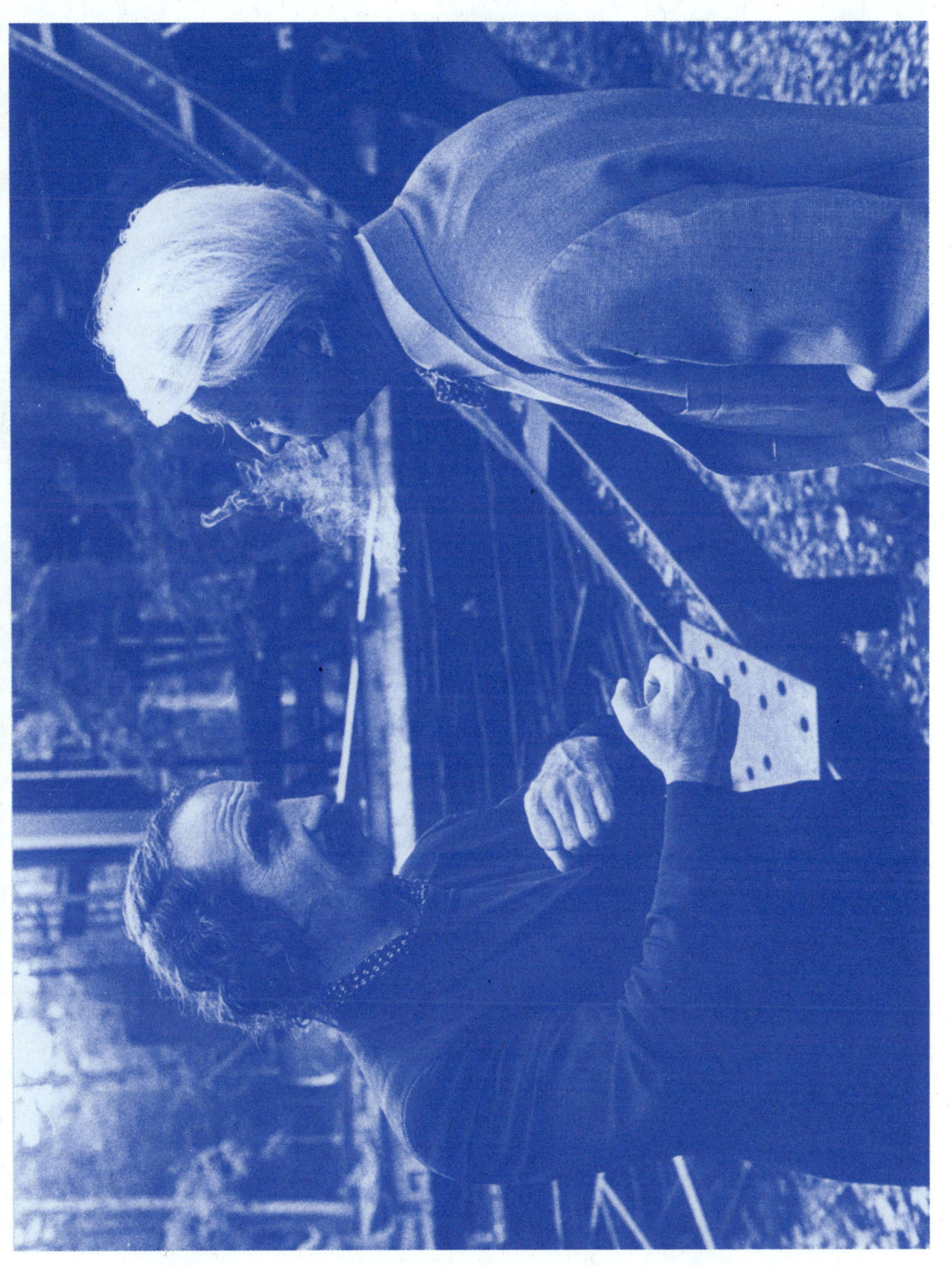

Jean Tinguely and Willem Sandberg, Milly-la-Forêt, 1973

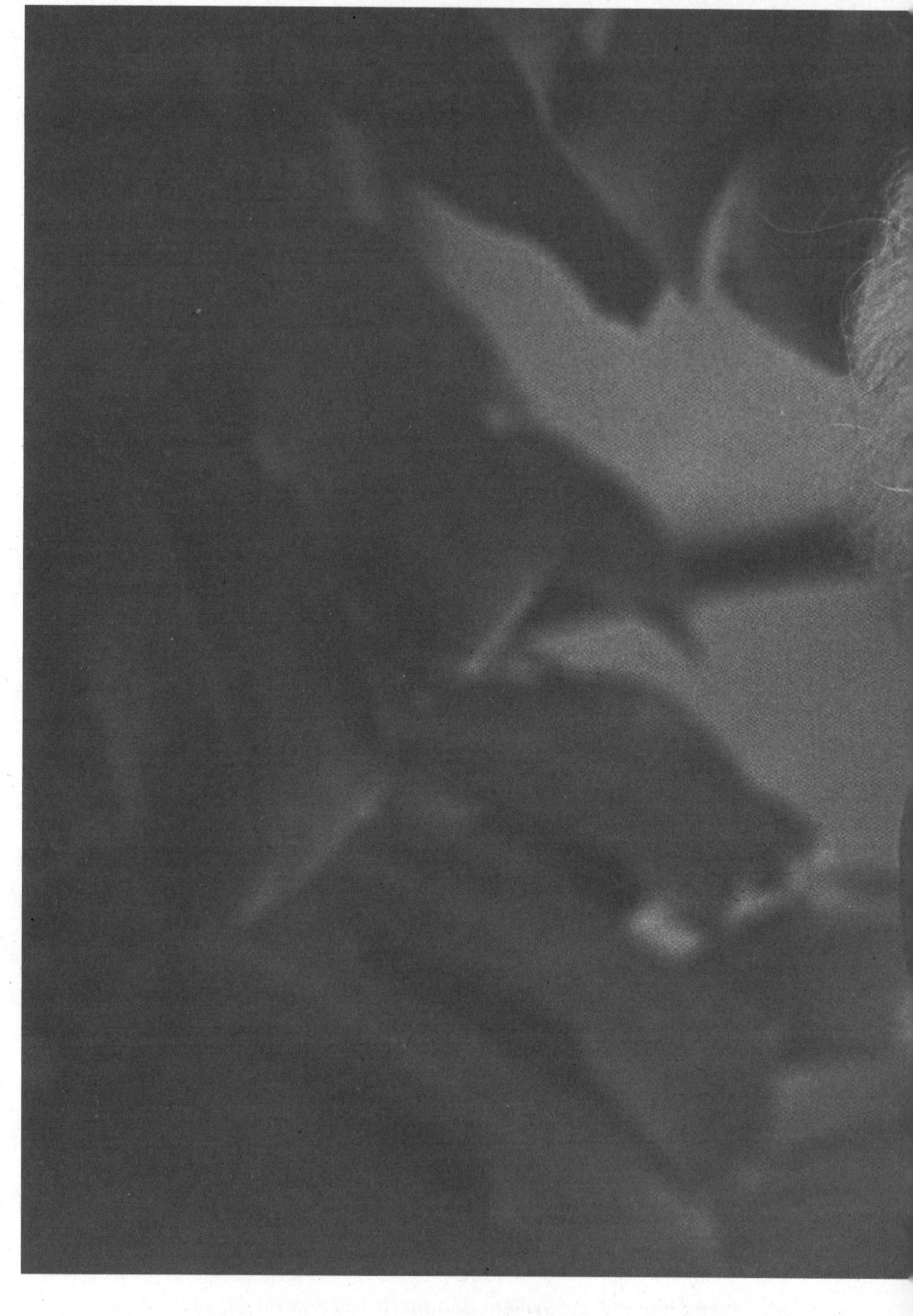

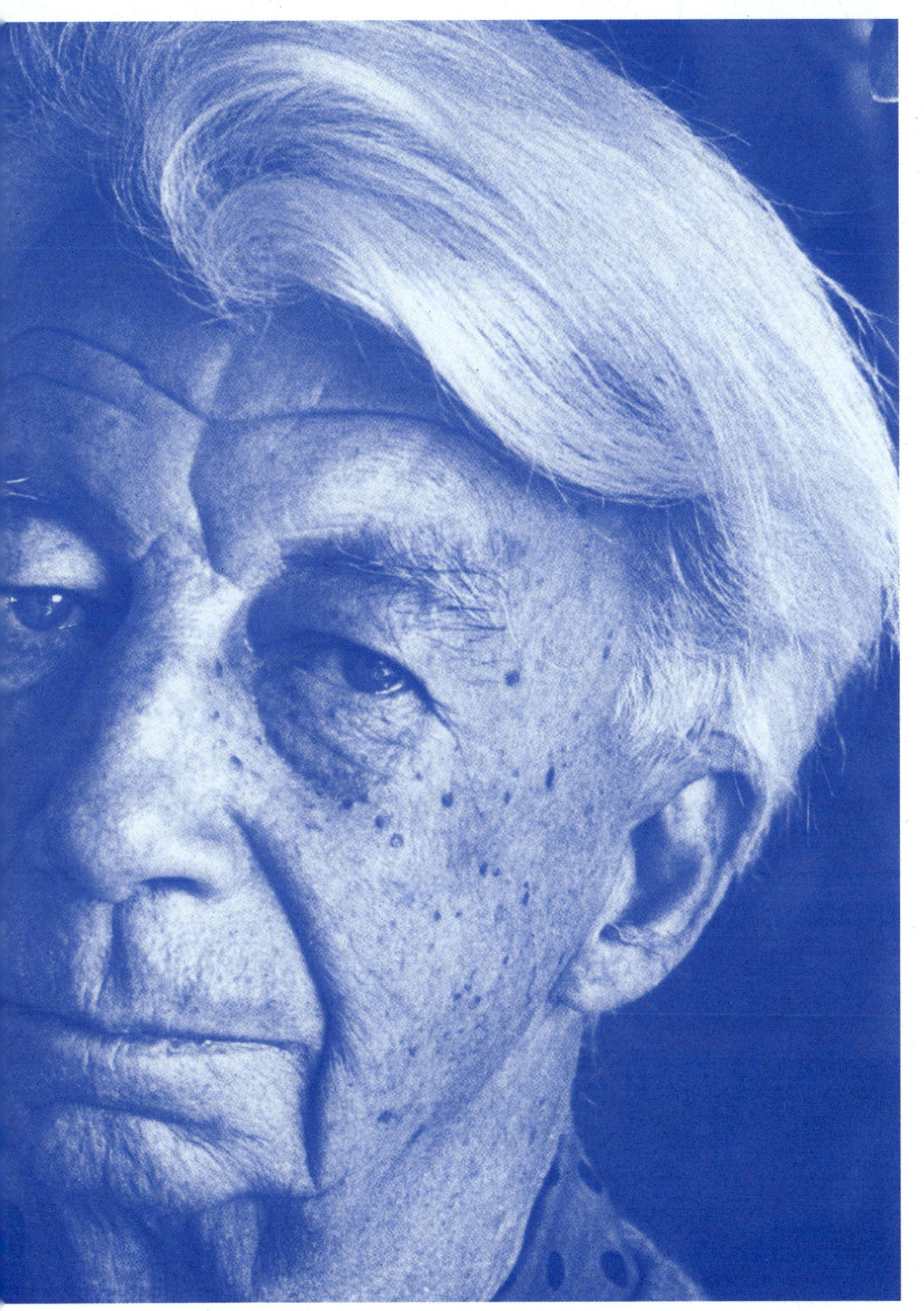

Willem Sandberg, Amsterdam, 1974

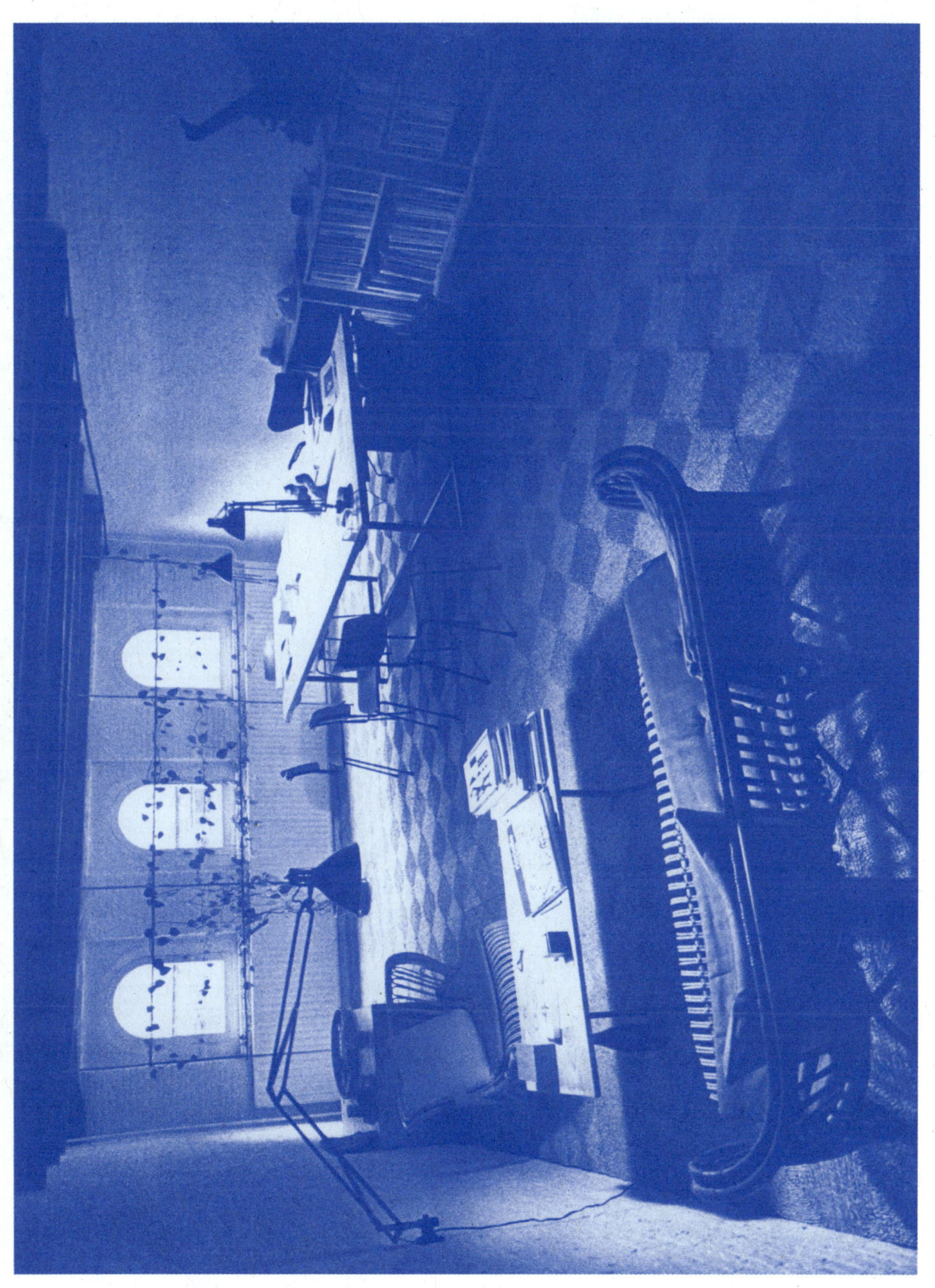

Studio Willem Sandberg at De Appel, Amsterdam, around 1974

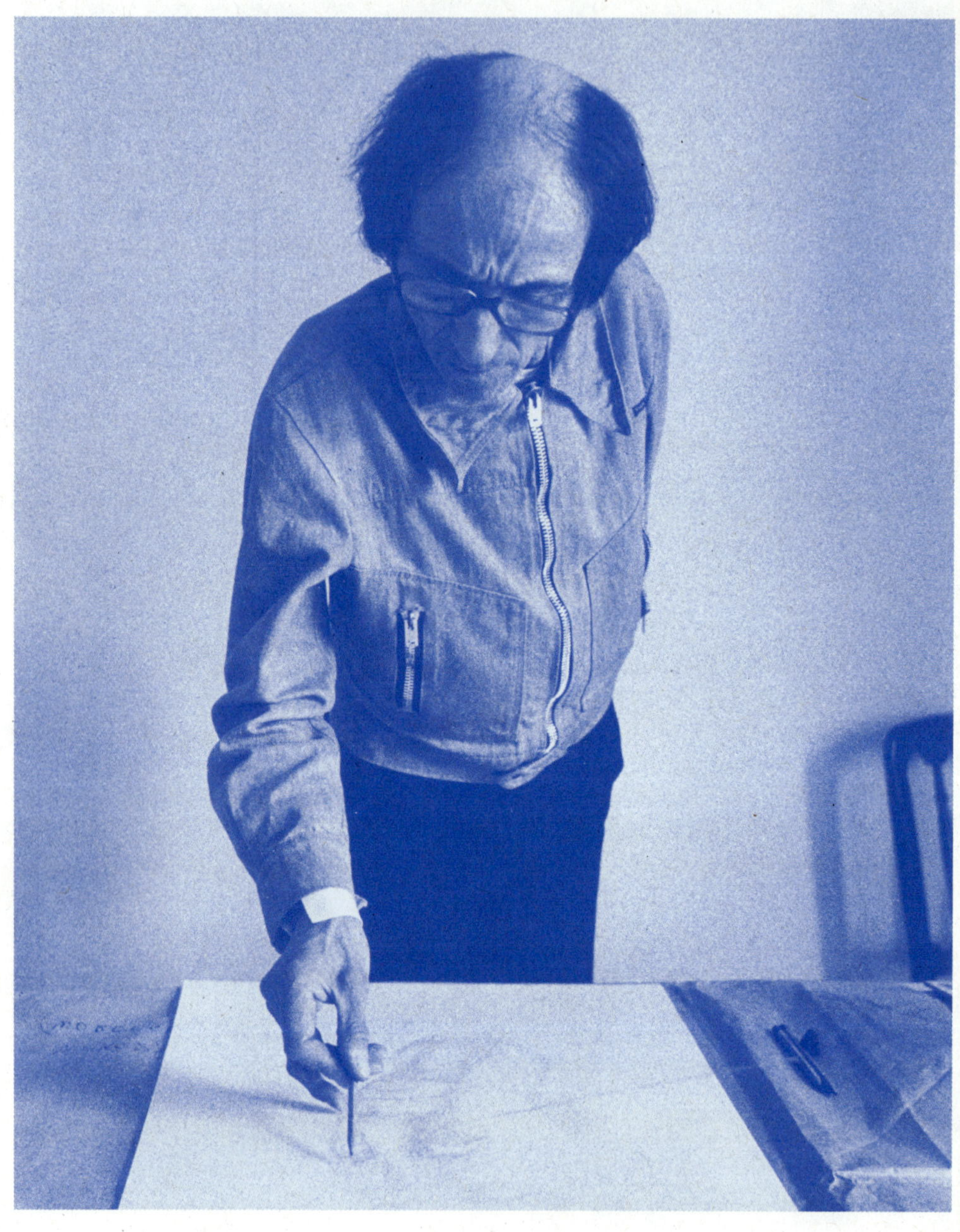

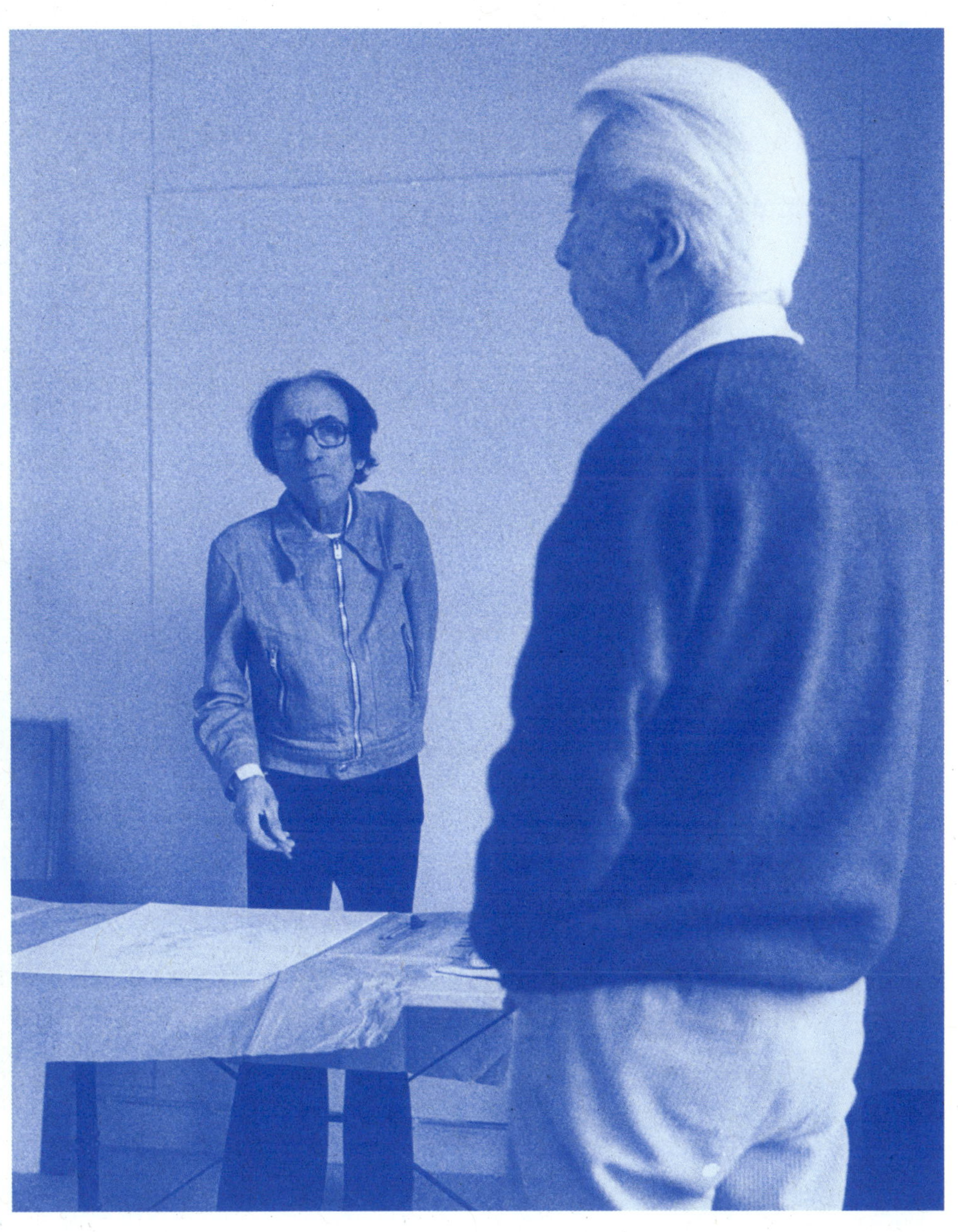

Wessel Couzijn drawing portraits of Willem Sandberg, Amsterdam, 1976

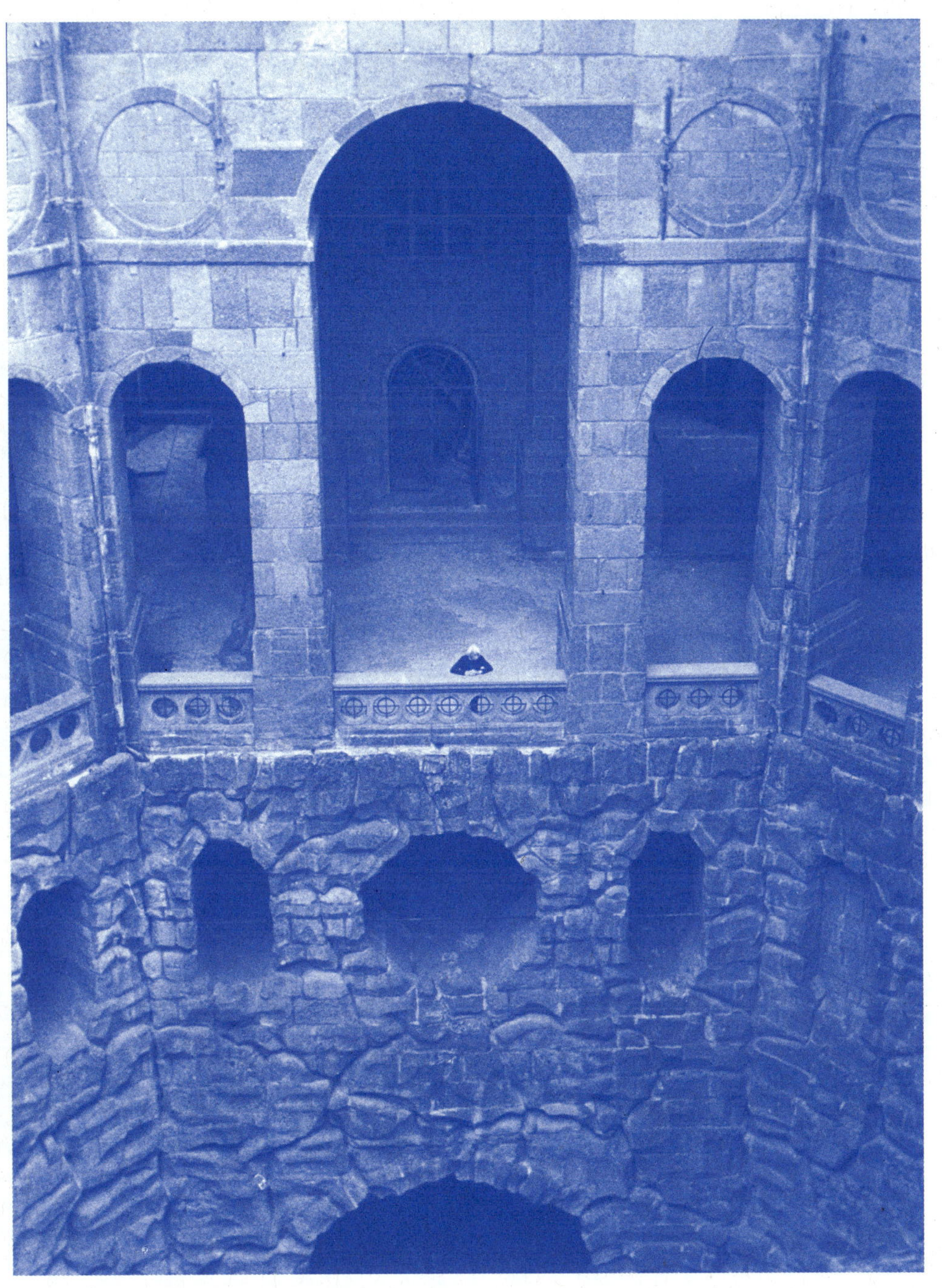

Willem Sandberg visiting the Herkules Castle, Kassel, 1977

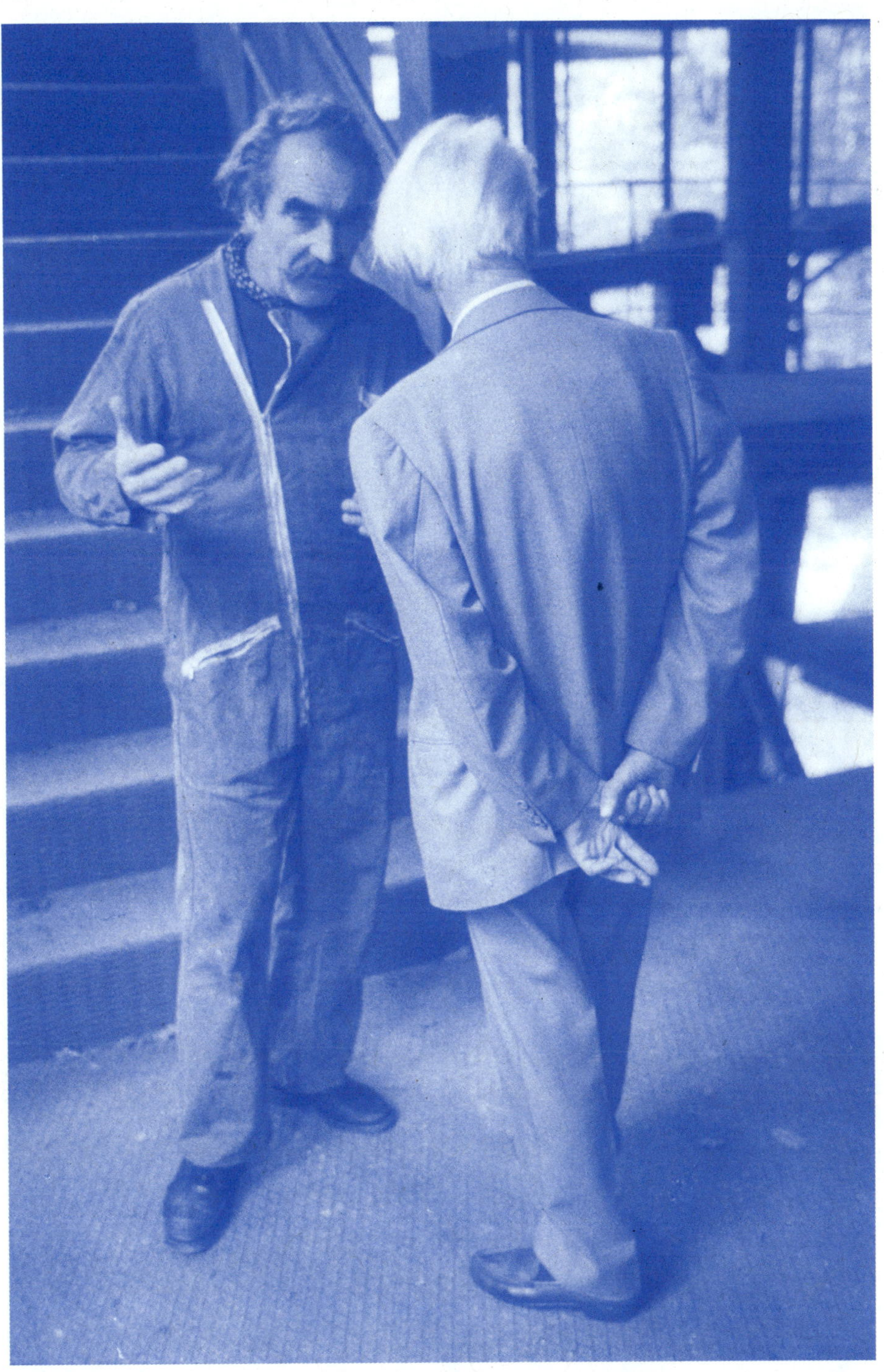

Jean Tinguely and Willem Sandberg, Milly-la-Forêt, late 1970s

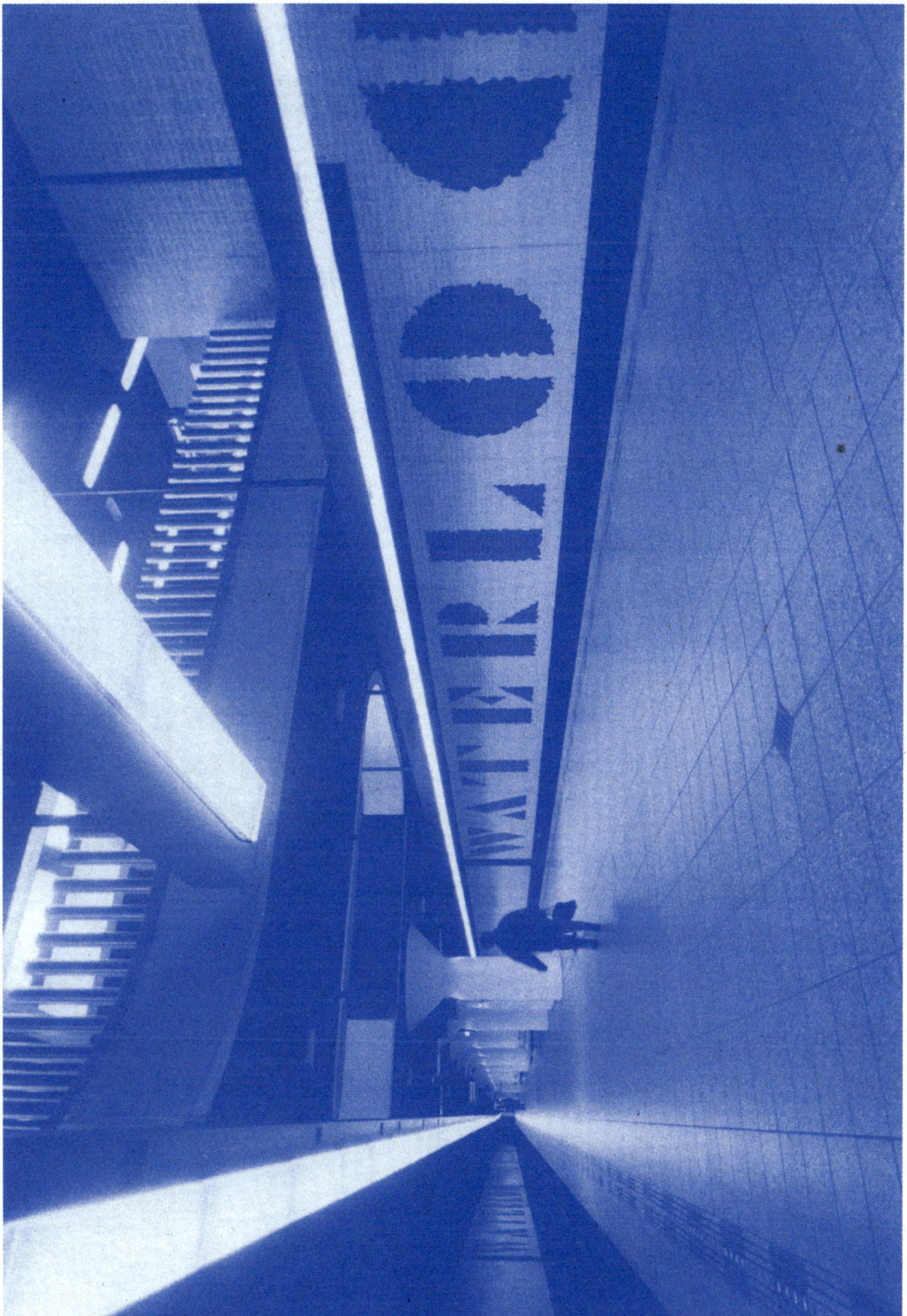

Metrostation Waterlooplein, Amsterdam, 1980

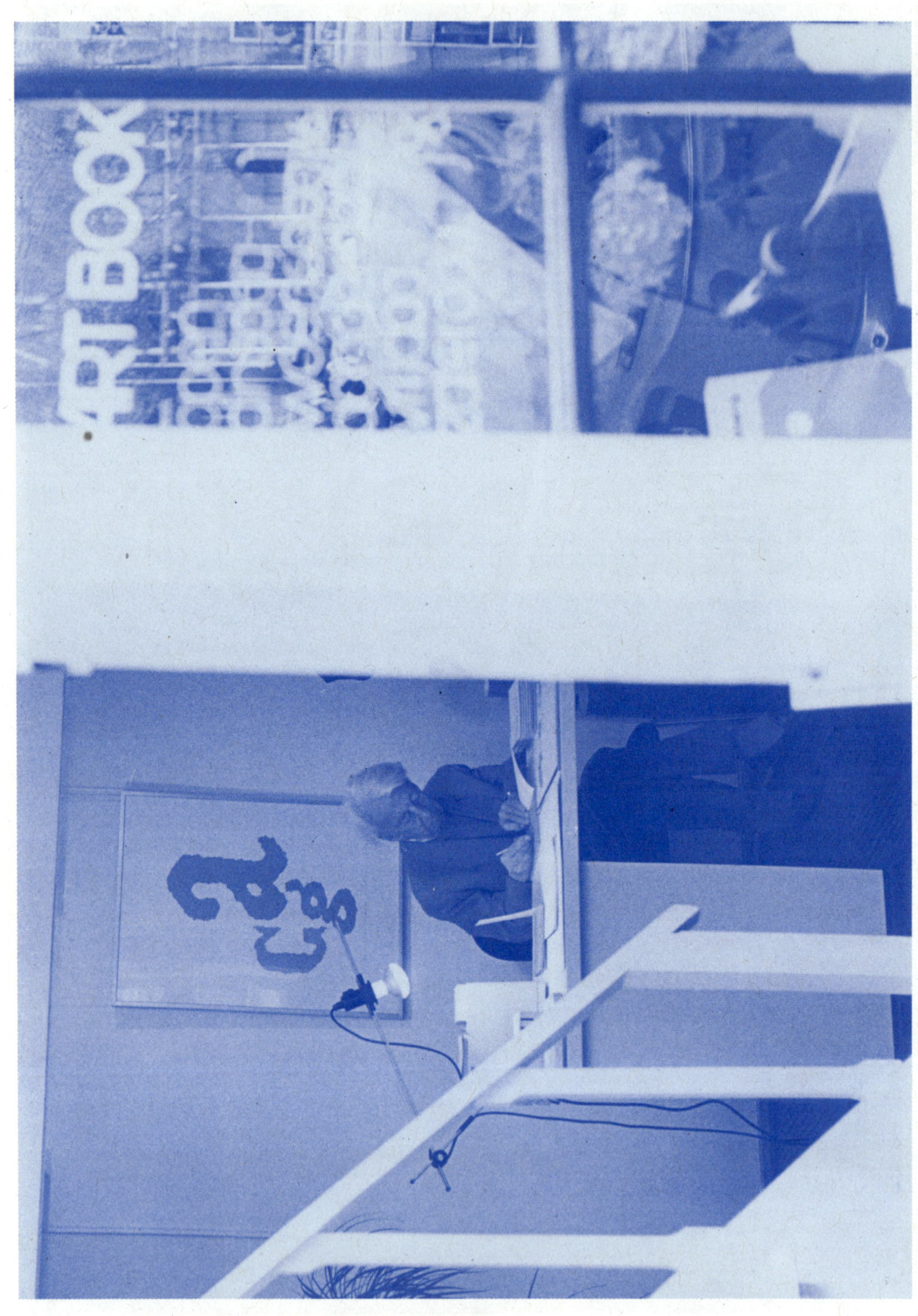

Presentation of "experimenta typografica" no. 4 at Art Book, Amsterdam, 1981

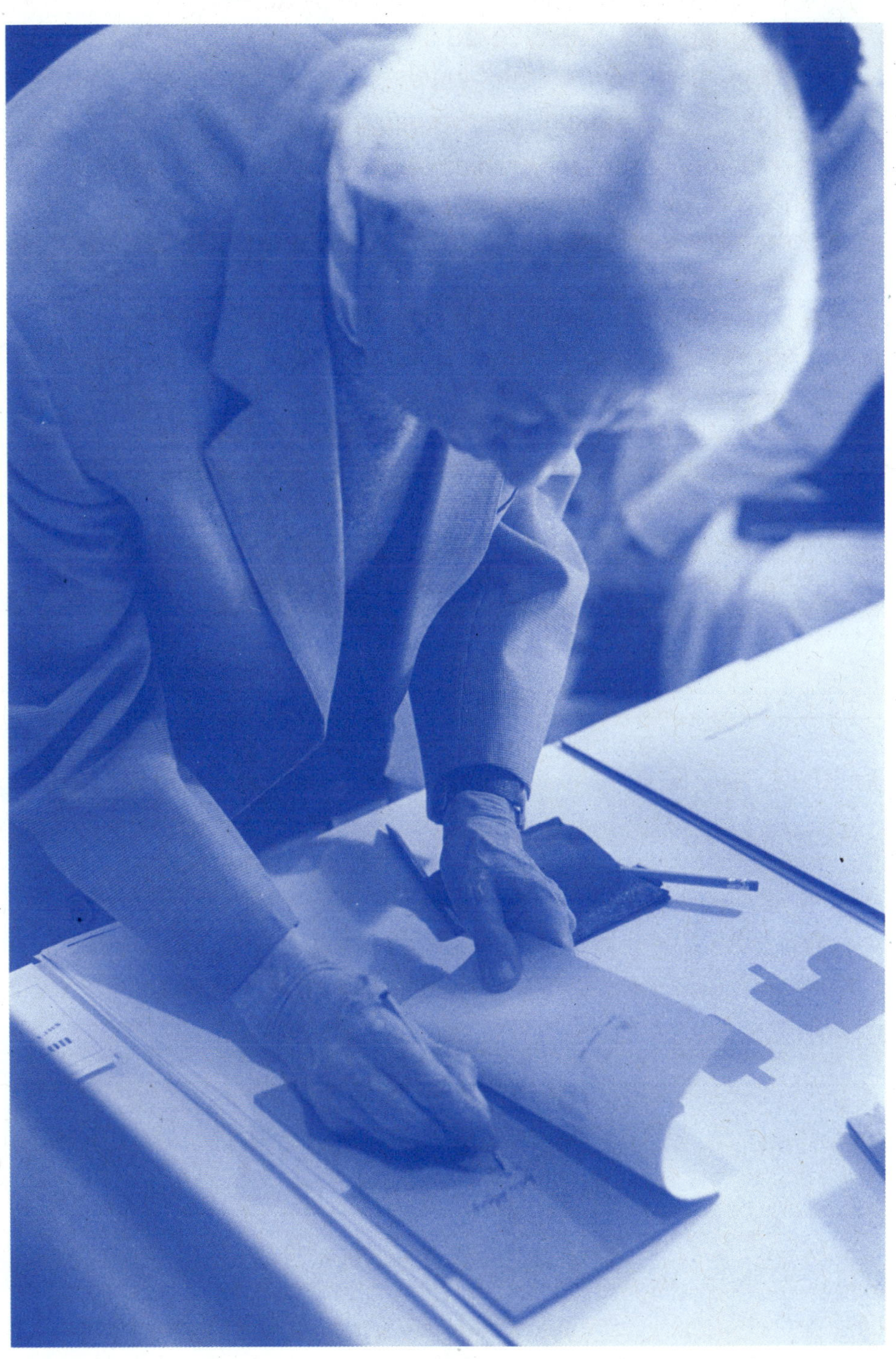

Willem Sandberg signing at Art Book, Amsterdam, 1981

Photographs of Sandberg, all photos by Ad Petersen
except pp. 283, 285, 286-287;
and pp. 298-299: © Han Singels

Ad Petersen (Zaandam, The Netherlands, 1931) studied
art history at the Universities of Utrecht and Groningen.
In 1960, when Sandberg was still director, he became a
curator at the Stedelijk Museum in Amsterdam, where he
left in 1990.
Petersen has also been active as a photographer
(books: ''A Curator's Camera'', Eindhoven, 1993; ''Les mille
lieux de l'art'', Basel, 2013). He is also the author of other
publications, including three on Sandberg: ''Sandberg:
a Documentary'', with Pieter Brattinga (Amsterdam, 1975,
English and Dutch), ''Sandberg, Designer and Director of
the Stedelijk'' (Rotterdam, 2004, English and Dutch) and
''Sandberg: graphiste et directeur du Stedelijk Museum''
(Paris, 2007, French).

POSTSCRIPT

designer of a museum

*looking back on my work in the 'stedelijk', i have
to say that i am pleased to have been able to work
there for 25 years, 18 of which as director — i started
after the war with 35 people and ended up with 167 —
after my entry i started to freshen up everything: whitewash everything! but i also started addressing everybody formally and then when i became director i
founded the employees' association — a participation
organ that turned all workers into colleagues — at the
same time, all tips were for the association, every year
we would use them for a four-day excursion with the
spouses — we visited nearby cultural cities such as
antwerp, bruges, brussels, and as far as paris by bus:
two days there and back and each time one day culture
and one day in the countryside — that considerably
stimulated fraternisation — everybody went from the
cleaners to the management and the leadership was
completely in the hands of the board of the association
— this is how we built a true museum community —*

*everybody could always walk in on the director but
the staff made sure that no misuse was made of this
— often people who left my office were confronted by
their colleagues with the question: why did you have to
keep the director from his work? i am grateful that i
have been given the opportunity to build up a socialist
company and i have to thank my alderman de roos for
that — he let me go my own way —*

Willem Sandberg
06.10.1981

INDEX

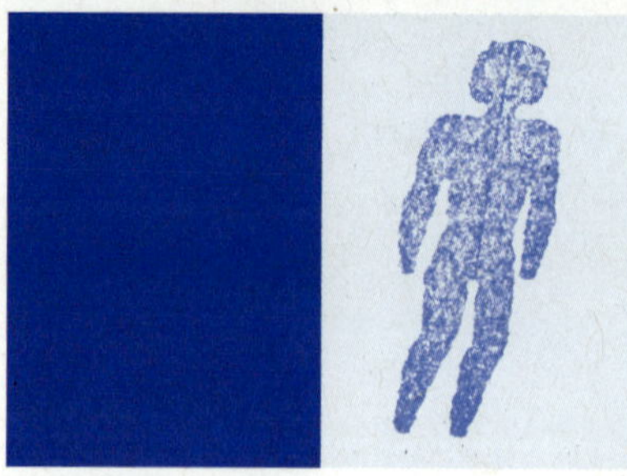

From: "Nu 2. Kwadraatblad"
1968, 25 × 25 cm

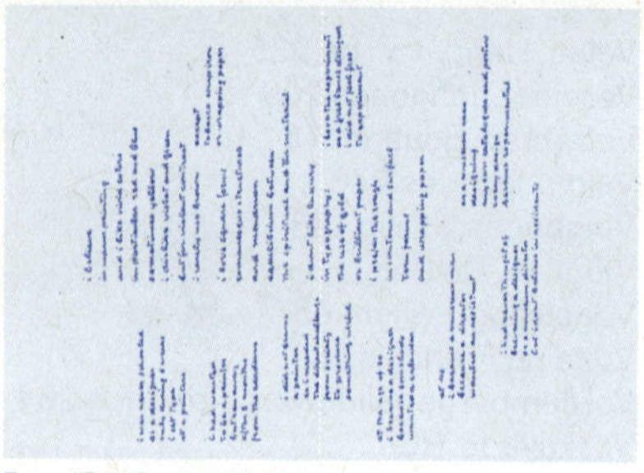

From: "Print", vol. XXIII, no. 1
1969

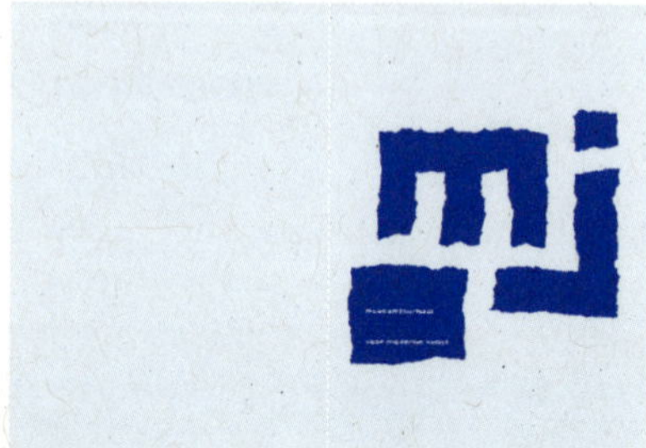

Cover "Museumjournaal voor moderne kunst", vol. 7, no. 1
1961, 25 × 19 cm

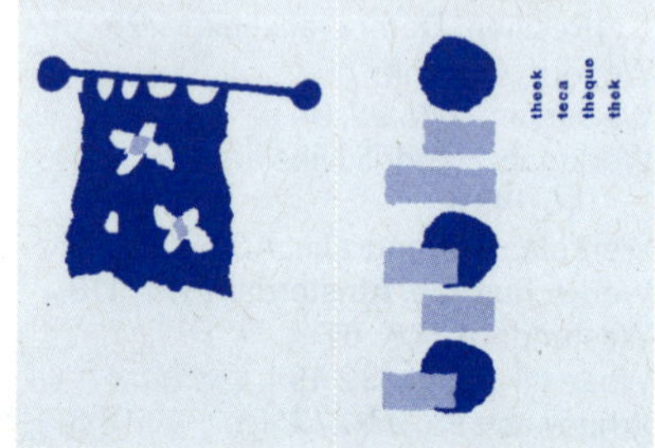

From: "STYL. Tijdschrift voor woninginrichting", no. 5
1938, 31.5 × 22.7 cm
Catalogue cover Stedelijk Museum Library
1957, 26 × 19 cm

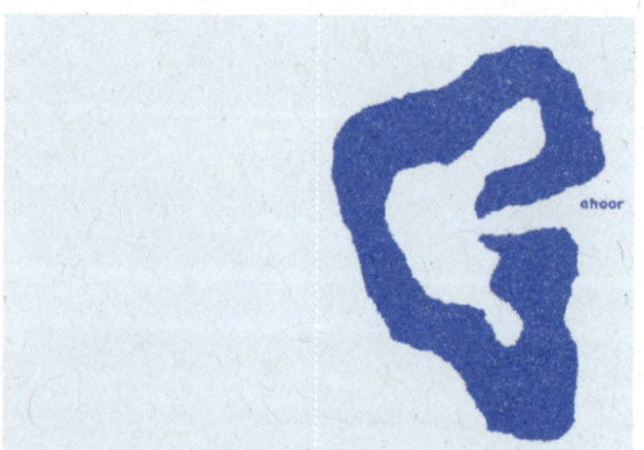

From: Piet Zwart, "Key-words"
1967, 21 × 18.5 cm

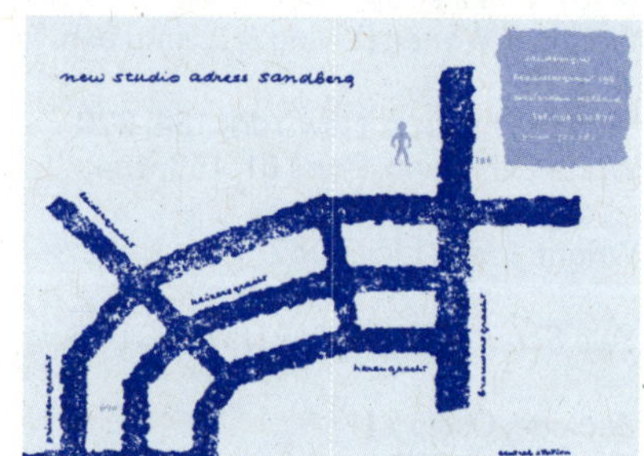

Change of address
1972, 22 × 30.5 cm

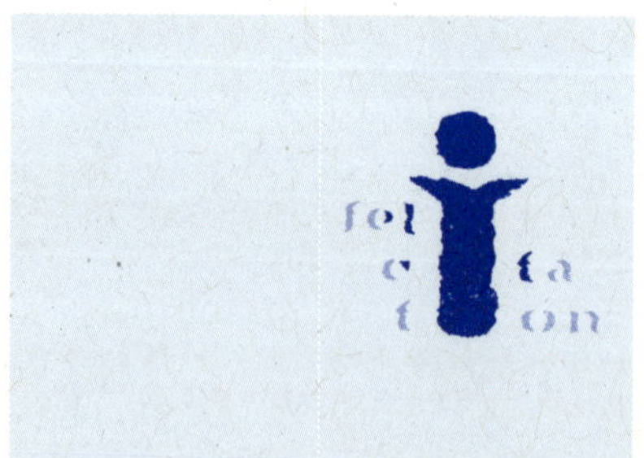

Birthday card (for Sonia Delaunay on her 90th birthday)
1957, 20.8 × 21 cm

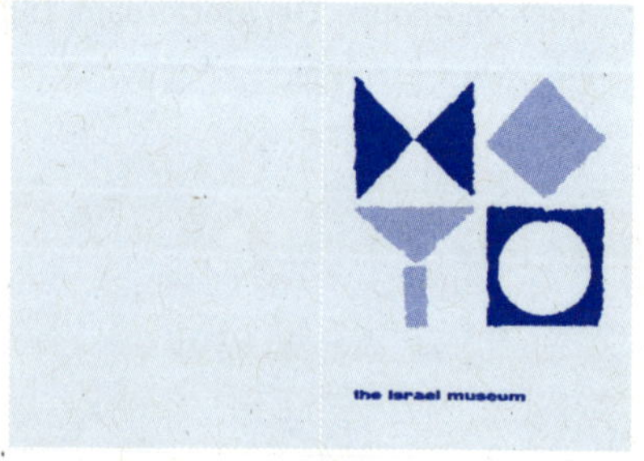

Catalogue cover The Israel Museum
1970, 25 × 19 cm

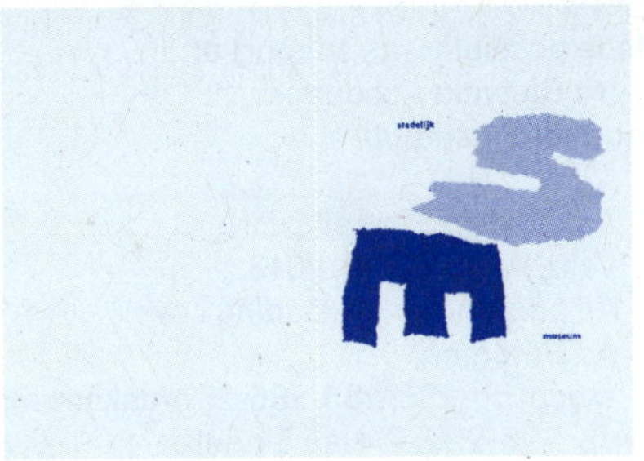

Logo Stedelijk Museum
around 1959

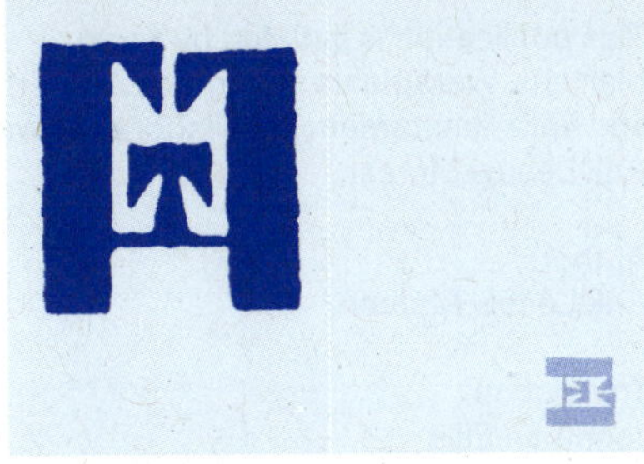

From: Piet Zwart, "Key-words"
1967, 21 × 18.5 cm

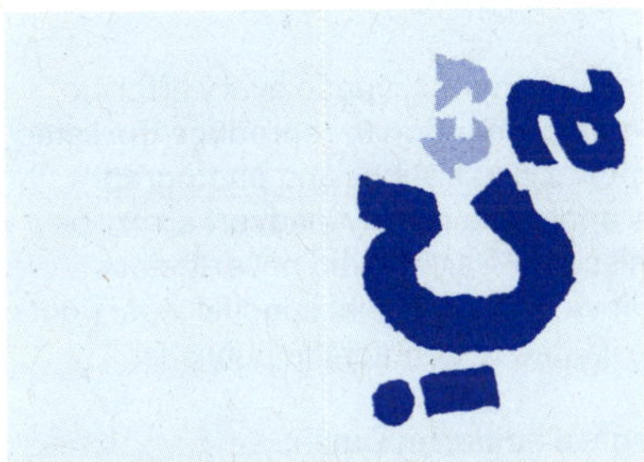

Leaflet International Center for the Typographic Arts
1961, 20.5 × 23 cm

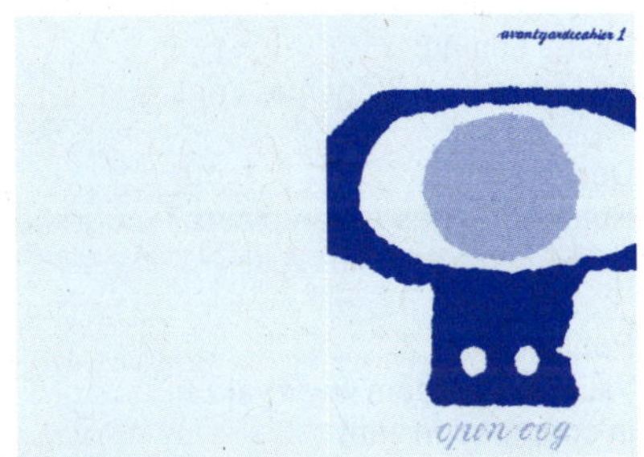

Cover "Open Oog", no. 1
1946, 24.8 × 19 cm

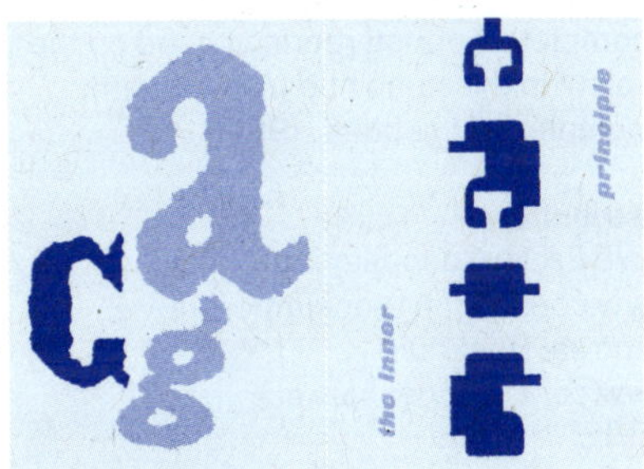

From: "Delta magazine", vol. 12, no. 1
1969, 22.5 × 15.5 cm
From: "experimenta typografica", no. 11
1956, 22.2 × 14 cm

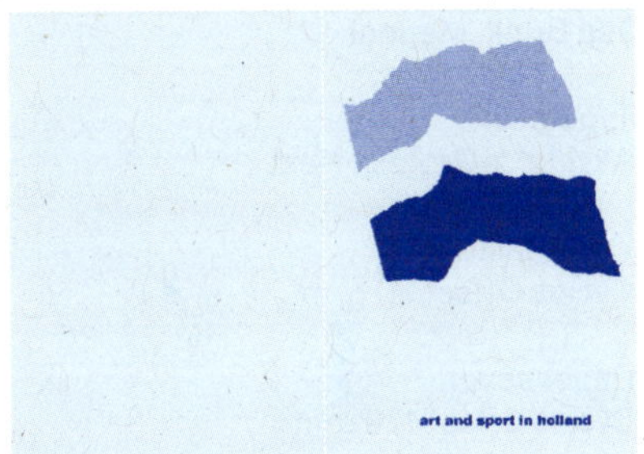

Leaflet Art and sport in Holland
Date unknown, 19.5 × 15 cm

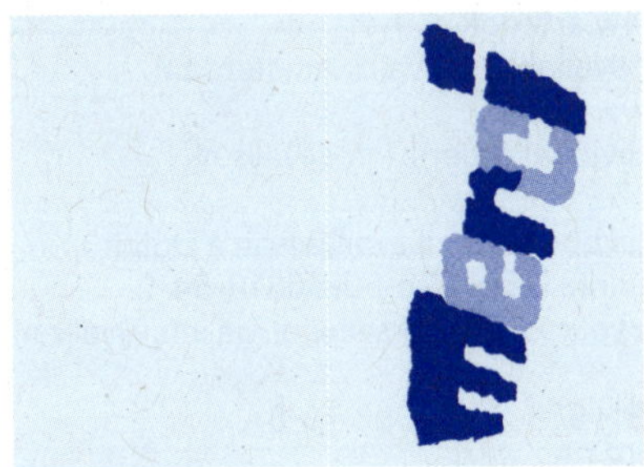

Thank you note
1968, 20.5 × 30 cm

This publication is initiated by Karel Martens, Werkplaats Typografie Arnhem and Valiz Amsterdam in collaboration with Ank Leeuw Marcar.

Author:
Ank Leeuw Marcar

Translation:
Jonathan Ellis

Copy editing and index:
Elke Stevens

Image editing:
Ad Petersen / Rutger de Vries

Design:
Rutger de Vries / Werkplaats Typografie
ArtEZ Institute of the Arts

Publisher:
Valiz, Amsterdam www.valiz.nl
in cooperation with
Werkplaats Typografie, Arnhem
www.werkplaatstypografie.org

Printing and binding:
Ten Brink, Meppel

Typeface:
Akzidenz-Grotesk Next

Paper inside:
Cyclus Offset 80 g/m²

Paper cover:
Cyclus Offset 170 g/m²

Structuring and designing this book was a project by Rutger de Vries, participant of the Werkplaats Typografie Year 13. He wishes to thank Anniek Brattinga, Roland Früh, Karel Martens, Armand Mevis, Maureen Mooren, Ad Petersen and Astrid Vorstermans.

Made possible with support of:
Gerrit Rietveld Academie
Sandberg Instituut

Original edition in Dutch:
Ank Leeuw Marcar, *Willem Sandberg: Portret van een kunstenaar* (Amsterdam: Valiz; Arnhem: Werkplaats Typografie; Rotterdam: Veenman drukkers, 2004), a completely edited reprint, based on the book with the same title (Amsterdam: Meulenhoff/Unieboek, 1981)

Distribution:
NL/BE/LU: Coen Sligting
www.coensligtingbookimport.nl
Centraal Boekhuis
www.centraalboekhuis.nl
GB/IE: Art Data
www.artdata.co.uk
Europe/Asia/Australia: Idea Books
www.ideabooks.nl
USA/Canada/Latin America: D.A.P.
www.artbook.com
Or available via Valiz, Amsterdam.
www.valiz.nl
Individual orders: info@valiz.nl

This book is also available in a Dutch edition: ISBN 978-90-80818-54-2 via your local bookseller or via info@valiz.nl

ISBN 978-90-78088-73-8
NUR 657, 640
Printed and bound in the EU